FROM MINNESOTA WITH MANNA

GOD'S PROVISION AND PROTECTION IN MY LIFE

Kathy Kramer

Trilogy Christian Publishers
A Wholly Owned Subsidiary of Trinity Broadcasting Network
2442 Michelle Drive
Tustin, CA 92780

For information, address Trilogy Christian Publishing
Rights Department, 2442 Michelle Drive, Tustin, Ca 92780.
Trilogy Christian Publishing/ TBN and colophon are trademarks of Trinity Broadcasting Network.

For information about special discounts for bulk purchases, please contact Trilogy Christian Publishing.

Manufactured in the United States of America

10 9 8 7 6 5 4 3 2 1

Library of Congress Cataloging-in-Publication Data is available.

ISBN 978-1-64773-776-4 (Print Book)
ISBN 978-1-64773-777-1 (ebook)

ENDORSEMENT

For over thirty-nine years, I was a prosecuting attorney in California, thirty-eight of them in Santa Barbara, where I met Kathy. We have continued to stay in touch as the years rolled on, and nothing has dimmed her ever shining star—a very bright light in a sometimes otherwise dull constellation of events... I am sure that people reading her book will have a good takeaway for their continued living despite the fact that life deals some terrible cards to people. Kathy's remarks will help some to navigate in the wake of tragedy...

—Patrick J. McKinley

"Kramer's work is yet another powerful testimony that speaks to the steadfast covenantal love of our King and Savior, Jesus Christ. God used her exposure to diverse denominations to ultimately point her back to the one true Church with Christ as its head."

—Pastor(s) David, Blake & Janessa Runyan, Canyons Community Church, Castle Rock, CO

CONTENTS

PROLOGUE

God is so good. Yet His ways are a mystery. When He reveals some of those things to us, we should share with others, since we gain wisdom through His divine help. As Jesus was about to ascend to heaven, He told his apostles to "go and tell the world" what He had taught them, but they had to be indwelled with the Holy Spirit before they could understand all He taught them. When the son of King David, Solomon, became king, the Lord asked what he wanted. He asked for wisdom. This pleased God, so He gave him wisdom and riches. Solomon wrote the book of Proverbs, which contains timeless wisdom and truth. I believe one of the weaknesses of our church bodies is that we don't share the trials we have faced and how we have overcome them. According to 2 Corinthians 1:3–4, "Praise be to the God and Father of our Lord Jesus Christ, the Father of compassion and the God of all comfort, who comforts us in all our troubles, so that we can comfort those in any trouble with the comfort we ourselves receive from God." I hope that my life stories and insights will bring comfort to others. Hope.

God also showed me the significance of people's names and why God said names were so important. Do you remember the first prayer Jesus taught His apostles? "Our Father, who art in heaven, hallowed be Thy name..." God has many names (Yahweh, I Am, Emmanuel, etc.), and He sometimes changed people's names to reflect His will for them. He changed Jacob to Israel. Jacob then demanded a blessing, and the being declared in Genesis 32:28 was that, from then on, Jacob would be called Israel, meaning "one that struggled with the divine angel; one who has prevailed with God; a man seeing God; he

9

will rule as God." He changed Simon to Peter. "You are Peter" (a small stone), but upon this Peter (a massive rock), referring to his confession of Himself being the Messiah, "[He] will build [His] church." So Jesus honored Simon by changing his name to Peter because he was the first to publicly confess Him as the Lord Messiah and Son of God.

This book is being written to honor God. This includes being broken from my pride to His will. "From everyone who has been given much, much will be demanded; and from the one who has been entrusted with much, much more will be asked" (Luke 12:48). God has given me much. God has also given me insight (looking in my rearview mirror) of all the ways in which He has protected me and given me insight along the way, like Moses and his followers as they spent forty years in the wilderness. By day, God protected them with a cloud. By night, He was there by fire. He also protected me along the way, from Minnesota (where I grew up) with manna, the food He gave to Moses and his people during those forty years. Hence the title for my book. Did you know Moses lived to be 120 years old? His first forty years were in the palace of the pharaoh in Egypt. The next forty years were in the desert where he escaped to after the murder of an Egyptian for killing a Hebrew slave. He was eighty years old when he led his people across the desert—his last forty years. If we were to split our life into three parts, I truly believe it is often the last third in which He can best use us. I have a friend who turns one hundred this year (Evelyn); she is a godly woman. I tease her that I plan to live to be ninety-nine. I just turned sixty-six this January, so I am now headed into the last third of my life. How can God use me? "They will still bear fruit in old age; they will stay fresh and green" (Ps. 92:14 NIV).

I love true books with *real* stories about *real* people. So I wanted to blend my insights into a fun book that is rather like *Chicken Soup for the Soul*, with a Minnesota beginning, for many to enjoy. Although I did not spend forty years wandering in a desert, I most certainly had a "desert experience" in which my life hit rock bottom (more on that later). While most books are arranged by topic or in chronological order, I thought I would put mine in alphabetical order, by the person, place, or thing that God used, just for fun and easy reference for the reader. I also wanted to thank those who have contributed to my story and to glorify and thank God.

Since the Bible often starts with a brief genealogy, I will do the same. I grew up in a small town in northern Minnesota as the eldest girl in a family of seven children. It is a place where most folks never move very far away. They often marry their high school sweetheart, settle down not too far from family, have kids, and relive the experiences they had as a child. They only move if a job takes them out of the area. Not me. I always had "wanderlust" and wanted to travel and see the world. My Italian father spent his whole life working in the iron mines and retired at age fifty-five. One year later, he died of a heart attack and never got to travel very far from home except to visit his "gypsy daughter," me, in places she lived. My German mom was a registered nurse, and she worked in hospitals and then in alcohol/detox until retirement, and then dementia took over and she lived in many "memory units" until she died at age eighty-nine. She was blessed with many children, grandchildren, and great-grandchildren, but she never had joy for life. Even though she grew up in the current location of *Lake Wobegon Days*, where we spent our summer vacations, her German Catholic upbringing made for all work and no play.

When I was in high school, I fell in love with a foreign exchange student from Rhodesia, now called Zimbabwe. That is a long way from Minnesota! So began my first of several long-distance relationships. I attended the same Benedictine Catholic College as my mom in one of the coldest places on earth, Duluth, Minnesota. I wrote to this sweetheart (Brian) all through college and thought for sure we would get married after college (him, too), but along the way, God had other plans for me. I clearly remember spring break during my sophomore year of college, where I traveled thirty-six hours nonstop on a bus to Daytona Beach, Florida, and thought I had died and gone to heaven. My "career goal" became finding a warmer place to live! I worked in a different state every summer, doing different jobs, from being a nanny to a Jewish family in New Jersey to selling cookbooks in Texas, then dictionaries in Pennsylvania, and finally getting to travel to twelve countries in twelve weeks for $1,200 (all expenses paid) upon my graduation from college, including time with my British boyfriend in England.

That summer clearly changed my view of our relationship. I came to love being an "American in Paris," and he disliked what he saw as "the ugly American" fun we had along the way. He never wanted to move to America, and I only wanted to live in the USA. You might say our point of separation was the Atlantic Ocean! So I came home to find a job. I also had made some new "Southern friends" during my trip, including two from Georgia. So I took my first real job with the Center for Disease Control (CDC) in Atlanta and traveled nonstop for one year on a large research project, moving every week, until I got tired of travel and our team was sent to Southern California.

While in the Los Angeles area, I scouted the *LA Times* for job openings and stumbled upon a job in Santa Barbara, one of the most beautiful places on earth. I was offered the job as the manager of the medical records department, so I packed everything I owned in my Chevy Malibu and moved there in 1977, not knowing one person west of the Mississippi River! I would start dating a guy (Gary) that I married two years later. That marriage only lasted five years (more later), but I stayed in the area we lived (Ventura). I got my master's degree at the University of Southern California (USC) in 1986 and was offered a job in Scottsdale, Arizona, in the fall of 1987. So after ten very interesting years in California, I moved to Arizona as a great career move and to live nearer one of my sisters with small children. I loved being Aunt Kathy! However, I hated the desert, and the job was completely wrong for me. I lost that job due to depression, and I returned to California in the spring of 1990, where I lived until 2006.

I always thought if I had a strong résumé, I could go anywhere and do anything. After all, I got straight As from grade school through grad school. Wrong. The apostle Paul (formerly called Saul, who persecuted Christians) also thought his great résumé would get him through life, until he had a conversion experience and was thrown off his horse (literally and figuratively) by Jesus. Paul said, "I was circumcised on the eighth day, of the people of Israel, of the tribe of Benjamin, a Hebrew of Hebrews; as to the law, a Pharisee; as to zeal, a persecutor of the church; as to righteousness under the law, blameless" (Phil. 3:5–6). In the end, his résumé was of no significance. He actually called it rubbish. All that mattered was being a servant of Christ. Jesus had a lot to reveal to him before he could become the apostle to the Gentiles, a journey including much pain but great joy.

My résumé (education and experience) was very important to my dad. In the summer of 1978, the hospital I worked for closed due to the passage of Proposition 13 (Jarvis-Gann Initiative). Since I was a manager, I did not lose my job but had to lay off most of my staff. Since our outpatient clinics remained open, I still had some supervision to do. After a few weeks, I became bored, so I took an administrative leave (retaining my health-care benefits) to work with a local Christian nonprofit that took local volunteers every other weekend to a location just north of Tijuana, Mexico. We traveled into that city to do outreach to the poor children who lived in the garbage dumps, as well as to orphanages where babies never cried since no one ever picked them up. During the week, I did the administrative work for the organization. My dad was appalled! He said I was "wasting my college degree." Really? To take time to help the poor?

I remember my primary math professor in college (with a PhD in math) also left his tenured position to go work for a national pro-life organization after *Roe v. Wade* passed, making abortion legal in the USA. I admired him for his strong convictions. It's the American way to be strong and self-sufficient. It's God's way to humble the proud and work through those who give Him their life to do His will.

Just like the apostle Paul, I was thrown off my horse, and one of those "things" that happened to me along the way: I lost my Scottsdale job since I was too ill to do the work. I suffered from two episodes of major depression accompanied with anxiety (including being hospitalized twice). I could not do anything. Thirteen months into my "frozen" life, all alone in the desert, my sister Sue called my best friends in Santa Barbara (Pat and Esther), and Pat drove to Arizona with a friend who had an RV and picked me up and took me back to their home. I was allowed to live with them for three months. During that time, I found a job as a hospital manager through a lead from a friend who had worked there herself.

This friend (Jean) had also suffered from depression—we both had moms with clinical depression. She introduced me to the Bible as the thing that brought her the most comfort. I joined her at a large community church and took my first Bible study in that body full of "ex-Catholics" seeking more in their lives, with an interesting beginning in the book of Revelation. So I began a spiritual journey as well. I met my current husband in the fall of 1993—he attended the same church as me. He called me his Proverbs 31 woman. Talk about great expectations! We married in February 1995 and adopted two foster sons in 1997 and 2000.

We always had golden retrievers as family pets (great therapy for everyone) and got very involved in our church as a family. I would suffer several job losses along the way, which was both painful and humbling (more later). Bill always worked for one company, and he was given the golden handshake (retirement) in 2003, and after the severance ended in 2005, we knew we had to find a better, more affordable place to raise two boys.

Along that journey, I got Bill to return to the hospital where he was treated for polio for over a year as a five-year-old. During this visit, he was diagnosed with post-polio syndrome, which qualified him for Social Security Disability. We also discovered our boys would get monthly Social Security benefits until they turned eighteen since their dad was disabled. So we had unexpected funds to make a big move. God provided for us in ways we could not imagine.

We moved to Douglas County, Colorado, in the summer of 2006, where some friends were doing a "church plant." We found a "house in the trees" with more windows and light than you can imagine. We have lived there ever since. We are blessed to live halfway between Denver and Colorado Springs and far (yet near) to two big cities—we have the best of both worlds. We are now at our fourth church (more God stories) and are deacons at a wonderful community church. I retired from my job in June (2020), so now I have time to listen to the Lord as He speaks to me about what mysteries He has revealed to me along the way. So here goes, my stories, His stories, His revelation. My crazy life…so far.

Note: To any persons of whom I write in this book, my reflections are to reveal stories that can help other people along the way. I didn't mean to "air any dirty laundry" or to "reveal any family secrets," but to briefly touch on some challenges we have all faced. Please know that I write every word in love to thank the Lord for the experiences we shared and to reflect what I learned along the way. Keeping secrets is what the evil one wants from us so they can eat us from within. I am releasing many "happy endings" to stories that were not always so pretty. My hope is that you will read every word as a piece of encouragement for others.

That's the funny thing about life: we learn more from our failures than we do from our success. A wise person once said, "It is not how many times you fall down in life, but rather how many times you get back up." (Right, Mat? We heard this from Grandpa Joe.) So I dedicate this book to each of you with my love. I also threw in some fun things I learned along the way. I hope many of you will be saying, "I didn't know that." Now you do! So enjoy.

CHAPTER A

Adoption (God to Us, Us to Our Boys)

This subject is close to my heart since we adopted both of our boys from foster care in California when they were ages three and four. Our first son came from a background of severe abuse at the hands of a schizophrenic mom. Our second son had a mom who was a heroin addict. We asked for children that had no local family, unwanted. We did this so we would not have to go through the horrible "visitation with birth families" ordeal. You see, the goal of foster care is "reunification with the birth parents." Not good. The reason I say this is that most children put into foster care are there because of severe abuse or neglect—alcohol abuse, drug abuse, or mental illness on the part of the parent. That's why reunification rarely works and why kids go from one foster home to another. Their life is completely unstable. They have a hard time trusting anyone or bonding with anyone. We think this system should be about what is best for the children. So we also became fost-adopt mentors to encourage more parents to give a permanent home to these kids.

In the same way, our life is completely unstable until we come to know the Lord in a personal way. The Bible says, "But when the set time had fully come, God sent his Son, born of a woman, born under the law, to redeem those under the law, that we might receive adoption. So you are no longer a slave, but God's child; and since you are his child, God has made you also an heir" (Gal.4:4–5, 7). Wow. We go from being slaves to sin to being heirs of the kingdom of heaven. That is truly amazing! Being adopted children of God took on a whole new meaning.

I have a sister-in-law that asked, "How do you do that love thing with kids that are not your own?" We told her that it was our choice to have these boys come into our family, just like God chose us when there was little "lovable" about us. Real love is a choice. The kind of love that thinks of others before ourselves (agape love). My mom had many grandchildren, but our boys were her favorites. Do you know why? Because she loved to "adopt pets" no one else wanted. In the same way, we took these boys in when no one else wanted them, and that warmed her heart.

The pediatric neurologist for our first son warned us not to adopt him because "he would never amount to anything." Really? What a prognosis for a three-year-old boy! They say foster kids are "unadoptable" after age seven, which is really sad. Many stay in a foster care institution until they reach the age of eighteen—that is when adoption assistance ends for foster parents. Many who consider this role to be a "job" end their relationship with the child at that age.

Can you imagine if you said to a normal eighteen-year-old during their senior year in high school, on their birthday, "Here's the door. Goodbye and good luck." What chance of success would they have? Very little. When you compound that with the many "conditions" that foster kids have, it is no wonder many end up on the streets or in jail. Another friend who adopted a "normal baby" who ended up being diagnosed with autism (Asperger's syndrome) in early life said, "You knew what you were signing up for, but I did not sign up for this." Some think we are "saints." Not so. We just had a heart to create a family through adoption. We were married in our early forties, so having our own children was not very likely. It seemed like a good choice.

Since Bill's job included having a territory that covered the whole West Coast, he was often out of town during the week. So I took the foster care training courses, first with the county, and then with a private agency. Along that journey, I was in class with the wife of Pastor Francis Chan (Lisa). Do you know that name? Francis Chan is an American author on Christian subjects and a teacher and preacher in evangelical churches and related settings. He is the former teaching pastor of Cornerstone Community Church in Simi Valley, California, which he founded in 1994. His wife was a student in a Bible youth group that Bill led in the church where we met. I do remember the Chan family deciding *not* to do foster care since they had small children and did not want to put them in "harm's way" since foster kids can get violent. (I believe they went on to adopt other kids later.)

It was friends from that very church who did the church plant in Colorado where we ended up moving. God connects those who serve Him, for sure! As they say, it is a small world. So adoption will always be close to our heart. Adoption, not abortion. We clearly are both pro-life and believe that unborn children need a voice, a family, a place to belong. It is the same for children who have no good parents—they, too, need a home. When we hear pro-choice, we laugh. The real choice is choosing life for all children and raising them up to know their Father in heaven. What a privilege it is!

America (A Country Blessed by God)

God bless America! It is a song we sing that I simply love. Here are some of the lyrics.

> *God bless America, land that I love*
> *Stand beside her and guide her*
> *Through the night with the light from above*
> *From the mountains to the prairies*
> *To the oceans white with foam*
> *God bless America, my home sweet home*

When I first traveled abroad (1976), it was the summer of the bicentennial of our country—a mere two hundred years since we got our independence from England. Imagine being twenty-two, just out of college, before taking a job, and traveling with a group of other like students from across the USA to twelve countries over twelve weeks. (Thank you to the University of Illinois–Urbana for this program!) Our first and last stop on that trip would be England, where my high school foreign exchange student boyfriend was in medical school. We had a "free week" in London, so I got to spend my time with him. What a fabulous week it was! It was romantic, but also my first introduction to British history, which I still love. In fact, my husband and I far prefer movies and series that are made in England to those in the USA. So rich. Good. Deep in meaning.

By the end of our twelve weeks, there was a girl in the group behind us that wanted to go home early, so I got a second week in England for free. By that time, my guy was on the south coast of England, doing an internship (Chichester), so I found a cute B&B and spent time with him and his fellow intern there. We were a merry threesome! However, when I started telling them the tales of all our crazy adventures across Europe (like jumping in the Trevi Fountain in Rome, skinny-dipping on the Greek Islands, and taking a midnight motorcycle ride around Athens), they thought I was just being an "ugly American." Brian clearly stated he had spent a year in America as a foreign student and had no desire to go back. After all, we were the largest consumers of everything in the world. I, on the other hand, had come to love being an American and could not wait to go home, to the land I loved, just like the song said. But we have stayed friends until this day, and I got to be godmother to one of his daughters and take my own family over there to visit on many occasions. God has a plan.

I must add a note about "proud to be an American" and what it means to those of my generation versus the current young people who are often taught in American colleges and universities to "hate America" for all the bad things done in our history. I find this so sad. I truly believe America is the best country on earth, a land of opportunity and freedom for peoples from across the world. That is why so many people want to move to the United States. No nation is perfect, but our republic is far and above any other national system in the world. When young people look at someone like George Washington and say, "He was a slave owner, so he was bad," I say, "What?" Everyone in the 1700s had slaves, but he treated his slaves very well (go visit Mount Vernon someday and see for yourself). He was a gentleman farmer and fought in two wars, including leading the American Revolutionary troops into victory despite all odds. They wanted to crown him king, but he said no; he would serve his term(s) and then go back to Virginia. He was a man of high moral standards and was clearly protected by God during the war. So I beg this younger generation to look at the whole picture in content and stop tearing down statues of great men like President Washington. If someone truly hates our country, rather than tear it down, they should move. So God bless America!

Ann (My Middle Name, Favored One of Grace)

So what's in a name? My middle name at birth was Katherine *Ann*. Anne, alternatively spelled Ann, is a form of the Latin female given name Anna. This, in turn, is a representation of the Hebrew Hannah, which means "favor" or "grace." In this incarnation, it is related to Germanic names and means "eagle." Isn't that cool? Part of my name means "favor" or "grace" and also "eagle"—one who soars. When I was reading a book on Martin Luther, I learned that German Catholics often prayed to Saint Anne. Who was she? Saint Anne was the grandmother of Jesus Christ. She was born from the house of David, the line that was prophesied to give birth to Christ. Saint Anne is the mother of Mary, the woman who gave birth to Jesus by virgin birth. The angel Gabriel came to Mary and told her that she would give birth to the Son of God. Germans considered her the patron saint of miners. I found this interesting since my dad was in mining. When Luther was nearly struck by lightning, he prayed to Saint Anne for help and vowed to join the priesthood.

Anna was also mentioned in the Bible at the time of Jesus's birth. "There was also a prophet, Anna, the daughter of Penuel, of the tribe of Asher. She was very old; she had lived with her husband seven years after her marriage, and then was a widow until she was eighty-four. She never left the temple but worshiped night and day, fasting and praying. Coming up to them at that very moment, she gave thanks to God and spoke about the child to all who were look-ing forward to the redemption of Jerusalem" (Luke 2:36–38 NIV). Anna and Simeon were in the temple when Jesus was brought by His parents to be dedicated. They both got to see the baby Jesus (Messiah) before they died. She must have been a very special woman. I wonder what "Grandma Anne" (Mary's mom) thought. Both special women.

Since our parents named each of their seven children after saints, I wonder if they knew the origin of this name (or just my first name, Katherine). I think that they probably did because so many of us had saintly middle names, especially the girls, Katherine Ann, Susan Mary, Joan Marie. When I got confirmed at around age twelve, we had to select a sponsor, and I chose the mom of a good friend of mine. The confirmation name I chose was Mary since that is about as high as you can go in the Catholic Church! Now I know I also had the name of Mary's mom.

Ironically, when my first husband got remarried (very shortly after our divorce), he married a gal named Anna. I do hope she brought favor to his life. I know they had twin girls. His older mom (Ellen) would have loved being a grandmother, especially since her only daughter died at age seventeen. Ellen's daughter was born with only one kidney and died in a hospital of kidney failure when Gary was very young. He was basically raised as an only child. His dad's heart was so crushed that he vowed to never die in a hospital. He ended up killing himself in 1982 (see *suicide*). I do hope Anna and her daughters brought great joy to Grandma Ellen—she deserved such joy. So Anna has some special significance to me.

One more note about "Annie's Song." John Denver wrote it for his wife and said it was the all-time favorite song he wrote. Here are the lovely words that would bless any woman:

> *You fill up my senses*
> *Like a night in a forest*
> *Like the mountains in springtime*
> *Like a walk in the rain*
> *Like a storm in the desert*
> *Like a sleepy blue ocean*

You fill up my senses
Come fill me again
Come let me love you
Let me give my life to you
Let me drown in your laughter
Let me die in your arms
Let me lay down beside you
Let me always be with you
Come let me love you
Come love me again

Thank you and bless you to all women named Anne.

Arizona (Desert Place of Sorrow)

It is interesting that God chose the land of Israel for His chosen people, since much of it is a desert. After being baptized by John the Baptist, Jesus fasted for forty days and nights in the Judean Desert. During this time, Satan came to Jesus and tried to tempt Him. With Jesus having refused each temptation, Satan then departed and Jesus returned to Galilee to begin His ministry (see Matthew 4:1–11). Even our Lord had to go through a period of temptation in the desert before He could begin His ministry. I find that comforting; He never asks us to endure more than He did. He fought Satan with the Word of God. I had no such tool.

Within the United States, Arizona is a desert state. I moved there in the fall of 1987 for a great job but only lasted until the spring of 1990 before I moved back to California. I never liked the desert heat or the brown surroundings. My sister lived less than two hours away with her husband and young children, so I loved my "Aunt Kathy time." However, the work environment was toxic—I was not liked from the beginning since I was the first female hired into the administrative ranks, something other women had tried but failed. I was completely resented and rejected, which led to major clinical depression and anxiety. It lasted nearly seventeen months, and many family and friends were very worried about me. I was rescued by a dear friend (Patrick).

I was living alone (career single) and did not find out that "two are better than one" until I got married. "Two are better than one, because they have a good reward for their toil. For if they fall, one will lift up his fellow. But woe to him who is alone when he falls and has not another to lift him up" (Eccles. 4:9–110 ESV). We had this passage read at our wedding. But in 1989, I was all alone and did not know the Bible.

I came to believe that Satan uses depression and anxiety to attack people. He can be such a good liar, and when you are weak, you are vulnerable. I did not know about the need for the full armor of God to fight Satan, so I had to learn the hard way—no weapons.

"Finally, be strong in the Lord and in the strength of his might. Put on the whole armor of God, that you may be able to stand against the schemes of the devil. For we do not wrestle against flesh and blood, but against the rulers, against the authorities, against the cosmic powers over this present darkness, against the spiritual forces of evil in the heavenly places. Therefore take up the whole armor of God, that you may be able to withstand in the evil day, and having done all, to stand firm" (Eph. 6:10–12).

I was on the board of the Franciscan Renewal Center in Scottsdale and also on a retreat team. That was where I made my friends. I never would have left my Catholic faith or discovered the Bible if I had not gone through this experience. It was only upon my return to California that a good friend/colleague helped to find me a job at a hospital where she used to work. She also invited me to her church and my first Bible study. Ironically, we both suffered from depression based upon poor serotonin uptake in our brains—something we each inherited from our moms. God sure works in mysterious ways.

I told my husband when we got married I would go anywhere with him but never again live in Arizona—it was the place I nearly died. But it became the basis for my new life in Christ as well. Ironically, my husband's mom bought a small mobile home in Lake Havasu, Arizona, so we did go there on occasion for summer fun.

But it was not to live, just to visit. To this day, I cannot see any beauty in the desert. But I know God does. He uses it to test people.

Avon (Sweet Summer Memories)

My maternal grandparents lived in a small town in Central Minnesota named Avon. We would go there for our summer vacations. It was a magical place. They lived on half a city block, just across from the Catholic church (where church bells rang 8:00 a.m., noon, 6:00 p.m.) and by the lake, where they had a dock and a pontoon boat. They had a two-story home, a three-bedroom cottage, a playhouse for us girls, an enclosed carport, and a big two-story air-conditioned candy shed since my grandpa was the local candy distributor for the region. It was all surrounded by a white picket fence and daisies and included a beautiful garden with vegetables and flowers. It had a big swing, on which four people could enjoy the summer days and listen to baseball on the radio. It was very special.

All children should have such sweet summer memories. Swimming all day at the beach or off the dock or off the pontoon boat. We also had picnics on that boat. We got to dig our own angle worms for bait and would use bamboo poles to fish off the dock. Grandma and Grandpa took me to a couple of Minnesota Twins games—I can still remember the names of nearly every player on that team. Grandpa (Ben) was a real character who grew up with many brothers; the Schmid boys worked very hard and practically ran the town. He would live his real childhood when he became an adult.

We would sometimes go to Avon for Easter as well. Grandma would cook homemade sausage for our breakfast, and Grandpa provided the biggest Brach's Easter baskets. Grandma sewed most of our clothing (the girls), and we got new Easter dresses and bonnets that we wore with our white gloves as we attended church together as a family. I also remember seeing Grandma on her knees every night in prayer. Later in life, other moms would ask, "Did your mom pray for you?" I could only answer that I was not sure, but I did know that my grandmother did.

In the Bible, there was a young man named Timothy who had a godly mom and grandmother who helped raise him up in the ways of the Lord. In 2 Timothy 1:5, the author tells Timothy, "I am reminded of your sincere faith, a faith that dwelt first in your grandmother Lois and your mother Eunice and now, I am sure, dwells in you as well" (ESV). Oh, the influence of those who raise us! I have become very active in an international organization named Moms in Prayer (see another chapter), and I thank the Lord for the dear influence of my grandmother. She was diagnosed with non-Hodgkin's lymphoma in the fall of 1985 and died in January of 1986. I was grateful that my sister and I chose to go home over Thanksgiving that year to see Grandma when she was still alive, rather than for her funeral. Those were some sweet memories.

It was sweet in the summer of 2018 when over four hundred members of this family had a grand reunion in Minnesota. So many stories. Extended family now in so many states, with the largest number ending up in California. Ironically, my husband's mom's maiden name was also Schmidt, so we have some unique roots. My mom had died in March 2018; her brother Chuck died several years earlier, but her remaining brother, Roger, was there with all his children. I was so grateful he got to enjoy this big reunion. Roger died in January of 2019, so the following summer, all his kids would once again gather to spread his ashes. God's timing can be so sweet. We were the only ones in my family to attend, and I am sure glad we did. You never know when it will be your "last time" to see someone.

It is now on my bucket list to visit Stratford-upon-Avon in England. More history to explore. More God moments to enjoy.

CHAPTER B

Belinda (My Sister-in-Law)

So what is the meaning of this name? Belinda is a feminine given name of unknown origin, apparently coined from Italian *belle*, meaning "beautiful." Alternatively, it may be derived from the Old High German name Belinda, which possibly meant "bright serpent" or "bright linden tree" (Wikipedia). I love that, Bella, beautiful, my favorite Estée Lauder fragrance! But I digress. One of my good friends in high school was named Belinda. She ended up dating my brother Paul, and when we were juniors, he got her pregnant. The summer between grades 11 and 12, we had a "shotgun" wedding in our family, and I was one of her bridesmaids. That was what you did in 1971. She gave birth to a beautiful daughter (Heidi) in February 1972, the year of our high school graduation. They went on to have three children. She became a young mom and had to put off any hope of going to college until her kids were in school. Years later, she did just that and got her elementary teaching degree and taught school for many years. I know she was an awesome teacher!

What I love most about Belinda is her great heart and the laughter we always share. We had a junior high teacher with a summer business as a canoe outfitter in the Boundary Waters area between Minnesota and Canada. We "adventure young women" were able to work for him in the spring and earn free canoe trips every summer for our three years of high school. If you like red licorice, you would have loved being in a tent with Belinda! Many years later, she would continue to be an "adventure woman" with other friends she made who loved the outdoors. Her mom (Rosemary) died too early in life, and her youngest daughter (Holly) also died tragically as a young mom with two children while living/working in Alaska as a nurse. They say the loss of a child is the hardest loss to ever experience—I know she grieved this loss a lot.

Her mom was an amazing woman. In high school, my brother spent more time at their house than ours, not just to be with Belinda, but also around her mom. She listened. She cared. She laughed and cried with you. It was a stark contrast to our mom, who was not that way at all. We learn a lot about what we want to be like as a mom from our early role models. We also learn what *not* to be like. Sadly, my mom never seemed to find joy in being a wife or mom, so I think we all vowed to do things differently when we grew up. Rosemary was one of "dear moms to everyone around her." Belinda has so many of her good traits. Thanks for being my friend.

Belinda and my brother got divorced after nearly thirty years of marriage, but she did remarry a wonderful man named Don (a widower), and she remains my "forever sister" in love for sure! These days, many families suffer from divorce, and there is always the question of relationships with the "ex-in-laws." Based upon my relationship with this special woman, I can only say they got her name right. She is beautiful, and my life is richer knowing her.

Bill (My Current Loving Husband)

Bill is a nickname for William, but I did not want to wait until the end of my A–Z chapters to talk about my dear husband, Bill. So what does William mean? The biblical meaning of William is "determined protector." I think he has that role toward me, our sons, and our dogs. Early in life, he was the one who needed "protection." At age five, he contracted polio and ended up spending a year in a rehab hospital named Rancho Los Amigos in the Los Angeles area (Downey, California). There is now a medical term named after this place. The Rancho Los Amigos Scale (RLAS), a.k.a. the Rancho Los Amigos Levels of Cognitive Functioning Scale (LOCF), or Rancho Scale, is a medical scale used to assess individuals after a closed head injury, including traumatic brain injury, based on cognitive and behavioral presentations as they emerge from coma. It is named after the Rancho Los Amigos National Rehabilitation Center, located in Downey, California, United States, in Los Angeles County (Wikipedia). It is interesting to note that our first adopted son had traumatic brain injury (TBI), so perhaps way back in kindergarten God was preparing Bill to "protect" our son James.

Early in our relationship, I was coordinator of a disability ministry at our church. I invited him to come to one of our group meetings, a time of encouragement and support. As he sat and talked with a young mom with three disabled sons, two in wheelchairs, I could see his heart ache for her. I remember him sharing from memory his favorite Bible verse that had to do with his own disabled body, Psalm 139:13–16 (NIV):

> For you created my inmost being;
> you knit me together in my mother's womb.
> I praise you because I am fearfully and wonder-
> fully made;
> your works are wonderful,
> I know that full well.
> My frame was not hidden from you
> when I was made in the secret place,
> when I was woven together in the depths of the
> earth.
> Your eyes saw my unformed body;
> all the days ordained for me were written in your
> book
> before one of them came to be.

I knew that this had become his "life verse," and he has shared it with many people we have met along the way.

Bill remembers being rushed to the hospital as he contracted polio, a disease for which he had *not* been vaccinated. The vaccine had just come out, and his parents did not believe he needed the vaccine. I know his mom felt guilty all the rest of her life, but she also "protected" this special-needs son of hers until the day she died. He was the "favorite" child in his family, just like me, but for completely different reasons—he had special needs. He was also second born, with one older sister (Karen) and one younger brother (Jack), and if you looked at the pictures of this threesome in early life, you would see a great resemblance to photos of me and my older brother (Paul) and younger brother (Tom). We were all baby boomers and shared simple, good childhood memories.

Years later, while in Washington, DC, as a grant writer working with a faith-based organization seeking federal grant funds, I went to see an exhibit at one of the Smithsonian museums about the history of polio and vaccine founder, Jonas Salk. I bought the book *Post-Polio Syndrome* and read about how the disease affected those who had it later in life. It became an accepted "disabling" medical condition that would allow Bill to get Social Security Disability after his retirement. That was new to both of us. It took me two years to get Bill to go back to Rancho Los Amigos for an evaluation, but he did. He was diagnosed with the syndrome. Since he qualified for Social Security Disability in his fifties, we found we would also get some benefits for our sons until they reached age eighteen. It was those very funds that provided a way for us to pay for a move from California to Colorado in 2006. God's ways are indeed an amazing mystery.

Because of his polio, Bill has a right arm three inches shorter than his left arm, and he had numerous surgeries as a child to create some ligaments around his "missing shoulder socket" so he could use his right arm. His dad made sure he could participate in sports and even made him a device to help him water ski. He swims. He golfs. He played basketball. He was the kicker on his high school football team, and several teachers and coaches that his mom knew "took care of him" during his school years, especially that awful time of "group showers." He was one of the most popular kids in his school, yet he did not have good luck with female relationships and longed to have a wife and family.

When I met Bill, he had a unique license plate on his car: Rom 5:3–5. "Not only so, but we also glory in our sufferings, because we know that suffering produces perseverance; perseverance, character; and character, hope. And hope does not put us to shame, because God's love has been poured out into our hearts through the Holy Spirit, who has been given to us" (Rom. 5:3–5 NIV). Another life verse! He had to glory in his sufferings and persevere with hope. That was just what he did through his Christian male friends.

As God would have it, an organization sprung up out of the University of Colorado–Boulder in March 1990 by a football coach named Bill McCartney. It was called Promise Keepers. Bill became very active as a leader of this group at the church where we met. Another leader took daily walks, during which he prayed. He added Bill's request to his prayer list, and lo and behold, we met in the fall of 1993 through a mutual female friend of his I met in physical therapy. (I blew out all my left knee ligaments skiing in Durango, Colorado, the last day of 1990.) We gals shared our frustration that there were very few "good, godly guys" out there to marry, so she introduced me to Bill. He wanted a girl who loved sports since his family had season tickets to UCLA football, and I loved sports. So our "dating" began every other weekend, going to the Rose Bowl for football, with a few dinners in between. My Colorado injury led me to meet him, and another Colorado ministry would draw us together and we would end up living in Colorado. God's ways are most unusual!

I got involved in helping at a big Promise Keepers event in Anaheim. It was at that event that some of the guy members of my church community group told me how this fellow Bill really liked me. What? He never told me. So I sent him a card that said, "I know how you feel about your dog, but not about me." He never responded, but we did get engaged in 1994 and married in February 1995. To this day, I tell people I married him for his dog!

At the time of our wedding, I was forty-one and he was forty-three. It was four days after Valentine's Day, and we had a glorious red-white-black theme, and many of my nieces and nephews were in the wedding, and our dog, Kelly, came to our reception. Our travel agent bought us a limousine ride to/from our reception and to/from the airport when we flew out for our honeymoon. That was a first for both of us, as well as those nieces and nephews! They all jumped in, and everyone got rides by the end of the reception. My mom flew in with her best friend, Loretta. They were both in AA together, and she was such a fun lady. My uncle Stan (Dad's youngest brother) gave me away at the wedding, and he said he had never seen my mom laugh so much—what joy that brought to my heart! My crazy brothers bought some carnival-type tickets and were handing them out to everyone as "drink tickets." We had a cash bar, so the bartender was quite confused and they were quite amused—ha! Our rings had two circles joined by a cross to signify that our lives were joined together by the Lord. It was one blessed day for sure. One of our wedding gifts was a plaque with the meaning of both our names. Here is what it said for Bill:

> *Assurance comes from within. No one can change his mind.*
> *Enjoys chasing his dream. Holds truth in high regard*
> *His deepest thoughts are those of love. Courageous enough to admit his mistakes.*
> *Expresses boldness and perseverance. Stress will never catch him off guard.*
> *Goodwill through good examples. I like this.*

Bill calls me his "gypsy woman," and we have traveled all over the place together. It started in New Zealand for our honeymoon; now that's a place everyone should get to see! We went to England several times to visit my former boyfriend, Brian, now married, with children. We even took our boys a couple of times—they had passports at a very young age. We got involved in an international mission's outreach at our church, including being the "American family" to several young men. The first was from Japan, and we took him golfing during late-afternoon cheap green fees. In 1997, we met a freshman at Cal Lutheran University near us. His name was Gabriel, and he was from Tanzania. He became an "adopted member" of our family, and to this day we have kept in close touch (see chapter G). It was the same year we met our first son, James.

This year we celebrated twenty-five years of marriage and continue to grow in our friendship and love. My sister once called him a keeper. She was right. He loves helping anyone and everyone, so that is one area where he needs better boundaries, so he does not wear out. Few women get to marry "a Bill," but I am sure God put us together. His plan unfolds every day.

Birth Order and Favored One

As I mentioned earlier, both Bill and I were second born in our family. In general, it is the firstborn that is the most highly esteemed, the one with the greatest inheritance. But God often chose the second born to be of greater importance.

Cain and Abel. Such is the case for the first two children born to Adam and Eve, Cain and Abel. "By faith Abel offered to God a better sacrifice than Cain, through which he obtained the testimony that he was righteous, God testifying about his gifts, and through faith, though he is dead, he still speaks" (Heb. 11:4). Cain was so mad at God for giving greater favor to his younger brother that he killed him. Talk about sibling jealousy!

Ishmael and Isaac. Then came Abraham and Sarah, who were told that they would conceive a son in their old age (both over age ninety). Sarah laughed. Then she became impatient and had her maidservant (Hagar) sleep with Abraham to produce a child. Ishmael was born, and Abraham loved him very much. He was firstborn, but not the promised son (Isaac) who would be the son of that promise, the second born. He was born when Ishmael was about thirteen years old. Then they both grew up.

The story from Genesis is quite remarkable.

"The child [Isaac] grew and was weaned, and on the day, Isaac was weaned Abraham held a great feast. But Sarah saw that the son whom Hagar the Egyptian had borne to Abraham was mocking, and she said to Abraham, 'Get rid of that slave woman and her son, for that woman's son will never share in the inheritance with my son Isaac.' The matter distressed Abraham greatly because it concerned his son. But God said to him, 'Do not be so distressed about the boy and your slave woman. Listen to whatever Sarah tells you, because it is through Isaac that your offspring will be reckoned. I will make the son of the slave into a nation also, because he is your offspring'" (Gen. 21:8–13 NIV).

The second born (Isaac) was the son of the promise, but the firstborn (Ishmael) was made into a great nation—he had twelve tribes that became the Arab nation. Isaac had twin sons, Esau and Jacob, and once again the second born (Jacob) was the favored one. He also had twelve sons, and this became the twelve tribes of Israel. The Arab-Israeli conflict of today goes all the way back to Genesis and these tribes! God has a most interesting and intricate plan, for sure!

Esau and Jacob. I can't help but tell a bit about the sons of Isaac, Esau and Jacob. They were twins, but Esau was born first and Jacob "grabbed his heel." Later, with the help of his mom (Rebekah), he would steal his brother's birthright and deceive his father into giving him the blessing normally bestowed on the firstborn. Yet God chose this deceiver to be the head of the tribe of Israel. Jacob fell in love with a gal named Rachel, but his father-in-law (Laban) tricked him on the wedding night and gave him the firstborn (Leah) as a wife. After seven days with Leah, he was also given Rachel as a wife, if he worked seven more years for his father-in-law. Once again, the second born was favored, this time by her new husband. Deceivers all!

These two women fought over giving Jacob children. Leah had six sons—whose descendants became some of the twelve tribes of Israel. She also had a daughter, Dinah. She also gave her maidservant, Ziplah, to her husband, and she bore two sons. When Rachel failed to have children, Rachel gave her maidservant, Bilhah, to Jacob as a concubine to bear his children. Bilhah gave birth to two sons, whom Rachel claimed as her own. Eventually, God opened Rachel's womb and she bore two sons, Joseph and Benjamin. Because Rachel was Jacob's favorite, so was her firstborn son, Joseph, even though he was number 11 of twelve sons! Joseph was not second born, but he was the favorite son, and this story is told in the last third of the book of Genesis. Yes, over 30 percent of the book was dedicated to this favorite son! (More later.)

Joseph versus His Eleven Brothers. I have to tell you about this "favorite son" of Jacob because his father gave him a "coat of many colors." When I went to see *Joseph and the Amazing Technicolor Dreamcoat,* I heard someone say, "That was one of my favorite Bible stories." "What?" I asked. "This is from the Bible?" Since I was my dad's favorite child (second born), I was despised by many of my siblings, especially my older brother, Paul. Joseph ended up being sold into Egyptian slavery by his jealous brothers, but through the providence of God, he became prime minister of Egypt and had many dreams, including one about seven years of good crops followed by seven years of famine. He had storehouses built during the first seven years, so Egypt ended up "feeding the world" during those second seven years. This included his brothers coming to Egypt to buy grain from him.

When they eventually found out that this guy was their brother, they were afraid of his retaliation. But Joseph forgave them. "You intended to harm me, but God intended it for good to accomplish what is now being done, the saving of many lives" (Gen. 50:20 NIV). This was *my* story. So being the "favored one" can be used in a mighty way by God! What a blessing to know the true Bible stories—God's ways don't always make sense, but His ways are the best.

Being second born and the favored one was not easy for me. But like Joseph, I was rather "clueless" about the favoritism and how it affected my relationship with my siblings. Joseph would tell his brothers about his dreams, including one where they would bow down to him. His dad said, "You better stop sharing such things." When I graduated from high school as one of four valedictorians in our class, my dad said he could pay something toward my college education ($100/month) or buy me a new car. I chose the $100/month for spending money to go with my full college scholarship. When I graduated from college, again first in my class, my dad went out and bought me that new car! What? Talk about sibling jealousy! I was so naive, a real Goody Two-Shoes (GTS), and I often had my antennae down and did not pick up clues all around me. Gratefully, my first job out of college with the CDC did not require a car (I was on a full travel per diem), so I guess my brothers and sisters got to use that car, for a while.

Many years later in life, I would "pay the price" for once again being the "favored one" in a work situation (Scottsdale), but again, as a Goody Two-Shoes, I did not know what was going on around me. It took a visit from a friend from California to say, as she joined me at work one day, "Boy, those folks really despise you!" The nursing director at that hospital also would call and ask if I was okay when she would see the glares at monthly staff meetings. What? I did feel "disconnected" from most of the folks around me at work but never knew I was falling deep into depression and loneliness and despair. Again, God showed me many years later how the two experiences were tied together, and I had held it all in (more later). The biggest lesson I learned was to never treat anyone as a "favorite," because horrible consequences can result. Yes, being second born or being the favorite or both can be quite a challenge.

I have to note that Bill was also second born, and he was favored by his mom. Ironically, it was because he was the child with a handicap (polio), so she always loved and protected him. Bill would say he was closer to his dad (whom I never met), but try being the daughter-in-law to one who thinks her son is perfect. It is not easy. I also had a handicapped brother, Michael, who had mental retardation. He would become my mom's favorite for the same reason, because she was protecting him. In both cases, siblings understood. It was a *different* kind of favorite child. It is funny how God works things out.

Books and the Bible

When I was a senior in high school, I was nominated for three awards by my classmates: (1) most likely to succeed, (2) hardest worker, and (3) most literate. I had to refuse the third one since I never read a book for fun until I was out of college. There were no books or bookshelves in our home. The only books I read were textbooks and some novels for school, and I did very well at that. I often was "teacher's favorite" and asked more questions than most everyone else. Again, my brothers and sisters got to hear, "You are Kathy's brother or sister. She was our favorite." (Ugh!) Many years later, I would hear about childhoods where people had a Bible from an early age and they knew every story there was. Now that would have been nice!

Once I was out of college, as I traveled with my CDC team, there were women who ordered room service and stayed in their room to read a book. Really? I wanted to explore and go out! I did start reading John Grisham novels, probably because they contained stories of adventure and romance. I did learn a lot from traveling to places—these adventures became my "books about the world." When I saw my brothers and sisters having families and reading to their children at night, I was pleasantly surprised. Where did they learn that? Not in our family while growing up! If you have never read the book or seen the movie *The Book Thief,* I highly recommend it. It is a historical novel by Australian author Markus Zusak and is his most popular work (Wikipedia). Set in World War II (when Hitter banned books), it was about a little girl who loved to read and had to steal books to read. Historical novels are my favorite kinds of books now. I love learning through reading. This young lady went on to be a great reader and writer.

The most important book ever written is the Bible. As Catholics, we never studied the Bible but did hear selected verses from the Old and New Testament in every Mass. The only Bible we had in our home was a large family Bible. It was kept in a closet and only taken out to record births or deaths. Many years later, I would inherit this Bible. As I began doing Bible studies, I learned that the standard Bible has sixty-six chapters (thirty-nine in the Old Testament and twenty-seven in the New Testament), but the Catholic Bible has extra chapters. What? Even the Bible was different for Catholics than for other faiths.

What books are unique to the Catholic Bible (Wikipedia)?

- Tobit
- Judith
- Baruch includes the Letter of Jeremiah as the sixth chapter or standalone book

- Sirach
- 1 Maccabees
- 2 Maccabees
- Wisdom of Solomon
- Additions to Esther

Wow. The church of Rome even added chapters to the basic Bible used by all other Christian faiths. The first church established by the apostles was called the Catholic Church because that term means universal, and it became a big organization led by the pope, who is considered the vicar of Christ. They believe Peter was the first head of the church. Through the years, the pope and his leaders would add things to the original Written Word of God and then "interpret" them for the laity since they believed only ordained priests could understand the complicated Bible. They teach that one has to go through a priest to reach God. How sad. When Jesus died on the cross, the temple curtain was torn in half from top to bottom, which meant that Jesus was now our way to connect directly with God. The era of priests offering sacrifices had ended. We can go to Jesus directly to know God.

I first visited the Vatican in Rome in 1976 during my twelve-country trip through Europe. I found the artwork to be amazing, especially the ceiling of the Sistine Chapel, done by Michelangelo. At that time, the colors of this ceiling were dull due to the smoke from the candles used inside this church. Twenty years later (1996), I made a trip to the Holy Land as part of a group led by our pastor, and we began and ended our journey in Rome. I was now more enlightened from the Bible. When we toured the Vatican, I noticed how much brighter the ceiling was—it had been cleaned. I had been enlightened,

I also noticed a statue of Saint Peter outside the church holding keys in his hands. Our pastor directed us to this passage in the Bible:

> "But what about you?" he asked. "Who do you say I am?" Simon Peter answered, "You are the Messiah, the Son of the living God." Jesus replied,

"Blessed are you, Simon son of Jonah, for this was not revealed to you by flesh and blood, but by my Father in heaven. And I tell you that you are Peter, and on this rock I will build my church, and the gates of Hades will not overcome it. I will give you the keys of the kingdom of heaven; whatever you bind on earth will be bound in heaven, and whatever you lose on earth will be loosed in heaven." (Matt. 16: 15–19)

Our pastor said this was one of the primary verses upon which the Catholic Church had been built, making Peter the vicar of Christ on earth. The first pope.

He then explained that the early church took this verse out of context. By going back to verses 15–17, you get the full meaning of what Jesus meant:

"But what about you?" he asked. "Who do you say I am?" Simon Peter answered, "You are the Messiah, the Son of the living God." Jesus replied, "Blessed are you, Simon son of Jonah, for this was not revealed to you by flesh and blood, but by my Father in heaven." (Matt. 16:15–17 NIV)

It was on this truth that Jesus started his church on earth, Christ followers, first called the Way, and later called Christians (not Peter followers). Not many Catholics know this history. I am glad I have had the chance to have my own Bible and study it now for years. I pray that many of my brothers and sisters will come to know the complete truth of His Word.

I have to add one more paragraph about a book that enlightened me about the difference between the Christian faith and the Muslim faith. It is called *Seeking Allah, Finding Jesus*, written by an American Muslim physician named Nabeel Qureshi. We studied this book in an adult Bible study. Muslims base their faith on a book called the Quran. Dr. Qureshi wrote his book to tear down walls, by giving non-Muslim readers an insider's perspective into a Muslim's heart and mind. It also helps equip a reader with facts and knowledge, the strength of the case for the gospel contrasted with the case for Islam. Finally, it portrays the immense inner struggle of Muslims grappling with the gospel, including sacrifices and doubts. Since one of the biggest struggles in our world is about Islam versus all other religions, it is good to read this book. Their beloved prophet, Muhammad, said, "If you are not with us, you are against us. Kill the infidels!" Yet many Muslims think of their religion as one of peace. Oh, the power of the *truth* and the power of which book we read and follow in our lives!

I had to note two book series I have read and highly recommend. The first is the Left Behind books, which were first published the year we got married, 1995:

1. *Left Behind* (1995)
2. *Tribulation Force* (1996)
3. *Soul Harvest* (1998)
4. *Apollyon* (1999)
5. *The Indwelling* (2000)
6. *The Mark* (2000)
7. *Desecration* (2001)
8. *The Remnant* (2002)
9. *Armageddon* (2003)
10. *Left Behind: A Graphic Novel* (2003)
11. *Left Behind: Graphic Novel 2* (2004)
12. *Glorious Appearing* (2004)
13. *The Rising* (2005)
14. *The Regime* (2005)
15. *The Rapture* (2006)
16. *Kingdom Come* (2007)

This is a series of sixteen best-selling religious novels by Tim LaHaye and Jerry B. Jenkins, dealing with Christian end-times: the pretribulation, premillennial Christian interpretation of the biblical apocalypse. Even though these are novels (fiction), they do contain a lot of reference to Scripture, so they make for a very interesting read. My biggest takeaway was, you could be "left behind" at the time of the rapture even though you said you were a Christian. Such was the case for the pastor in the very first book.

The other is the Killing series by Bill O'Reilly and Martin Dugard. These are history stories that are very well researched, with stories very well told. You will love them!

1. *Killing Lincoln* (2011)
2. *Killing Kennedy* (2012)
3. *Killing Jesus* (2013)
4. *Killing Patton* (2014)
5. *Killing Reagan* (2015)
6. *Killing the Rising Sun* (2016)
7. *Killing England* (2017)
8. *Killing the SS* (2018)

Books can teach you a lot and give you insight. I like that.

Of course, the most important book of all is the Book of Life. That is the book that we all want our names written in; it contains the names of those who belong to the Lord Jesus. According to Revelation 20:11–15 (ESV), "Then I saw a great white throne and him who was seated on it. From his presence earth and sky fled away, and no place was found for them. And I saw the dead, great and small, standing before the throne, and books were opened. Then another book was opened, which is the book of life. And the dead were judged by what was written in the books, according to what they had done. And the sea gave up the dead who were in it, Death and Hades gave up the dead who were in them, and they were judged, each one of them, according to what they had done. Then Death and Hades were thrown into the lake of fire. This is the second death, the lake of fire. And if anyone's name was not found written in the book of life, he was thrown into the lake of fire."

This is the one book in which you want to see your name!

Brian (British Boyfriend and Doctor)

Falling in love is so much fun, especially at age seventeen! Such was my relationship with Brian. What does this name mean? Brian (sometimes spelled Bryan in English) is a male given name of Irish and Breton origin, as well as a surname of Occitan origin. It is common in the English-speaking world. It is possible that the name is derived from an Old Celtic word meaning "high" or "noble" (Wikipedia). So Brian was my "noble love"—such a gentleman that when we played golf together, he would even carry my clubs (my brothers could not believe it!).

We met while attending a high school (Catholic) retreat. I met Brian, a foreign exchange student from the neighboring high school. Handsome, intelligent, well-mannered. And such a sweet accent! We only spent three months together before he flew home to Rhodesia (1971). His American family was a doctor that my mom worked with, and they all knew we were falling for each other. So much happened so fast!

We started writing "love letters" for the next five years. Everyone should have such an experience! I still have all those letters he sent to me. Having someone out there really helped me get through four years at a Benedictine Catholic College with 80 percent females! As I said earlier, I got to reunite with Brian the summer after college as the first and last stop on my European adventure. I can still remember the flowers he left at the hotel where our group was staying. "Welcome to London! Please rest and refresh yourself, and then we can get together." Which was what we did for the next week!

He showed me around London, and we had such fun together. I did stay with him, but "no hanky-panky," since we were both good Catholics saving ourselves for marriage. I learned a lot about English history during those days, including much about King Henry VIII. We even saw a play where the men were naked. *Equus* is a drama play by Peter Shaffer written in 1973 telling the story of a psychiatrist who attempts to treat a young man who has a pathological religious fascination with horses. Shaffer was inspired to write *Equus* when he heard of a crime involving a seventeen-year-old who blinded six horses in a small town in Suffolk (Wikipedia). I was shocked, so naive, but my world was expanding! To this day, I love all things British! The main building at the college I attended was called Tower Hall. It looks just like Westminster Abbey.

During our eleven weeks apart as I traveled through Europe with a group of other students from across the USA, I learned how special it was to be American. It was the bicentennial year (1976), and we spent July 4 in Italy, where we taught our waiters American patriotic songs! I got to climb mountains, jump in the Trevi Fountain, get a special gondola ride from an Italian who liked this American blonde, take a motorcycle ride around Athens at night, and skinny-dip in the Greek islands! Let's just say it was the first time I got to "let my hair down" and had an amazing summer! Among the small group of friends I hung out with, I met Steve from Atlanta, a Georgia Tech football player. Again a very handsome, sweet guy. We would get to rendezvous again during CDC days (another story).

We were in groups that summer, and the group behind us had a young lady who wanted to go home one week early, so I gave my ticket to her and got to stay one more week in England—fun! I joined Brian on the south coast of Great Britain, where he was doing a medical internship with a friend named David. We were the three musketeers and did many fun things together when they got off work. I stayed in a B&B and found it so charming. But when I told them of my adventures in Europe, they scoffed at my "annoying American behavior." Brian said one year in America was enough; he would never move there because we were a country that had so many of the world's resources and were quite spoiled. So my love for him cooled down, and I went back home to the land I loved, America.

I had "fallen out of love" with Brian, but I am not sure he ever fell out of love with me—not at first. As God would have it, he had an older brother (Paul) who was marrying a gal from Santa Barbara, the very place where I was living! I got to meet them when they came to explore the possibility of living in America. Brian sent a gift with them, and they were so kind. Paul and Berta decided to move to Northern Ireland. I think Brian thought I would make such a "right choice," but I never did. I started dating a guy in Santa Barbara

43

(Gary), again handsome and very intelligent, who proposed marriage one year into our relationship, and we got married one year later (1979), living in one of the most beautiful places on earth, Santa Barbara. That marriage fell apart (1983) the very year Brian married one of his fellow medical students (Janet). God's timing is so interesting.

By 1986 (ten years after my European adventure), I got to return for a three-week trip to England, Scotland, and Ireland, and I stayed with Brian and Janet in the northern part of England, near the Lake District. We had great fun together! We all became good friends, and I got to finally meet Brian's mom and dad, who lived nearby. I remember the night Brian took me to dinner at their home. They got to meet "the one who got away," the one they had heard about all these years. It became a sweet relationship. I felt like I was part of the family. Ironically, a few days after my arrival, that other medical school friend who I met in southern England (David) showed up for a visit, and as I opened the door, he exclaimed, "What? Your old flame?" I had to chuckle since I was now returning as a "dear friend." I dated several men in those years after my divorce, and several would say, "I am too attracted to you to just be friends." Somehow, Brian and I managed to do it, and I even got to be the godmother to one of their twin girls (Fiona) in 1993—so I did become part of the extended family.

When I got engaged to be married to Bill in 1994, we invited Brian and Janet and family to come to the wedding (February 1995), and they all came, including two young boys and twin girls under the age of two! It was such a delight for me. As God would have it, one of Bill's best friends from Promise Keepers (John) was also raised in Rhodesia, and we got to sit him at the table with Brian and Janet and family. How sweet is that! It was Brian and Janet who told me one of their favorite places in the world was New Zealand (where she had a sister living), so that was my choice for a honeymoon. One of the first things we did when getting there was to visit John's parents, who had fled Rhodesia to South Africa, then New Zealand, when all the apartheid began. They were also delighted to meet us! So two guys raised in Rhodesia ended up having families that accepted both of us. God is so good!

After we adopted two sons from foster care—one at age three in 1997 (James), and one at age four in 2000 (Josiah)—we took our young sons on several trips to England, and they got to play with Brian and Janet's children. We took long walks across the Lake District and had a dear time. I was given the honor to be one of the twins' (Fiona's) godmother. Many years later (2009), Janet died of breast cancer, and I was able to fly back to England to spend some time with Brian and his children. I know my brothers and sisters thought that was "an old love rekindled" (bad), but nothing could be further from the truth. We had a sweet time, and I got to know the children even better. Ten years later (2019), Brian found a new love, named Dolly, and we can't wait to meet her when we hope to go visit, hopefully in 2021.

So Brian will always have a special place in my heart. He raised his children in the Catholic Church (Janet had no particular faith), and if we had ever married, we would have done the same. I think it was God's choice that I would leave the Catholic Church and find an evangelical faith and get to study the Bible. I smile because the Catholic-versus-Protestant struggle in England had huge historic significance. Brian's mom was a Protestant, and his dad was a Catholic. When she found out Bill was also a Protestant, we all had a good laugh together. Brian's parents drove Bill and me to Edinburgh one day, and we had a tea party along the way. Such sweet memories! To this day, I look at the broach she gave me (her family crest), and I smile. A part of my wonderful life, friendship with the noble one, Brian. Thank you, dear Brian. You will always have a special place in my heart.

One final note about England and its religious struggles. King Henry VIII was a devout Catholic and loved his first wife (Catherine), a marriage that lasted twenty-five years. Since having a male heir is so important to royalty and she could not give him a son, he wanted to get an annulment for their marriage. (Note: she did give him a daughter, named Mary, who did become a queen in England.) He chose to divorce her and marry another woman (Anne Boleyn) in order to have a male child. (Note: she also gave him a daughter, the first Elizabeth, who would become queen.) The Roman Catholic

Church did not believe in divorce, so they would not grant him his wish. So he started his own church, the Church of England, also called the Anglican Church, where the king was head of both church and state. Yes, we all know Henry went on to have many wives, often killing those who could not give him a male heir. Once he finally got a son (from Jane Seymour, who died in childbirth), he accomplished his goal, but this young man (Edward VI) was a very weak king and was only on the throne for a few years. The English Rhyme about King Henry and his wives: divorced, beheaded, died, divorced, beheaded, survived.

This is not to be confused with a song that came out in 1965 by Herman's Hermits called "I'm Henry VIII, I Am." My brother Michael loves to sing these lyrics:

I'm Henry VIII I am
Henry VIII I am, I am
I got married to the widow next door
She's been married seven times before
And every one was a Henry (Henry)
She wouldn't have a Willy or a Sam (no Sam)
I'm her eighth old man, I'm Henry
Henry VIII I am
(Second verse same as the first)

How's that for some fun sixties music from England!

The Anglican Church is "Catholic light." We have attended such services in the London area, which very much resemble the Catholic Mass—just no affiliation with the church in Rome. We also love visiting the large cathedrals, such as Westminster Abbey and Saint Paul's Cathedral, so historic and beautiful. The war between the Catholic Church and the Anglican Church in Great Britain caused much bloodshed, including the split of Northern Ireland from the rest of Ireland (hence the Irish Republican Army, IRA). Brian has a brother who lives in Northern Ireland as a doctor married to an American gal—so interesting!

It is also fun to note that the Puritans were called dissenters and also called separatists, and they left England to start a new country (America), where the first order of business was freedom of religion. They left for America to escape religious persecution and have an opportunity for them and their children in a new land and to evangelize the native peoples. That is now part of the First Amendment of the Constitution of the United States. Scotland had very fierce Catholics who fought for the crown. Ironically, the Presbyterian Church was founded in Scotland and continues to be a very strong, conservative Protestant church. This church was started by John Calvin in Geneva. It was the first Protestant church started in Scotland under John Knox, who fought against the Roman Catholic queen Mary, queen of Scots.

So I have gone from being one of those devout Catholics to being a Presbyterian. How I love history! My life just seems to be wrapped up in this eternal conflict. Brian, my noble British suitor, and the churches that once connected us now are split, just like England. One final irony: Bill and I love British shows on TV—serials like *Downton Abbey*, *Poldark*, *Reign*, and *The Queen*, just to name a few. So when we watch these shows, we brew a pot of tea and enjoy our time watching these shows we find superior to anything made in America. Sometimes we even toast Brian! So, Brian, you are right about one thing better in England than America: the television shows and movies! God bless you, dear friend.

CHAPTER C

California

The places that we live can really affect our lives in more ways than we ever imagined. Such was my time living in California for twenty-six years. California—in his popular novel *Las sergas de Esplandián*, published in 1510, writer Garci Ordóñez de Montalvo named an imaginary realm California. The state name also relates to the English word *florid*, an adjective meaning "strikingly beautiful," from Latin *floridus* (Expedia). Yes, California is a beautiful state. The golden state economy would make it the seventh largest country in the world! It is big and diverse and has the highest population of any state. Sadly, the large cities of Los Angeles and San Francisco make the state politically left-progressive, which has tarnished the state a lot. When the whole state becomes a sanctuary state, laws are ignored, criminals are set free, and everyone gets "free stuff" regardless of being a citizen, it changes everything.

Although my introduction to this state came through my temporary CDC job in Los Angeles, the first place I lived was Santa Barbara. Now that is a place of striking beauty! As I said in my introduction, I stumbled upon a job there through the *LA Times* and moved there in the summer of 1977. I was amazed to learn that much of the state was settled by Father Junipero Serra, a Franciscan priest. Saint Junipero Serra was a Roman Catholic Spanish priest and friar of the Franciscan Order who founded a mission in Baja California and the first nine of twenty-one Spanish missions in

California from San Diego to San Francisco, in what was then Alta California in the Province of Las Californias, New Spain (Wikipedia).

So many of the large beautiful coastal cities are named as saints: San Diego, Santa Monica, Santa Barbara, etc. I knew the Franciscan order well since I served on the board of directors for the Franciscan Renewal Center in Scottsdale and then at the retreat center in Malibu, California. Ironically, two of my best friends in Santa Barbara were married at the mission in Santa Barbara, and one of those Franciscan priests (Gino) did a reading and final prayer at our wedding. The other irony is that this order with a vow of poverty owns some of the most valuable land in the state! I know they have been approached to "sell" (for quite a profit), but most have said no—they chose to offer a place of retreat.

In the church where we met (Calvary Community, Westlake Village), our pastor used to say the two books of the Bible, 1 and 2 Corinthians, could be named 1 and 2 Californians! So what was Corinth like in the Bible? When Paul arrived in 51 CE, the Corinth he saw was little more than one hundred years old but was five times as large as Athens and the capital of the province. Ancient Corinth, the original Corinth, founded in the tenth Century BCE, had been the richest port and the largest city in ancient Greece (Wikipedia). The Corinthians' life theme could be summarized as "eat, drink, and be merry and do whatever you want!" The place was full of moral corruption. Sounds like Los Angeles and San Francisco? No more to be said.

In the fall of 1991, I purchased a Chrysler convertible and learned to drive "with my top down." Everyone should have such an experience! There is nothing like taking in the sights and sounds as you drive along the coast of California, but one has to beware of sudden changes in weather, such as hail—yes, I got hit with my top down the first week I owned my car! This experience made me appreciate being aware of all that is around you; it made me a better driver and a better human being. Once married, with two golden retrievers and boys, we even entered a couple parades with both dogs in the back seat and our young son in the middle. They never even thought to jump out—they just loved it. Oh, to be a dog, with the wind blowing in your face! We traded in that vehicle for a minivan and have now owned three of them, to be able to bring dogs, kids, and others on outings or for family trips. My hope is to once again buy a convertible. It brings one closer to the glory of nature all around. I think God invented convertibles!

If you move away from California, as we did in the summer of 2006, people will say, "Do you miss it? What to do you miss?" I laugh when I hear folks say, "I miss the beaches." The majority of long-term California residents I know never go to the beach! We found a dog-friendly beach in Summerland, California, and loved to go there with them and our boys, so we do miss that. We miss friends and family but try to go back regularly, at which time we create "mini reunions" for folks to gather together. Who wouldn't miss the mild weather? We must say that the four seasons of Colorado are much more to our liking. Even my California-born-and-raised spouse enjoys our winters here! A covering of soft white snow can be quite peaceful. We sure don't miss the earthquakes, including the one that hit in January 1994 just thirty miles from where I lived—the Northridge earthquake. The aftershocks were just as scary as the first quake.

We lived all our married life in Ventura County, where the number 1 industry is agriculture. We do miss all the fresh fruits and vegetables and the roadside stands, especially the fresh large flats of huge strawberries! Our friend Patrick has multiple avocado trees on his property, and we miss getting to go out and pick them at will. That goes for citrus fruit as well. We had season tickets to UCLA football at the Rose Bowl—we miss those weekend adventures. But we do go to a couple Air Force football games in the fall and sure enjoy the polite, family-friendly atmosphere (not a bunch of drunk college coeds—ha!) We loved Dodger baseball but have come to enjoy the Colorado Rockies at Coors Field and the ease of using light rail to get to/from the games. Overall, given the cost and quality of living in California today, we would never go back. But it is a place everyone should visit—quite a large and diverse state! Can't you just hear the Beach Boys singing, "I wish they all could be California girls"? I guess I was one, for a while.

Catholic Priests and the Church

I can just hear the reader saying, "What does this mean?" Good question. I grew up in the Catholic Church, and our local Saint Kevin's Catholic Church in rural northern Minnesota had the same priest for all the years I could remember. Our priest came from Yugoslavia with his parents, who had survived WWII. They all lived in the rectory together. They were very kind, humble people. When we did a building project to build a new church, I remember that every family had to make a pledge for a certain amount of money. As part of that donation, every family had their name on a pew. Ours was the front pew on the right side (facing the altar), so all nine of us (seven kids, two adults) sat there every Sunday. That was our "norm."

Growing up in the sixties and seventies, we saw a lot of change in the Catholic faith, including going from the Mass in Latin to English and the priests facing the congregation instead of the altar. My brothers were altar boys, and I was one of the first female lectors (reader of the Word). That was a big deal back then! I loved when nuns would come in the summer to teach us, a form of vacation Bible school, and I even considered becoming a nun because of my love for these dear, sweet women. I came to find out there were all kinds of religious orders and types of priests—something I never knew growing up.

I attended a Benedictine College that had just hired their first male president, a Jesuit priest from the East Coast. So what is a Benedictine? Benedictine life is based upon the gospel of Christ and is lived in witness to this good news in peace and simplicity. It strives to create surroundings permeated by Christian vision and an attitude of openness to the Spirit. Benedictine education draws its inspiration and values from the rule and monastic tradition. They follow the *Rule of Saint Benedict.* Saint Benedict's rule organizes the monastic day into regular periods of communal and private prayer, sleep, spiritual reading, and manual labor—ut in omnibus glorificetur Deus. "That in all [things] God may be glorified" (Wikipedia).

My maternal grandfather was named Benedict. Their church was Saint Benedicts. So I came to love this spiritual meaning.

So how did a Jesuit priest (versus years of Benedictine sisters) become the president of the college? It happened in 1972, as the college was becoming coed and wanted to attract more students and become more a part of the city in which it was located, Duluth. That included the first male sports team on campus—a hockey team—and I got to be a cheerleader! We were the Scholastica Saints and had a Saint Bernard as our mascot. It was great fun. But what about that Jesuit priest and his order? The Society of Jesus is a religious order of the Catholic Church headquartered in Rome. It was founded by Ignatius of Loyola with the approval of Pope Paul III in 1540. The members are called Jesuits (Wikipedia). Now that sounds pretty high and powerful!

The Jesuit order played an important role in the Counter-Reformation and eventually succeeded in converting millions around the world to Catholicism. As I studied the life of Martin Luther and the Reformation, I found this to be very interesting. By joining the Protestant faith, I had joined "the other side" that the church fought in the sixteenth century. I came to appreciate Luther (himself a Catholic priest) for opening the Bible to laypeople and let them read and study it for themselves—in many languages, not just Latin. This truly was an important part of history for me. I grew up during an "ecumenical" movement, where all faiths could come together to worship. I now know there is a difference.

Luther, a Catholic priest, taught that you could not earn your way to heaven or buy your way (indulgences), as the church was teaching, but rather you would earn salvation through "five solas."

- Sola scriptura ("by Scripture alone")
- Sola fide ("by faith alone")
- Sola gratia ("by grace alone")
- Solus Christus, or Solo Christo ("Christ alone" or "through Christ alone")
- Soli Deo Gloria ("glory to God alone")

The Roman Catholic Church, which was full of rules, had failed to teach about the importance of a *relationship with Jesus* as the key to everything (more later). This was eye-opening to me. My dad called me his "dutiful daughter." I was good at following rules. No one taught us about the importance of relationships with Jesus. I have heard it said that following rules will not change your heart. One has to remember that the early church was full of Jewish folks who chose to follow Jesus. They still had many Jewish traditions that some wanted to include in this new faith. The apostle Paul chastised Peter for doing this. "When I saw that they were not acting in line with the truth of the gospel, I said to Cephas in front of them all, 'You are a Jew, yet you live like a Gentile and not like a Jew. How is it, then, that you force Gentiles to follow Jewish customs?'" (Gal. 2:14 NIV). The leaders in Rome became much like the Pharisees of old, forcing customs on followers. Jesus did not teach this.

When I moved to California, I discovered that most priests were diocesan priests, trained by the diocese in which we lived. I lived in the diocese of Los Angeles, and our local parish priest in Ventura was a personable young guy who loved to surf! When I went through my divorce in 1984, he helped me with my annulment. An *annulment* is a legal procedure that cancels a marriage. Annulling a marriage is as though it is completely erased, legally, and it declares that the marriage never technically existed and was never valid. Mine was based upon the infidelity of my husband. Later, I would become a part of a "divorce recovery group" in that church. One of the guys told me it was hard for Father Dennis to be around me because he was so attracted to me. What? A priest having feelings for a woman? I was shocked and naive.

Through the years, I had met many priests who became my friends, and a few former priests who also became my friends. I now wonder, Did any of them find me attractive too? I sure hope I did not cause any to want to break their vows or for me to break their heart.

It is the strangest requirement of the faith to me for priests to be celibate. *Celibacy* is the state of voluntarily being unmarried, sexually abstinent, or both, usually for religious reasons. Mostly used in terms of abstaining from sexual relations. It is often in association with the role of a religious official or devotee (Wikipedia). Where did this come from? It is certainly thought that the first pope (Saint Peter) was married since he had a mother-in-law (Luke 4:38). So it did not go back to the early church. I later read that the Roman Catholic Church added this requirement for financial reasons. If a man joined the priesthood and he died, all his family inheritance would go to the church. Now that is interesting. I do know the endowment at our college is greatly helped by nuns who die and leave all they have to the college. So perhaps it is true. It is most certainly true that the Roman Catholic Church is one of the richest organizations in the world! I do hope the rule gets changed someday.

So yes, the Catholic Church and many priests had a great influence on me. One final note about our college chaplain, Father Whit. He called me Botticelli'. What did that mean? He thought I looked like a portrait done by an Italian painter from the early Renaissance named Botticelli. During my twelve-week summer tour of Europe, I visited Florence, Italy, and saw some of those Botticelli paintings. It made me feel very special. Another priest attracted to me? I guess I will never know. But I visited him on many trips to Minnesota, and he remained my friend until his death. Picnics on the north shore of Lake Superior. Precious.

One final note about the priesthood. In the book of Hebrews, Jesus is called "our great high priest."

> Therefore, since we have a great high priest who has ascended into heaven, Jesus the Son of God, let us hold firmly to the faith we profess. For we do not have a high priest who is unable to empathize with our weaknesses, but we have one who has been tempted in every way, just as we are— yet he did not sin. Let us then approach God's throne of grace with confidence, so that we may receive mercy and find grace to help us in our time of need. (Heb. 4:14–16 NIV)

In the Old Testaments, priests were selected by God. The priesthood of ancient Israel was the class of male individuals who, according to the Hebrew Bible, were patrilineal descendants from Aaron (the elder brother of Moses), who served in the tabernacle, Solomon's Temple and Second Temple, until the destruction of Jerusalem in 70 CE (Wikipedia). We no longer need priests to offer sacrifices for us since Jesus offered the final total sacrifice, himself, by dying on the cross. We don't have to go to a priest to reach God. We can directly go to Jesus, who then will advocate with God on our behalf.

> My dear children, I write this to you so that you will not sin. But if anybody does sin, we have an advocate with the Father—Jesus Christ, the Righteous One. (1 John 2:1 NIV)

Jesus also said he had to leave earth (his ascension) so he could send a "helper/advocate."

> And I will ask the Father, and he will give you another advocate to help you and be with you forever—the Spirit of truth. The world cannot accept him, because it neither sees him nor knows him. But you know him, for he lives with you and will be in you. (John 14:16–17 NIV)

Martin Luther understood that the role of a priest was really to be a pastor-teacher and not one that was needed to advocate to God on our behalf. Although I respect Catholic priests as "pastors," I do not think they really fulfill the role of a "priest" in biblical terms. I hope and pray that other Catholics will come to understand this significant difference. We have one high priest named Jesus, and we can approach Him directly in prayer. How special is that?

Churches and Their Impact

As you may have guessed, I have belonged to several churches since my 1990 departure from the Catholic Church and my awakening to read and study the Bible. Each has had a different influence on my life. I have been part of a nondenominal Community Church, a Brethren Church, a Grace Chapel, a Baptist Church that renamed itself a Community Church but held many Baptist concepts, a Calvary Chapel, and now a Presbyterian Church. I have to reflect on how each church has influenced my life. I have also made friends across many Christian faiths, and I am so grateful for all I have learned. I think Jesus would weep at all the *denominations* that have been formed as Christian Churches. He wanted us all united. It says in 1 Corinthians 12:13 (NIV), "For we were all baptized by one Spirit so as to form one body—whether Jews or Gentiles, slave or free— and we were all given the one Spirit to drink."

The Catholic Church

This church taught me the value of having a "family faith" and attending church on the Sabbath Day, Sunday. We learned that we had to repent of our sins (confession), and the importance of receiving communion. The odd thing that I learned much later was that this "consecration" of the body and blood of Christ (host and wine) was unique to the church. It is called transubstantiation—actually turning bread and wine into the body and blood of Christ. Clearly, at the last supper, Jesus taught His disciples to break bread "in remembrance of [Him]."

> For I received from the Lord what I also passed on to you: The Lord Jesus, on the night he was betrayed, took bread, and when he had given thanks, he broke it and said, "This is my body, which is for you; do this in remembrance of me." In the same way, after supper he took the cup, saying, "This cup is the new covenant in my blood; do this, whenever you drink it, in remembrance of me." For whenever you eat this bread and drink this cup, you proclaim the Lord's death until he comes. So then, whoever eats the bread

or drinks the cup of the Lord in an unworthy
manner will be guilty of sinning against the body
and blood of the Lord. (1 Cor. 11:23–27 NIV)

I never really thought much about this meaning for Holy
Communion. After all, it was just part of one of the seven sacraments
for which we were *obliged* to honor. I believe the whole turning of
bread and wine into the body and blood of Christ was misinterpreted
by the early church.

The seven sacraments include the following:

1. *Baptism.* We were baptized as infants and sprinkled with
holy water, we had sponsors that promised to raise us as
Catholics if the parents died, and verbiage includes "We
renounce Satan and all his evil ways." Rarely is Satan mentioned after that from the pulpit in Catholic churches. This
sacrament was one of two that Jesus actually asked His disciples to follow. "Therefore go and make disciples of all
nations, baptizing them in the name of the Father and of
the Son and of the Holy Spirit" (Matt. 28:19 NIV). These
were among Jesus's final words before ascending to heaven.

2. *Eucharist.* This is Holy Communion. We made our first
Holy Communion around age seven and, after studying
the catechism, were allowed to take communion. It was
included in every Mass as an important sacrament to participate in if you had first confessed your sins and repented
of them. The words spoken by anyone receiving communion is, "Lord, I am not worthy that You should enter
under my roof, but only say the word and my soul shall be
healed." I once heard a Catholic priest tell all members of a
wedding party that unless they came to him with their confession, they could not receive communion during the
wedding Mass. Really? Clearly, different priests have different interpretations of this. Jesus also commanded His disciples to "do this in remembrance of [Him]." In the
Protestant Church, it is usually only done about once a

58

month, not at every church service. I think this sets apart Holy Communion as something special. It includes bread and grape juice (not wine, since that is not allowed). I think Jesus liked wine, so I will just say the celebration of communion with fellow believers is very special and important.

3. *Confirmation.* This sacrament was done around age twelve. We were then mature enough to confirm our Catholic faith. We also had a confirmation sponsor. I think this sacrament is like baptism in the Protestant Church, an adult declaration that you have accepted Jesus as your savior. You have made a "choice to follow Jesus." There is no mention of confirmation in the Bible, but clearly, there is a lot to say about not being ashamed of your faith—you need to boldly proclaim you are a Christ follower.

4. *Reconciliation.* This was known as going to "confession"; you had to go to a priest to recite your sins and be given absolution after saying some Hail Marys and Our Fathers; it was a pretty rote exercise for most of us. Confession of sins is, however, important.

5. *Anointing of the sick.* This is done when someone is very ill and near death—to anoint them with holy oil and ask forgiveness from any sins so they can go to heaven.

6. *Marriage.* This is the sacrament uniting one man and one woman in a bond for life. It is performed by a priest. One must promise to raise their children in the Catholic faith, especially if one spouse is not a Catholic. If one member of this union is unfaithful, you can apply for an annulment (more later).

7. *Holy orders.* This is the sacrament by which a man is ordained as a priest; he takes a vow of celibacy and is, in effect, "married to the church."

So these became the basic sacraments of our faith that we were obliged to follow. We never talked about the Bible or studying the Bible; we just followed the faith of our family. We never thought of things like our free will while following Jesus. Most Catholics believe people are basically good and will go to heaven. Clearly, the Bible teaches that we are all born in sin and need to be "born again" with the indwelling of the Holy Spirit. People are not born "good." It is also a faith full of rules. Among them were holy days of obligation. These were days we *had* to go to church (Mass). The holy days of obligation in the Catholic Church include the following:

January 1: The Feast of Mary, the mother of God. Mary is revered in the Catholic Church, and we were taught to pray to Mary, who would then intercede with her Son (Jesus) on our behalf. Once I began to study the Bible, I learned that there is only one way to heaven: by believing in Jesus, who paid the price for all our sins, and giving our life to him. "Jesus answered, 'I am THE way and THE truth and THE life. No one comes to the Father except through me" (John 14:6 NIV). We have to go directly to Jesus to get to the Father. Praying to any saints (including Mary) will not help. Yes, praying to Mary is a big issue in the Protestant faith; it was something "made up" by the early church leaders. So are indulgences—you pay to get favors for your family who have died and need to get to heaven, sprung from purgatory. Another made-up place. These practices made Martin Luther crazy!

Once you read and study the Bible, you are told one thing, to *not* add anything to the Word of God. Such is the misinterpretation about Mary being "holy." "In a loud voice she (Elizabeth) exclaimed: 'Blessed are you among women, and blessed is the child you will bear'" (Luke 1:42 NIV). So the first part of the Hail Mary prayer is okay: "Hail Mary, full of grace, the Lord is with thee; blessed are thou amongst women and blessed is the fruit of thy womb."

The second part is not from the Bible and was added by the early church: "Holy Mary, mother of God, pray for us sinners now and at the hour of our death."

The early church created a whole system of deeming people to be "saints," and Mary was one of them. It is interesting to note that in the Acts of the Apostles, when people approached Peter to bow before him, he was quick to say, "Stand up!" No one is holy except God. This is true for Mary as well.

One final note about praying to Mary and the rosary. This is another tradition created by the Roman Church, where you say ten Hail Marys and then one Our Father. You do this five times, using a string of beads. When Catholics pray the rosary, they often say it very fast, repeating the same words over and over. In the Bible, the apostles ask Jesus to teach them how to pray. Before He gives the words to the Our Father, he tells them how *not* to pray.

> And when you pray, do not be like the hypocrites, for they love to pray standing in the synagogues and on the street corners to be seen by others. Truly I tell you, they have received their reward in full. But when you pray, go into your room, close the door and pray to your Father, who is unseen. Then your Father, who sees what is done in secret, will reward you. And when you pray, do not keep on babbling like pagans, for they think they will be heard because of their many words. Do not be like them, for your Father knows what you need before you ask him. (Matt. 6:5–8 NIV)

When I now hear the rosary, it sounds like folks "babbling on." Such prayer does not please God. We must approach Him with our own words, from our own heart, to ask His forgiveness and His guidance in our lives. One should never "hail" someone who is not holy. I don't mean to offend my Catholic family, but these prayers are not biblical.

Forty days after Easter Sunday, Ascension Thursday. The church teaches that forty days after Easter, Jesus ascended to heaven. This is very scriptural.

August 15, assumption of Mary into heaven. The church also says Mary was assumed into heaven. This is not biblical. Again, the early church created this holy day to honor Mary as one nearly equal with Jesus, who was assumed into heaven. This is very sad.

November 1, All Saints' Day. As stated earlier, the early church created a big system for declaring humans to be "saints," including those who died for their faith, the martyrs. This was another man-made tradition. Interestingly, the day before this is All Hallows' Eve (Halloween). They say the church created holy days close to Satan's holy day to offset his curse. I even remember in college, if we had a Halloween dance, we would stop at midnight to have a Mass so we did not have to get up early the next day. We were just following the rules. It is a great irony that Martin Luther tacked his thesis to the church door on Halloween.

December 8, the Feast of the Immaculate Conception. When I was growing up, we thought this meant Mary had a baby without having intercourse with a man. The actual meaning the church assigned was that Mary was born without sin. This is completely made up. From the time of the original garden of Eden, all people are born into sin, including Mary. "For all have sinned and fall short of the glory of God" (Rom. 3:23 NIV).

December 25, Christmas, the nativity of our Lord. The birth of Jesus should be celebrated by all Christians! Jesus was probably not born in December, but the early church chose this date since "light came into a dark world" and this is near the winter solstice, the darkest day of the year.

We accepted these as law and went to Mass on these six days. It was only later in life that I would unpack what each one meant in the overall Christian world. Somehow, Good Friday got taken off the list. I am not sure when or why, but the Roman Catholic Church doctrine can certainly be changed/updated by the pope and his cardinals.

One more interesting note about the Catholic Church in the Holy Land. About three hundred years after the death of Jesus, the mother of Emperor Constantine made a trip to the Holy Land and bought all the land where Jesus did his holy work. On each site a Catholic church was built so that land would never be desecrated. Such churches include the Church of the Nativity (Bethlehem) and the Church at Gethsemane (garden where Jesus spent His last night on earth), and a church in Capernaum (where Jesus lived and taught

62

with His apostles). I discovered this during our trip to the Holy Land in 1996. Gratefully, these churches were owned/operated by the Franciscan Order. These monks are very humble men. In fact, they say, outside of Jesus and His Bible, more books have been written about Saint Francis of Assisi than any other man. Interesting. (See in chapter F, more about Saint Francis).

The basic creed of the Catholic Church, the Apostles' Creed, is the foundation of the Catholic Church. It is also the creed of most Christian churches where the word *Catholic* means "universal." The basics of the first church were pure and good. Over time, the papacy became more powerful and rich, and that was when it "added on" all these traditions. I believe it became a way of maintaining power over the people. I am encouraged that many Catholic priests now allow the Bible to be studied. There is always hope for those who believe in the Lord Jesus as Savior. Lifelong learning!

Calvary Community Church

This "megachurch" in Southern California was the first non-Catholic church I attended, from 1990 to 1999. During those nine years, I began my baby steps to learn the Bible. Pastor Larry called his church "the second biggest Catholic Church" in the area since so many Catholics flocked to this church. When he preached from the Bible on Sundays, I would often feel that he was talking directly to me (a stirring in my spirit). I began my study of the Bible in this church. I joined a community group, and we met every week. It was composed of a lot of adult Christian singles. It was called White Cloud, and we also did fun events together, such as skiing and camping together— wonderful fellowship and also a place we could discuss our questions about the Word.

I got married to my husband in this church, and a year after our marriage, we joined our pastor on a trip to the Holy Land. Before our journey, we met for several months to study the history, geography, and biblical significance of each place we would be studying. This was an amazing preparation for our trip to visit the places where Jesus walked and talked. We went via Rome. At the beginning of our trip, we visited the Vatican, and my view of Saint Peter's Cathedral and my views had changed from twenty years earlier. As the Sistine Chapel had been cleaned (now brighter), my understanding of the Bible also had brightened, and I could see where the statue of Saint Peter holding keys to the kingdom came from. Wow. Then to find out that every holy site now had a Catholic Church on it was amazing. I thank God that our pastor was never one to "bash" the Catholic Church. He just explained the source of their beliefs and traditions.

A special note about the first Bible study I took at this church, in the book of Revelation. It was taught by a lay leader, and he did have a personal agenda against the Catholic faith. He told us that the antichrist would come from the Vatican and that all Catholics would go to hell because they prayed to Mary. What? I asked about Mother Teresa. Would she also go to hell? Yes, he said, because she prayed to Mary. I knew something was wrong, so I communicated my concerns with our pastor. He made sure this man never taught another Bible class at that church. Thank goodness. I never recall the Catholic Church ever teaching about end-times issues, so this book was an interesting place to start. I am glad I was given a discerning heart. The other Catholics in our group often went home in tears. I have now studied this book three different times, and I am glad to know, in the end, Jesus defeats Satan and all his minions. Believers win.

Grace Brethren Church

Once we decided to adopt a second child from foster care, we knew we had to buy a larger home with a separate bedroom for the child. We ended up moving from the town of Moorpark to neighboring Simi Valley and decided that we needed to find a local church that offered family-friendly programs (versus the big megachurch). One such church was located very near the hospital where I worked, Grace Brethren Church. Our hospital used their parking lot during the week as needed as an overflow area. We came to find out they had a program called AWANA, Approved Workmen Are Not Ashamed, that made learning the Bible fun for young students. This came from 2 Timothy 2:15 (NIV), "Do your best to present yourself to God as one approved, a worker who does not need to be ashamed and who correctly handles the word of truth." Our boys loved Awana! They also had a K-12 Christian school and youth sports program, so the boys were in a baseball and soccer program run by the church. Bill was one of the coaches—it was a great experience for our family.

I also attended numerous women's evening Bible studies and expanded my knowledge of the Word. My favorite memory was one teacher telling us that when we got to heaven, God would be wearing an apron that said, "Fruit inspector." The evidence of our faith would be based on the fruit of our lives. We participated in a couple of family camps with this church at a boy scout camp in the Sequoias. During one such camp, the theme was "fruit of the Spirit," with nine elements to one fruit. "But the fruit of the Spirit is love, joy, peace, patience, kindness, goodness, faithfulness, gentleness and self-control. Against such things there is no law" (Gal. 5:22–23 NIV). To easily memorize this, we were taught the first three had one syllable, second three had two syllables, and final three had three syllables. This was fun! I came to envy those who grew up learning this stuff.

After Bill got the golden handshake from his employer in the fall of 2003, he started to volunteer at this church. He spent hundreds of hours working for the church that even took away from his family time. He took his uncle Don on a men's retreat with this church. I clearly remember when Uncle Don told me, "What a strange bunch of guys. All they talked about was that they could not get their wives to submit to them in all things." He said he had a strong marriage with his wife and this was not the formula they followed—they were partners. I came to see that this was one of those churches that was very male dominant to the point where the leader of women's ministry (a pastor's wife) could not even give her annual report on the altar; it had to be done by her husband. No women teachers or deacons allowed. You could not approach the pastor about anything in your marriage unless you first got your spouse's permission. They used the Matthew 18 model of discipline and would call out people from the front of the church who would not turn from their sin.

> "If your brother or sister sins, go and point out their fault, just between the two of you. If they listen to you, you have won them over. But if they will not listen, take one or two others along, so that 'every matter may be established by the testimony of two or three witnesses.' If they still refuse to listen, tell it to the church; and if they refuse to listen even to the church, treat them as you would a pagan or a tax collector" (Matt. 18:15–17 NIV).

Most people found this to be very harsh. By the time we decided to move to Colorado in the summer of 2006, I was more than happy to leave this church. We escaped.

Grace Chapel

Our friend who did a church plant in Castle Rock referred us to this church. It was also family friendly, and we enjoyed the people. I attended a class for women in the new area, and it was filled with lots of good information for me. The book used was *After the Boxes Are Unpacked: Renewing the Heart*. This is a great book I highly recommend. Among our speakers was a woman (Cheryl), who gave us an introduction to the ministry called Moms in Touch, moms who gathered once a week to pray for their kids and schools. Ironically, it was started in Southern California, and I had never heard of it. I ended up starting a group for our local elementary school in the spring of 2007 and have been involved in this ministry ever since. It is now called Moms in Prayer International. Using a simple format of ACTS—adore, confess, thanksgiving, and supplication—we pray our kids into Scripture. What a great way to learn the Bible and learn to better pray! This was the biggest gem from this church for me (more later).

After one year at this church, the pastor left. We were told by some he was going into mission's work and by others that he was asked to leave. What? There was a church split happening in our midst, something we had never experienced. We spent the next year with guest speakers every week as they did a search for a new pastor. We belonged to a community group called the Free Birds (empty nesters), and even though we had two boys in school, we were the right age to fit their group. This kept us involved, but eventually we went shopping for another church so we could have some consistency in our church home.

Creekside Bible Church (Baptist)

Again, we were referred to this church by some new friends, so we checked it out and became members. We came to find out that it was previously a Baptist Church but had changed the name to include a broader range of members. We enjoyed the pastor's teaching and the Bible studies. We also got involved in the mission's committee and children's ministry. I grew up near a small Baptist Church, and we felt sorry for our friends who attended the church. They could not listen to music or watch TV or participate in school dances. How sad was that? Our new friends in this church did not seem so rigid—perhaps there were different types of Baptists? Yes, we learned about that as well. We became involved in a community group and made some great, lifelong friends. The following true story does *not* reflect on this sweet church; it was a situation that caught us all by surprise, and no one knew what to do.

Just two years into attending this church, I volunteered to help with Vacation Bible School (VBS) and brought our younger son with me to help. He had helped with children's ministry during the year, so this seemed like a good idea. He was then accused of touching a young lady in an "inappropriate way." What? We were asked to leave the church. The accusing family was making a big fuss and had hired an attorney. So did the church. They advised us to do the same. So we did. Through our attorney, we contacted the mom's ex-husband, and he asked, "Who is she accusing of something now?" Nearly every time I gave the kids a bath, she would call protective services and tell them I was touching our children inappropriately. He indicated he filed for divorce if she would remove all the restraining orders against him. She did, and they divorced and she got remarried and moved to a new state, Colorado.

As a family, we went through everything from diversion to lie detector tests to special counseling, community service, and paying restitution. The DA overcharged our son as a "person in a position of authority," so it was a felony. Let's just say it led to many years of a long, expensive legal case where our son was finally found not guilty and the charges were expunged from his record. This was a painful process for us, but we did learn a lot about the justice system. Our attorney told us from the beginning that if a four-year-old girl makes an accusation against a fourteen-year-old boy, no jury or judge would find him not guilty. In our society, when a female accuses a male of something wrong, they are often presumed guilty instead of inno-cent. We certainly saw this in the national case of a supreme court justice trying to be confirmed and nearly ruined by lying witnesses. I often wondered if the DAs of the world were making up for all the cases not brought against the Catholic Church for pedophilia.

We did not have bad feelings for the church leadership since they were as challenged as we were. Many of the church members that we knew approached us to apologize and say the incident was not properly handled. Every parent in that VBS was interviewed, with no corroborating testimony from anyone. Through the years we have heard of others accused of such things and are able to listen with great empathy and let them know we had gone through a similar ordeal. I think Christians should be more vulnerable to share such experiences so others won't feel alone or ashamed if it happens to them. We often appear to be "perfect" on the outside, so when we do share, we open doors to healing for others. So we had to find another church. The key factor was one where our boys had friends who accepted them.

Calvary Chapel

We joined a Calvary Chapel in our local area. It was a place that had a lot of programs for kids and teens. We liked the teaching pastor, verse by verse teaching from the Bible. I came to learn more about the founding of this church. Beginning in 1965 in Southern California, this fellowship of churches grew out of Chuck Smith's Calvary Chapel Costa Mesa. Doctrinally, Calvary Chapel is evangelical and charismatic (Wikipedia). The first such churches were often attended by hippies. The leaders wore blue jeans and played guitar; they often came out of broken lives, involved in drugs and alcohol. Very interesting. We were part of this fellowship for five years.

Our best experience with this church was becoming part of the Open-Door Team that went to Denver once a month to serve a Sunday-evening meal to the homeless. The leader of the team changed several times, and we even led it for a few years. Since it was not a Calvary ministry but rather an inner-city ministry for which Calvary had a team, we continued to be part of the team for over ten years. We loved serving these folks and came to know some of them very closely. The first pastor of the Church of the Open Door was Pastor Curtis and his wife, Mavis. When he retired, we continued to be friends and supported them both in their role as prison ministry chaplains. We also have had them at our home for Thanksgiving, Christmas, and Easter dinners. Bill drives to/from Denver to get them except one Christmas snowstorm that came suddenly for which they stayed at our home overnight. We also got to know a homeless man named Kevin, and we would include him in these meals as well as an annual treat to take him to a Rockies game for his July birthday. We learned how those who have so little appreciate your love and friendship so much. Jesus had a lot to say about serving the poor.

> When the Son of Man comes in his glory, and all the angels with him, he will sit on his glorious throne. All the nations will be gathered before him, and he will separate the people one from another as a shepherd separates the sheep from

the goats. He will put the sheep on his right and
the goats on his left.

Then the King will say to those on his right,
"Come, you who are blessed by my Father; take
your inheritance, the kingdom prepared for you
since the creation of the world. For I was hungry
and you gave me something to eat, I was thirsty
and you gave me something to drink, I was a
stranger and you invited me in, I needed clothes
and you clothed me, I was sick and you looked
after me, I was in prison and you came to visit
me." (Matt. 25:31–46 NIV)

Participating in the Open-Door Ministry also helped teach our
boys the importance of sharing all the blessings He has given to us.
Planting the seeds of compassion for those in need was a precious
experience for us. I am now trying to introduce Moms in Prayer into
the women's prison, working with Mavis. I have had her talk at
Moms in Prayer state events, and she once said, "When I grow up, I
want to be like Kathy." Since I am in my sixties and she is in her
eighties, that made me laugh. We also helped with Angel Tree, where
we delivered gifts to kids whose parents were in prison/jail. During
one such visit, we encountered three boys with one mom but three
different fathers. So I told them the story of the apostle Paul, who did
much of his writing of the New Testament from jails. They smiled.
God connected all these ministries, joining the hearts of those who
serve Him.

We eventually left Calvary Chapel over some doctrinal issues
that were dear to my husband's heart. He loved to read the works of
John Calvin and follow the teaching of RC Sproul, both who believed
that we were chosen by God.

For those God foreknew he also predestined to
be conformed to the image of his Son, that he
might be the firstborn among many brothers and
sisters. 30 And those he predestined, he also

called; those he called, he also justified; those he justified, he also glorified. (Rom. 8:29–30 NIV)

Once Bill shared this sentiment at a Calvary Men's Bible study, he was called a heretic! That was pretty hard to take, so we began searching for another church. We had a local Christian friend we knew through our membership with the Larkspur Chamber of Commerce, and he brought us to a new church in town. Once again, we moved to another fellowship of believers.

Canyons Community Church (Presbyterian)

It was the fall of 2015 when we first visited Canyons Community Church. It was a church plant from a larger Presbyterian church in South Denver, and it had a small number of members. It was and is the friendliest church we ever attended! We accepted the Westminster profession of faith—it matched the teachings of a Scottish pastor we heard on the radio (Alistair Begg,) and we felt right at home. Within six months of being there, Kathy was asked to be a deacon. They even had women elders! (I had to laugh at the memory of Grace Brethren—how different this was!) Bill became involved as a leader in men's ministry and also as a deacon. We also both got to sing in the church choir and learned a lot about music. We are now in a building project and may open a new church building by the end of 2020. We have quite a few members in their seventies, eighties, and nineties, so we feel "young." We feel so blessed to be part of this body of believers. We continue to help those in need through a Good Samaritans ministry there. Who knows how God will use us, as we are now in our fifth year there?

One fun note about a certain Presbyterian elder from Houston. He was one of the first men to land on the moon, and the first thing he did was to give thanks to God. According to Fox News, Buzz Aldrin, seated next to Neil Armstrong, became the first person to celebrate a religious sacrament on a heavenly body outside Earth. The ordained Presbyterian elder wrote in a piece for *Guideposts* in

1970 he chose Holy Communion because his pastor at Webster Presbyterian, Dean Woodruff, often spoke about how God reveals Himself through the everyday elements.

"I wondered if it might be possible to take communion on the moon," Aldrin recalled a year after the mission, "symbolizing the thought that God was revealing Himself there, too, as man reached out into the universe. For there are many of us in the NASA program who do trust that what we are doing is part of God's eternal plan for man." Isn't that cool?

Having been a member of so many different and varied churches has helped us to grow as a couple and as a family. It has helped us to discern the meaning of the Bible better. We have had our share of challenges along the way, but that was also for our good. One of the fun results of having been in four different churches in our area is that whenever we are at a community event, such as the noon gathering on the National Day of Prayer, we know just about everyone at the event! We have made lifetime friends and know that the church is not about any building or denomination but rather the people who love and serve the Lord Jesus. We are His church. I have to say a few words about other churches I have experienced secondhand.

The Church of Jesus Christ of the Latter-Day Saints (Mormons)

No, I never joined a Mormon church, but since we had extended family who lived in Salt Lake City and we went to see the great Mormon Temple there several times, we became familiar with this church. Our eldest son had a birth brother (Paul) whose family moved to the Salt Lake City area around 1998 as a Christian family surrounded by Mormon families. They told us that the Mormons did not accept federal or state funds to run the public schools—the Mormon church gave the primary support. As such, they could use the last hour of each day as "mission preparation time" since all their seniors were expected to go on a mission trip upon their graduation from high school.

Both our boys had friends who were Mormon with an LDS church near every high school in our town. When they attended Job Corps in an area just north of Salt Lake City, they came to have more LDS friends and learned more about this religion. It was interesting to note that the young people from America were sent on missions overseas, and it was the overseas youth who came to America as evangelists, including working at the Mormon Temple. To visit the temple and listen to these sweet young people and listen to their movie *The Story of Joseph Smith.* You would think this was just one more Christian denomination. Not so.

As one pastor friend said to us when they came to his door, he would say, "My Jesus has a capital *J*, but your Jesus has a little *j*." He said this because their church doctrine taught that Jesus was the brother of Satan and they had a fight in heaven. Jesus won. Satan got kicked out of heaven. What? They all had Bibles, but I guess they missed the part that said Jesus was the *only* begotten Son of God. Satan was a fallen angel, a created being.

> Then war broke out in heaven. Michael and his angels fought against the dragon, and the dragon and his angels fought back. But he was not strong enough, and they lost their place in heaven. The great dragon was hurled down—that ancient serpent called the devil, or Satan, who leads the whole world astray. He was hurled to the earth, and his angels with him.
>
> Then I heard a loud voice in heaven say: "Now have come the salvation and the power and the kingdom of our God and the authority of his Messiah. For the accuser of our brothers and sisters, who accuses them before our God day and night has been hurled down. They triumphed over him by the blood of the Lamb and by the word of their testimony; they did not love their lives so much as to shrink from death.

"Therefore rejoice, your heavens and you who dwell in them. But woe to the earth and the sea, because the devil has gone down to you! He is filled with fury because he knows that his time is short." (Rev. 12:7–12 NIV)

Yes, you have to wait until nearly the end of the book (the Bible) to hear about what happened "back in the beginning." This was a revelation to me since we never studied this stuff in my home. By contrast, the Mormons teach that when they die, they will be given their own planet to rule; it will be separate from Earth. How strange. Yet the Mormons I have met are very nice people. They have strong family values. They live in areas called their stake to which they give a required tithe. When Mitt Romney ran for president of the USA, the LDS Church did a great job marketing their faith as "just another Christian church," but if you don't believe Jesus is the only Son of God and is part of the Trinity (Father, Son, and Holy Spirit), you are not a Christian. How easily we can be deceived!

The Seventh-Day Adventist Church (versus the Puritans)

I worked for an Adventist hospital in Southern California and learned a bit about the Seventh-Day Adventist Church that started these hospitals. The largest one was Loma Linda University Hospital in Loma Linda, California. The motto of this hospital, which opened in 1905, is "to make man whole." Pure Adventists do not drink caffeine or drink alcohol and do not eat red meat. I came to learn that the church celebrated their Sabbath Day on Saturdays (just like the Jews). I was told the church had broken away from the Puritans (many founders of our countries) because they thought that Sunday was not only a day of rest but also a completely serious day in which no one could have fun.

The Adventists decided the Lord wanted this day to be one of joy, so they started their own church. Saturday became their "seventh day" of rest. Ironically, the hospital where I worked had less than 5 percent Adventist staff and an administrator (who was Adventist) who loved to drink wine—he even retired and moved to the wine country! So every faith has its "rules," but not everyone follows the rules in the same way. I can certainly see this in most *all* the churches I have attended. Gratefully, as part of my job, I held cancer screenings on weekends, and I was able to convince the leaders that folks would not come on Sundays—we had to screen on Saturdays. So I guess it is a flexible rule. I did love the saying on the back of our business cards: "To continue the healing work of Jesus." Paintings of Jesus looking over a surgeon's shoulder while he performs an operation are common in these hospitals. I think that is precious.

The Jewish Faith

My dad had a Roman, hooked nose. He grew a beard. When you combined the two, he could pass for a Jewish man. Such was the case when he traveled to Miami for an American Legion convention. The Jewish men accepted him as one of their own. Ironically, my dad's all-time favorite play was *Fiddler on the Roof.* He was rehearsing to play the lead role at a local playhouse in Minnesota when he died in June 1986. Ten years later (1996), when we traveled to the Holy Land, we bought a poster/painting just outside the town of Joppa. It is a painting of a fiddler on the roof, with the entire book of Ecclesiastes and Song of Solomon written in Hebrew! It now hangs in our guest powder room, with a reminder that life can be as shaky as a fiddler on a roof unless you have Jesus as your rock! Dedicated to my "Jewish Catholic" dad.

The summer after my freshman year of college, I took a job as a "mother's helper" (governess) for a Jewish family in New Jersey. They must have thought the eldest girl in a family of seven children would know a lot about taking care of young children! I felt a bit like Maria in *The Sound of Music!* They had four kids, and the eldest son was about to have his bar mitzvah, a very big deal in the Jewish culture. So I got to attend this event, more lavish than any wedding I had ever seen! We also spent a month on the Jersey Shore in a six-bedroom home on the coast, and Uncle Bernie would come down from New York City in his Mercedes convertible (the things we remember) and we would eat steamer (steamed clams). He even let me drive his car! I think it was that moment that I decided someday I would own a convertible! (I had to wait until 1991.)

So I got a taste of some Jewish culture. Great food and wine. Bagels. I never liked the lox on the bagels, though. Challah bread. Sweet and yummy. Gratefully, I kept in touch with this dear family for many years afterward. Steve and Carole eventually retired and moved to Stowe, Vermont. In the summer of 2015, while on the East Coast for a wedding, we took a side trip to Vermont to visit them. What a delight! Carole said Bill was the nicest guy she ever met (just after Steve, of course). Remember my *The Sound of Music* governess moment? Well, the real Von Trapp family singers moved from Austria to America just after the war, and the family settled in Stowe, Vermont! We visited the Von Trapp Family Resort, and I found out that the granddaughter of the real Maria was now a friend of Carole's. Such a sweet touch to my Jewish family story. This family did not celebrate the Sabbath on Friday nights or attend the synagogue regularly, so I think their faith was modern American Jewish.

I must digress. I have known several married couples where one is Catholic and the other is Jewish, and it seems to be a good blend. Why? I believe it is because both faiths are filled with traditions (one of my favorite songs from *Fiddler on the Roof*). It makes sense. The first Christian church was the Roman Catholic Church. It was founded by a group of Jews from Israel—those apostles. During my time as a hospital manager in Ventura, California, I had an assistant who married a Jewish doctor who had just completed his family practice residency at our hospital. She took all the classes to become a Jewish wife. Both their sons had a "bris" (circumcision) eight days after birth. She shared with me the meaning of keeping a kosher home, especially during the Jewish high holidays. I learned more about this faith.

During the summer of 1996, when we went to the Holy Land with our church pastor (who had lived in Israel for a while), he also taught us a bit about the Jewish faith. While sitting in a restaurant, he would point out the Hassidic Jews (long sideburns, black hats, very conservative), and he told us about their "ritual" of a girl's engagement before marriage. Very interesting. They were completely different from my New Jersey Jewish family. We also learned of old biblical traditions that, when a Jewish man died, if he had an unmarried brother, that brother was supposed to marry his widow. More tradition.

Our pastor taught us from the Old Testament about the Shema of the Jewish faith, the affirmation that there is only one God. Here are the words from Deuteronomy 6:4–9 (NIV). "Hear, O Israel: The Lord our God, the Lord is one. Love the Lord your God with all your heart and with all your soul and with all your strength. These commandments that I give you today are to be on your hearts. Impress them on your children. Talk about them when you sit at home and when you walk along the road, when you lie down and when you get up. Tie them as symbols on your hands and bind them on your foreheads. Write them on the doorframes of your houses and on your gates. You have to love this devotion to God!" According to the Bible, the Jews are the "chosen people." Only some are "Jews for Jesus" (Messianic Jews) I know at the end of the age; a remnant of these people will be preserved by God. I pray that many of our Jewish friends will come to realize that Jesus is *the* Messiah. They don't have to wait any longer. I just love these people of faith. I am so glad that our country stands with Israel in most all matters in the Middle East. We are Judeo-Christian brothers. That is very special.

The Methodist Church

One more Maria story that links to the United Methodist Church. While working as a grant writer in Simi Valley, California, I met a female Methodist Hispanic pastor named Maria. I helped write grants for her organization, which did outreach to the local Hispanic people. She was their shepherd. She was the first female pastor I ever met (that's okay with me, but not all strict Protestants). And she was a hoot! She and her husband were separated for many years—I am not sure they ever divorced. But she told me she had a Jewish boyfriend. "Really?" I asked. Who was he? She said his name was Jesus and he was Lord of her life! Now that was a new way of addressing Jesus Christ to me!

It was during the time George Bush was US president and they had a faith-based initiative conference in Washington, DC, so I made a trip there with her and some of her staff. We attended a Hispanic National Day of Prayer, and I met many prominent folks in the faith-based world. It was an eye-opening adventure. One afternoon, when we had a break, I strolled over to the Smithsonian Museum and took in their current exhibit on polio. I learned more about Jonas Salk, who came up with the Salk vaccine, and I bought a book about post-polio syndrome. That book helped me to get Social Security disability benefits for my husband, Bill, who had polio as a child. You just never know how God is going to connect you to special resources when you are doing His will and helping others in His name. I will never forget you, Maria. A real sister in the Lord. More manna. More of God's provision.

Church of God in Christ

By now you are saying, How many churches did this woman attend? Well, this is another grant-writing story. I was working with the local Hispanics, doing public health grant work, and met a guy named Paul who introduced me to Gabriel. He was a black pastor who also was a high school principal in our area. His church was called the Church of God in Christ. He asked me to take a trip with him to Muskegon, Michigan, to meet the head of their church on the west shore of Lake Michigan. They, too, were seeking federal grant funds to do "social justice" work like day-care facilities, prisoner job placement, food banks, and low-cost housing. The latter was what we hoped to develop in Ventura County, California.

So I learned about the "social justice" movement among black churches just north of Chicago, the home of a future president, Barack Obama. I gained special insight into the work that propelled this man into office and what social justice meant to the black community. This understanding still helps me dissect political and social movements in our country.

WOW, I have learned more about churches than I ever realized! My experience with each one is part of my story, which makes my life quite colorful compared to only knowing one church, the Roman Catholic Church. The church is not a denomination. It is not a building. It is the followers of Jesus Christ as Lord and Savior. Oh, how He must weep when He sees how the word *church* has been used in our society. I am still learning.

Evangelicals versus Reformist Christians? My husband loves to dig deep into these type of subjects. Perhaps in retirement we can dig deeper together and have some good conversations, but we do not plan to major on the minors. We are Christians. Christ and Bible followers. Amen.

Colorado (High Place of God)

We are now in our fourteenth year in the beautiful state of Colorado. Most, including John Denver, consider it the Rocky Mountain state, but that is *not* the real state name. Colorado has been nicknamed the Centennial State because it became a state in the year 1876, one hundred years after the signing of our nation's Declaration of Independence. Colorado is also called Colorful Colorado, presumably because of our magnificent scenery of mountains, rivers, and plains. We live east of the Rocky Mountains, at an elevation just under seven thousand feet. It is called the Front Range. Some of our extended family with respiratory challenges (smokers) can't tolerate our thin air, but outside of that, we love being part of a state with fifty-six peaks over fourteen thousand feet high! In the Bible, God is often seen as one who resides in "high places." I think that is so for our state.

I have been drawn to Colorado ever since my junior year of college, during which I took a winter break to go skiing at a place called Steamboat Springs. I joined a group of guys I had met as a team leader, selling books door to door the previous summer (they were all from the South), and we laughed a lot as they learned how to navigate chair lifts and falling down in the snow! I was the token female in this group of highly moral guys (they sold Bibles). It was fun to note the amazing snow, soft and fluffy, like powder. Having grown up in Minnesota, where the snow was wet and heavy and cold, I found it a real treat to discover the mountain difference. I also ventured back to Colorado during the final days of 1990 with a guy I was dating. We went to a ski area near Durango called Purgatory. Now, as a good Catholic, I should have known better than to go to a place with such a name! Sure enough, on New Year's Eve, I fell down on the last run of the day and blew out the ligaments in my left knee. I ended up with four knee surgeries in 1991 and over eighteen months of physical therapy, but that adventure would lead to me meeting my husband, Bill, through a friend of his I met at PT. Yes, our beginning was a Colorado connection.

Through various Bible studies, I have heard that Satan is alive and well along the front range of Colorado. Why? Because he loves to copy God and to go after believers in Jesus Christ. I have heard that Colorado Springs is home to more Christian nonprofit organizations than anywhere else in the USA. I think it all started when Dr. James Dobson moved his organization, Focus on the Family, from California to Colorado. (Just like us!) He also figured out there had to be a more affordable place to live and work. A great many organizations have chosen Colorado for their headquarters. Among our favorites is Greater Europe Missions (GEM), for which we have supported several missionaries. We also love Glen Eyrie Castle. Glen Eyrie is an English Tudor-style castle built by General William Jackson Palmer, the founder of Colorado Springs. The castle is now owned by the Navigators. We also support a missionary with the Navigators. It's even on the registry of national historic sites!

The original state song for Colorado is "Oh Columbine" (named after the state flower), but no one knew the words or the song. So they decided the "co-state song" would be John Denver's famous tune "Rocky Mountain High." We love that song! Here are the interesting words:

He was born in the summer of his twenty-seventh year
Coming home to a place he'd never been before
He left yesterday behind him; you might say he was born again
You might say he found a key for every door
When he first came to the mountains his life was far away
On the road and hanging by a song
But the string's already broken and he doesn't really care
It keeps changing fast and it don't last for long
But the Colorado rocky mountain high
I've seen it raining' fire in the sky
The shadow from the starlight is softer than a lullaby
Rocky mountain high (Colorado)
He climbed cathedral mountains, he saw silver clouds below
He saw everything as far as you can see
And they say that he got crazy once and he tried to touch the sun
And he lost a friend but kept his memory
Now he walks in quiet solitude the forest and the streams
Seeking grace in every step he takes
His sight has turned inside himself to try and understand
The serenity of a clear blue mountain lake
And the Colorado rocky mountain high
I've seen it raining fire in the sky
You can talk to God and listen to the casual reply
Rocky mountain high
Now his life is full of wonder but his heart still knows some fear
Of a simple thing he cannot comprehend
Why they try to tear the mountains down to bring in a couple more
More people, more scars upon the land
And the Colorado rocky mountain high
I've seen it raining' fire in the sky
I know he'd be a poorer man if he never saw an eagle fly
Rocky mountain high
It's Colorado rocky mountain high

I've seen it raining' fire in the sky
Friends around the campfire and everybody's high
Rocky mountain high
Rocky mountain high, Colorado

I believe the song has two meanings. One is a tribute to the beauty and solitude of Colorado. Unfortunately, as the last stanza says, "Friends around the campfire and everyone is high" relates to his love of marijuana, the drug that has been legal in our state for quite a while. It has become one of the most famous things about Colorado—weed. So sad.

When I went to work for the local school district, I found out every April 20 they have a paid day off called Columbine Day. It, too, has a sad meaning. It is in memory of the first major school shooting in Colorado in 1999 at Columbine High School. It is celebrated in Denver as "weed day." No kidding. It also happens to fall on the birthday of Adolf Hitler, a hero to one of the shooters. Creepy. (Some say Hitler was one of the antichrists.) So Satan has been able to weave his evil into this state in a unique way. Yes, we do believe in good and evil and are glad we are on the winning side! While doing some work for the Fellowship of Christian Athletes (FCA) at our local high school, we helped to get speakers for the monthly meetings. Among them was a great guy named Casey. He was in ninth grade at Columbine High School at the time of the shooting. He now has a ministry called From Tragedy to Triumph, and what a story he has to tell! (You can check out his YouTube channel, called Becoming Dangerous; his outreach to youth is amazing.)

One more thought about Colorado that was unexpected for us: the weather! Our realtor told us that the saying in our area is, "If you don't like the weather, just wait ten minutes and it will probably change." She was right! I guess it is the mountain effect—weather can turn on a dime. In the winter it is wonderful since it can snow one day and melt the next day, completely. (Not like Minnesota, where snow stays for six months.) You really have three seasons here, summer, fall, and winter/spring, since there is melting that goes on all winter long.

In summers it is the sudden thunder and lightning storms that scare our dogs to death. Douglas County, where we live, has the most lightning of any county in the USA except one small spot in Florida. When it strikes near our home, it makes everything shake! We also have lots of hail that comes down hard and fast, but just for short periods. It kind of reminds me of all the stories I have heard about the Sea of Galilee, where Jesus did a lot of His ministry—the weather could turn wicked in an instant and capsize boats. It certainly is a constant reminder of being able to weather all the "storms" in our life with faith in God that He will protect us. God's provision once again!

Coronavirus (The Power of Fear)

My first job out of college was working for the Centers for Disease Control (CDC) in Atlanta, Georgia. I was assigned to work on a project called the Study Efficacy of Nosocomial Infection Control (SENIC). This was to determine how often patients get hospital-acquired infections. I joined this federal agency the year that Jimmy Carter was elected as US president (1976), so it was an exciting place to be at that time. I even got my swine flu shot there! I never would have imagined that a communicable disease could shut down our entire world forty-four years later! But that is what happened in mid-March 2020. A virus that was believed to come from a lab in Wuhan, China, had made its way around the world, causing folks to get sick and even die.

As a result of inaccurate "models" that were made to predict high death rates, the government decided to shut down the economy and tell people to stay home. Shelter in place. Practice social distancing. Wear masks in public. Only *necessary* businesses were allowed to stay open, such as grocery stores. That included marijuana dispensaries. A huge fear came over our nation and the entire world. I heard a great analogy to hurricane models: they are often wrong and only used as estimates; people know how to respond. The world does not stop.

As one who worked in health care for many years, I was skeptical of the way this virus was treated as an international pandemic since death rates were lower than those of the regular flu. The response should have been more surgical in nature, to target the hot spots like New York City and not the entire country, and also the elderly. I guess in my old age, I could not help but think there was a political agenda behind these huge decisions. Many democrats in Washington, DC, loved the idea of controlling the lives of people and getting them to depend on big government, creating a welfare state. Even some governors took advantage of their new power to control the lives of people in their state (i.e., Michigan, where you could not have elective surgery but abortion was okay).

The Bible says "Fear not" and "Don't worry" a lot. The phrase "Does not be afraid" is written in the Bible 365 times. That's a daily reminder from God to live every day being fearless. I remember when I went through a long period of anxiety and depression in my mid-thirties, fear ruled my life due to an imbalance of serotonin in my brain. I would go to the grocery store and try to buy something as simple as a head of lettuce and be filled with fear that I was making a mistake, so I would leave without making a decision—no lettuce. A good friend sent me a book called *Feel the Fear and Do It Anyway* (by Susan Jeffers), published in 1987, the very year I moved to Arizona. It tells you that making a decision—any decision—even if it is wrong, is better than living in limbo. I remember that same advice years earlier from a marriage counselor when I was trying to decide whether to file for divorce. He told me you cannot live in limbo; just make a decision and do something. As I write the draft of this book, I feel like I am living in a world of fear. What if we go back to work and more people get sick or die? I can only say that living in a state of "wait" is not a good place to be. I truly believe our God loves order and action. Satan likes to instill fear in people and create chaos. Don't let him do it to you.

I was pleased to see that President Trump led a movement to "open up America" in a safe way but to end the horrible economic and physical/emotional toll staying home was having on a lot of people. Gratefully, the jobs numbers started to increase in June 2020, so it looked like we had turned the corner as a nation. But wait, the leftists had another plan to get Trump. They turned a police shooting in Minneapolis over Memorial Day weekend to start protests and riots in the streets of our largest cities. Complete anarchy and chaos was the result, and state governors and city mayors would not let the police do their job to shut it down; instead, they were told to stand down. This led to a radical movement to "defund the police." When Trump offered to send in federal assistance, such as the National Guard, he was asked not to come into their states. Really? Many lives and businesses were lost. The Black Lives Matter movement seemed to join with the Antifa crowd as paid rioters continued to burn down America and even tear down statues of historical figures. The left hoped to blame Trump. It did not work.

I recently read on Facebook, "Fear does not stop death. It stops life" (Laurie Buchanan, author).

And worrying does not take away tomorrow's troubles; it takes away today's peace.

The overresponse to the coronavirus stopped life in the world (and America) for a while, but the resilience of human beings allows us to carry on after such times. I truly hope the entire world will get back to normal and never be put into a place where life stops ever again. I have now taken my work with the CDC off my résumé. It is sad to see that they have become a political organization with so much power. The same is true for the World Health Organization (WHO). Their political ties to China prevented the world from knowing the truth about this virus created in a Wuhan lab at an early stage of the disease. In the year 2020, people believe what they hear on the news—much is biased opinions only. It is often the truth that follows later. I pray that changes someday. Fear gives way too much power to those in charge at any level of government. It is truly sad, especially for one nation under God.

I must add a note about opening up schools in the fall of 2020 (starting in August). Even though the CDC and National Association of Pediatricians recommended letting all kids go back to school, this did not happen in most states. The fact is that young people rarely get the virus, and if they do, they do not die and they are not carriers.

Safe. By comparison, staying home from school for more months on end was not a good choice. Suicide. Depression. Lost learning.

In Douglas County, Colorado, our district decided to try a hybrid model, where students could come to school Monday to Thursday and then have online classes on Friday or opt for complete e-learning. What about working parents with young children? No one seemed to address this issue, so many parents became very upset at the fearmongering going on among school boards and teacher unions to the detriment of their families. Once again, fear seemed to be the driving factor for the decision. And politics. I did return to the high school from which I retired to help train my replacement and do some substitute teaching. The building feels empty. Very few students walk about. Erie. Most fall sports were postponed. Yes, football is now scheduled for January. Really? Football in the snow?

I find it all so sad. So unnecessary. Some states and countries have gone back to school "as normal" without any huge negative impact. Good for them. The Democrats want to use COVID as a way to attack Trump once again. I hope and pray intelligent voters will see the truth and not allow this amount of government control over their lives. To me it is not a matter of right versus left, but rather of right versus wrong. I pray for eyes to be opened.

David (Effect of Jealousy)

When I first read the Bible, I was drawn to this king in the Old Testament named David. He wrote most of the psalms in the Bible and was called "a man after God's own heart." I have known several Davids in my life. So what does this name mean? From the Hebrew name דָּוִד (David), which was derived from Hebrew meaning "beloved" or "uncle." David was the second and greatest of the kings of Israel, ruling in the tenth century BC. Several stories about him are told in the Old Testament, including his defeat of Goliath, a giant Philistine (www.behindthename).

What I appreciate about King David is that he was not perfect but he was hated for something completely out of his control. After being anointed king in his teen years by the prophet Samuel, he had to run for his life from the first king (Saul), who was very jealous of how much all the people loved David.

> When David returned from killing the Philistine, the women came out of all the cities of Israel, singing and dancing, to meet King Saul, playing songs of joy on tumbrels. The women sang as they played, and said, "Saul has killed his thousands, and David his ten thousands." Then Saul became very angry. This saying did not please him. He said, "They have given David honor for ten thousands, but for me only thousands. Now

what more can he have but to be king?" And Saul was jealous and did not trust David from that day on. (1 Sam. 18:7–9 NIV)

He spent years trying to kill David, so David had to run for his life for over ten years.

Once again, the issue of jealousy raises its ugly head, just like Joseph with his multicolored dream coat and very jealous, angry brothers who wanted him dead. Both Joseph and David were considered precursors to the real King of Kings, Jesus, who was killed by the Jewish high priests out of envy.

For he knew that it was out of envy that they had delivered him up. (Matt. 27:18 ESV)

Wow. This is a human emotion that has to be conquered, or someone might get killed!

This, of course, was my own story, of brothers that hated me out of jealousy, since I was my dad's favorite child. I have seen women with very jealous husbands who don't want them to have any relationships outside of the marriage. It is certainly a green-eyed monster.

I have to take time to make note that King David was first a shepherd. I believe this is the primary role of all church pastors, and not an easy one at that, since sheep are so stupid. But they do listen for their master's voice. We had a Pastor Dave in our last church. He was a good teacher of the Word, but we did not think he was a good shepherd of his flock. When we approached him with concerns about the actions of fellow believers and its impact on our family, we were chastised and told we were in sin to make any "accusations." Really? By contrast, our current church also has a Pastor David. He is a good shepherd of his flock. He listens. He cares. He teaches. And we listen to his voice and follow him. I am grateful that King David was a shepherd before he was a king. He learned a lot of good leadership skills in this lowly role. We, too, learn some of our best lessons in lowly roles.

Deborah (She Knows)

I had a cousin named Debbie. I also have a good friend who is a praying mom named Deb. The first one let me borrow her wedding dress to get married. The second one introduced me to a career within the public school system. I also liked the biblical character Deborah, who was one of the first judges. So what does the name Deborah mean? The name Deborah is a Hebrew baby name. The meaning of the name Deborah is "bee." Deborah was the biblical prophetess who summoned Barak to battle against an army of invaders. After the battle, she wrote a victory song, which is part of the book of Judges. Deborah's name meaning and origin is "she knows" (www.sheknows. com). I had to laugh that Judge Deborah had an assistant that was afraid to go into battle without her. His name was Barack.

I wanted to include this name in my book because Deborah was the *only* woman judge named in the Bible, and she was such a strong leader. I like that! Who were the judges? They were the ones who ruled Israel before the time of the kings.

> In those days Israel had no king; everyone did as they saw fit. (Judges 17:6 NIV)

They compromised their convictions and disobeyed God. Deborah was the fourth and only female judge. She had special abilities as a mediator, adviser, and counselor. When called on to lead, she was able to plan, direct, and delegate, even to men who were not as strong as her. She also wrote songs. Her life showed that wise leaders are rare. They accomplish great amounts of work without direct involvement because they know how to work through other people. It reminded me of something Ronald Reagan once said that I think he borrowed from Harry Truman: "It is amazing what you can accomplish if you do not care who gets the credit." I would love to be a Deborah.

My cousin Deb is daughter to my dad's youngest brother, the one who gave me away during my marriage to Bill. She would say I was the "religious" one in the family, but I have to refute that claim since I happen to find it to be an insult. What? I do consider myself to be a strong Christian conservative, and our annual Christmas letters always quote Scripture, but Jesus Himself found greatest fault with the religious leaders, and I would do the same, given what *religious* means to so many people. It often means "self-righteous," and that certainly is not a Christian trait! So I do hope very few label me as religious. Thanks, cousin.

My friend Deb is a quiet lady of grace. She is a real prayer warrior. When her husband died of cancer (as I took over her job on the audiology team), she went back to school to get her master's degree in computer science. Yes, she is also smart. Given such a strong degree on which to earn a great living, she turned instead to mission work. She attended a class called Perspectives (three times) and encouraged me to take it as well. So I did. Perspectives is a fifteen-week course designed around four vantage points or "perspectives"—biblical, historical, cultural, and strategic. Each one highlights different aspects of God's global purpose (www.Perspectives). This was a life-changing class for her, and I think, eventually, it will be the same for me. "Blessed to be a Blessing." What a great life goal. Deb now works for Greater Europe Missions (GEM) and lives in Germany as a prayer encourager. Thanks, Deb, for all you shared with me during our many times of prayer. You have made a difference in my life.

Dogs (Unconditional Love)

Now you may say I have lost my mind. In the midst of talking about someone as important in history as King David and the judge Deborah, talking about dogs is pretty crazy. Did you know that *dog* spelled backward is *god*? I really think God created dogs to teach us about unconditional love of one's master. That has been the case in our family.

I often say I married Bill for his dog. She was a beautiful golden retriever named Kelly. She was a gentle, sweet dog. We bred Kelly to have two litters of puppies. In her first litter, she had six puppies. We had created a pen in our garage using old bricks, and one little guy dropped a brick on his foot and it had to be wrapped and he had to be separated from the other puppies. By the time we could return him to the litter, the others would have nothing to do with him, so we kept him and named him after his dad, called Billy by his old friends. One such couple had a little boy who could not say Billy, so he called and asked for "Booly." Cute. So we chose that name for our new little puppy.

Kelly and Booly were our dogs when we started our fost-adopt process. Both our boys fell instantly in love with these two dogs. I believe they provided the unconditional love that the boys had never had before. We found out early two dogs are better than one, since they have each other as companions when we adults are at work. So here is our dog legacy:

- Kelly: She was the runt of the litter, female, sweet, well-behaved. Our groomer used to say she is the nicest golden she had ever known; everyone loved her. *Kelly* is a very popular Irish name meaning "war, lively, and aggressive." She did not match her name at all. Kelly died at age thirteen of cancer. When we had to put her down, it was the most tear-filled day of our family. As God would have it, *all* our dogs would contract cancer and have had to be put down. If you have ever read the book or seen the movie *Marley and Me*, you will know just how much a dog can mean to any family.
- Booly: He was son to Kelly, a mama's boy; he followed her everywhere, and he really didn't like water but would jump in and follow Kelly and swim in tandem. Folks thought we taught them that trick—not so. They also died at age twelve of cancer. More tears.
- Buddy: He was an adopted large red male golden retriever; he had a bark like a seal and was an "old man" since we knew him, and would wander off and get lost (dementia). We still loved him, and he also died of cancer at age twelve.
- Sammy: She was a female golden retriever rescue. She was a Denver street dog, our first Colorado dog. Very skittish at

first but became a sweet pet. We also had to put her down from cancer.

- Capone: He was a dog rescue mutt, mostly terrier, adopted just before Christmas one year. He had been adopted before to another family with a Doberman pinscher. Capone would stand under this dog and chew on its legs to say "Let's play," but the bigger dog gave him the look "Do that again and I'll eat you," so they returned him. Capone and Sammy loved to play; he is quite cute and all personality. We call him our most expensive dog since he came with cataracts, blind one eye, skin allergies, parathyroid condition—lots of vet visits and medicines. We even took him to the Colorado State University (CSU) Veterinary Hospital, and everyone said he was their favorite! Clearly, he is our most spoiled dog and is also a mama's boy, but I am his mom. (See photo of these two dogs.)

- Amani: Some friends had a litter of goldens, and we got the female runt; we gave her a Swahili name that means "peace," Amanai. (Swahili is the national language of Tanzania—another place we love.) She and Capone play like crazy! She sleeps with our son James and thinks she is a lapdog; she gets overexcited when folks come to visit, but once she calms down, she is one affectionate dog, and we love her.

When Kelly had her first litter, we surprised our sister Sue's kids and brought them one of her female puppies for Christmas (Katie). They loved her! When they moved from Arizona to Minnesota, that dog was run over by a car (so sad). So we gave them one from her second litter (Daizee Mae) and had to buy her a plane ticket in warm cargo from LA to Minneapolis one very cold Minnesota winter day. She was picked up by my brother John (his kids got to love on her), then transferred to sister Joan (her kids loved her too), and finally to Sue's kids as a Christmas surprise. She became Sue's walking companion, and she got to live a long life and then died at home in peace. Sue saw a shooting star that day, and it forever reminded her of Daizee.

Whenever one of us is sick, the dogs come and lie by the bed to watch over us. We have taken some on vacations, including camping trips, and they always add joy to the venture. We once took off on such a camping trip and got twenty miles from home before we noticed that one of our dogs was missing. So we went home, and sure enough, he (Booly) was waiting on the front lawn for us.

My parents had a small dog in their retirement named Buddy. When my dad retired, he bought a van and took that dog with him everywhere as he visited all his kids and grandkids. When Dad died at fifty-six of a heart attack (June 1986), the van went to my brother Tom. When he returned to our home a year later, Buddy ran to the window to see if it was Dad. How heartbreaking is that picture! Dogs know.

So *dog* spelled backward is *god*, and I know God puts them into our lives for special reasons at special times. We are grateful for these gifts.

Donald (A Good Man)

I dated a wonderful man named Don. Bill has a wonderful uncle named Don. So what does this name mean? It comes from the Gaelic name Domhnall, meaning "ruler of the world," composed of the old Celtic elements *dumno*, "world," and *val*, "rule." This is the name of one of Walt Disney's most popular cartoon characters, Donald Duck (www.Behindthename.com). The two primary Dons in my life were sure "rulers" in their world. The third is an interesting story. I am not sure about the duck.

It was the summer of 1990 that I met *my* Don at an auction where townhouses were being sold. We sat next to each other, and he asked if I would like to join him for a celebration dinner after he bought a townhome. So we enjoyed a lovely Italian dinner with red wine and tiramisu (my favorite Italian dessert). The next day at work, a huge bouquet of flowers was delivered with a note: "I'd like to see you again." Charming. So we began to date. He helped me at an auction later that year, where I bought my own townhome. He made me feel alive again (after a year of depression). It was very special. I felt like he was an angel sent by God.

He was a successful stock broker and going through a divorce—his wife just left, saying she didn't want to be married anymore. He had two young children (boy and girl), and he was in the process of selling their magnificent home. He also used to play professional football, and he took me to a couple of NFL games at the LA Coliseum, including a game between the LA Rams and the Minnesota Vikings (my team). He loved the fact that I loved to eat, have fun, and enjoy sports. Something his wife never did. She suffered from an eating disorder and ate very little. Oh, the things we learn along the road of life! Yes, I ate everything on my plate—with gusto!

When the Christmas season arrived, I invited him to our hospital staff dinner dance. He took me to Nordstrom's to buy a black evening dress for the occasion. I had never been in this amazing and expensive store. Just one year earlier, I had seen the movie *Pretty Woman*, and I felt just like Julia Roberts in the presence of a prince charming. We flew to Durango, Colorado, to go skiing over New Year's weekend, and that was where I blew out all the ligaments on my left knee. In 1991, his wife hired a new divorce attorney, and he could not manage a "wounded girlfriend" going through four knee surgeries and a new divorce battle, so we parted ways. I was sad but understood.

Since he attended the same church as me, he saw my "announcement of engagement" in the fall of 1994 and called to congratulate me. He said, "Your husband is a very lucky man." He told me he was also getting remarried to a gal who had two children in youth sports with his kids. I was touched. That was a very sweet moment for me. I will be forever grateful for having *my* Don at just the right time in my life. Thank you for all you did for me.

So what about Uncle Don? He was married to the sister of Bill's dad (Jean), and they lived very close to where his mom lived. We call him Uncle D. He is a character! His mom was too poor to raise him, so she put him in an orphanage—that was where he grew up. He lied about his age to join the US Navy in World War II, where he met Bill's dad. He and Jean were married for over fifty years. Their only son, David, got married the year before Jean died. They ended up having four girls, so Uncle Don is now surrounded by females!

I don't know if he knew that there is a Saint Donald in the Catholic Church. Saint Donald of Sheridan was an eighth-century Scottish saint who lived at Ogilvy, in the former Forfarshire. Upon the death of his wife, Donald converted his home into a hermitage, where he lived a monastic life with his nine daughters (known as the nine maidens or the holy nine virgins). Upon his death, they entered a monastery in Abernethy. Churches throughout Scotland were dedicated to the nine maidens. Their feast day is July 15 (Wikipedia). So how about that, girls?

When we adopted our two boys from foster care, Uncle Don took a real liking to them and would tell them stories of having been raised in an orphanage. He told them they had it really good! He continued to attend the Lutheran church where Bill's mom had belonged. We made it our goal to always go to church with him when we visited California after our move to Colorado. Uncle D celebrated his seventy-fifth birthday on September 11, 2001, the day the World Trade Center was bombed. So we can always remember his birthday! He had amazing woodworking skills, and we have a beautiful grandfather clock in our home that he made. Our Christmas tree is also adorned by several wooden ornaments that he carved. So Donald is pretty special to us. The name must have been special to Walt Disney, too, since he named one of his favorite characters Donald Duck. Do we have a fondness for the name Don?

One more Donald story I just have to add. I recently heard about an event in Scotland in the late 1800s called the Hebrides Revival (on the Isle of Lewis). Two old ladies held church in their home and prayed for revival. The local church was struck by lightning and burned up, but one young teen, named Donald, helped the church and began doing public prayer. A cousin of these old ladies immigrated to America in 1936. Her name was Mary Ann Smith McCloud. She met a guy named Fred, and they got married and had four children. The first was named Fred, after his dad; the second Mary Ann, after her mom; the third Elizabeth; and the fourth Donald, after that young man back in Scotland during the revival.

The mom gave her family Bible to this youngest son, Donald, because it was the Hebrides Bible and his name came from that era. That Bible now resides in the Oval Office since Donald is the forty-fifth president of the USA, Donald J. Trump. Donald was raised in the Presbyterian church but got away from his church as an adult. He became interested in Christian prayer around 2006 as he watched a lot of Christian TV. When he decided to run for president, he surrounded himself with many evangelical Christians who began to pray for him. Many believe God raised him up "for such a time as this," to bring America back to the moral values of our Founding Fathers. God uses unusual people to do His work, that is for sure. Many "wall builders."

It is like King Cyrus (of Persia). According to the Bible, Cyrus the Great, King of Persia (modern-day Iran), was the monarch under whom the Babylonian captivity ended. In the first year of his reign, he was prompted by God to decree that the temple in Jerusalem should be rebuilt and that such Jews as cared might return to their land for this purpose. The leader of this effort was Nehemiah. He was a prophet during the third return to Jerusalem after captivity, telling how the walls were rebuilt and the people were renewed in their faith (since the temple was surrounded by walls). One of Trump's biggest campaign promises was to "build a wall" on the southern border of the USA. He is fulfilling that promise as I write. A modern Nehemiah? Maybe. A very interesting Donald with a very special Bible now in our White House. Precious. Thank you for giving us all this manna, Lord.

CHAPTER E

Educational Systems (Teach Up a Child)

As I stated in my introduction, I grew up in rural northern Minnesota. Our only option for education was public schools. So I attended K-12 public schools and think I had a very good public education. The mining companies put a lot of money into schools. I heard that the neighboring high school (Hibbing High School) was the number 1 school in the world in the 1950s because of all that was poured into this school by the mines. For example, I grew up thinking that all middle schools and high schools had indoor swimming pools and free busing for every sport and extracurricular event imaginable—at no cost. Not so. So what makes education in Minnesota so unique? I found this in Wikipedia.

Education in the US state of Minnesota comes from a number of public and private sources and encompasses prekindergarten to postsecondary levels. Minnesota has a literate and well-educated population; the state ranked thirteenth on the 2006–2007 Morgan Quitno Smartest State Award and is first in the percentage of residents with at least a high school diploma. In 2007, Minnesota students earned the highest average score in the nation on the ACT exam. While Minnesota has chosen not to implement school vouchers, it is home to the first charter school, the City Academy High School of Saint Paul.

The state supports two public university and college systems, including thirty-seven institutions in the Minnesota State Colleges and Universities System, and five major campuses of the University of Minnesota. It is also home to more than twenty private colleges and universities, six of which rank among the nation's top one hundred liberal arts colleges, according to US News and World Report. Wow. My college was one of those six colleges. Teachers are well paid, and higher taxes support good education and roads. I was blessed to grow up in such a state.

It wasn't until I moved to California that I realized how different public education can be. When I moved there in 1977, I was shocked to find out that state residents get free college education if they attend a California State school. But I believe due to open borders and a big influx of foreign immigrants, the elementary schools are now very crowded, which is not good. You get paid more if you are bilingual because so many students have a primary language that is not English (Spanish is the most common). Over 50 percent of the state budget is spent on education. As such, the teachers' union has a very powerful voice in California. In large urban areas, gangs have a big impact on the atmosphere for teaching—you get battle pay in the inner city.

My husband grew up in an environment similar to mine—great public schools in the old days of California. He got a very good education. California was once at the top of the list for great universities. Sadly, when we decided to leave California in 2006, things had changed. Our local elementary school was so crowded that a classroom meant for twenty students now had thirty-nine, and half the kids could not speak English. Most teachers were not bilingual, nor did they have an aide in their classroom, so it was not a good learning environment for our "average kids." When we moved to Colorado, we were told the school district into which we were moving was one of the top ten in the USA. We were glad our realtor gave us this fact.

When I graduated from high school, my favorite subject was math, so I selected it as my major in college. I briefly considered becoming a math teacher, until I became a calculus tutor. The students I worked with (including many in premed or nursing) often had a perplexed look on their face that said, "What are you talking about?" To which I would think, *It's only calculus!* So I decided that was probably not a good career for me.

After we had lived in Colorado for nearly six years, I was praying with a group of women for the kids and staff at Douglas County High School. One of these moms, Deb, had a husband who was dying of cancer, so she decided to take a one-year leave of absence at her job working on the audiology team for the school district. While helping to fix up her home to put on the market for sale, I met her boss (Donna), who asked me if I wanted to come and do Deb's job for a year. So I applied and I was offered this interim job by her boss (Donna) and began in February 2012. Deb's husband died within three months, but she decided not to return to work, so my temporary job became permanent. In my role as the lead person for our Castle Rock Schools, I began to travel to every school in the district—a journey that included both public and charter schools. Our county was exploding in population with a lot of new housing, and the district had no capital budget to build new schools, so a lot of new charter schools were approved (K-8).

During our vision and hearing screening times, we relied on parent volunteers to help with our work. During our breaktimes, I came to find out that staff/volunteers at public schools greatly resented the charter schools. They felt as if their neighborhood kids had been "stolen" by the charter schools, who seemed to promise a better education. In turn, the charter schools' staff and volunteers often felt their type of education was more personalized and their students did better academically when they entered high school. I understood both sides, but I felt as if I were in the middle of a war zone. To top it off, we had a new superintendent and a board of education that seemed to favor charter schools. What a mess! Along the way a legal battle had begun about school vouchers, whereby parents were given vouchers to offset their child's cost of private education. I think the battle went all the way to the US Supreme Court, and public education and the teachers' unions won. The school district could no longer offer such vouchers. What a time to be immersed into the educational system!

Also along the way, homeschooling became popular, and a special home education department was created. I had a cousin whose first wife had homeschooled their children on a remote farm to "protect them" from the big, bad world. Gratefully, by the time I joined the school district, I had met quite a few Christian moms who home-schooled their kids with great results, so my impression changed a lot, for the good. This was followed by an online school. I never knew so many forms of education were possible! Each one had its pros and cons, but clearly, the standard public school, K-12, wanted to retain its dominance and most of the funds per pupil allotted by the state Department of Education. I went on to work for the inter-national baccalaureate (IB) program at one of our high schools, and this program was in competition with the advanced placement (AP) program (more later). I never knew such "competition" existed within school systems!

The reason I include this in the "persons, places, and things" that have had an impact on my life is that I see how influential teach-ers and types of schools can be in the way a student looks at the world. I also came to realize that 90 percent of college and university professors are liberal and that conservative opinions (including Christian values) find very little room at most of these schools. This is where young people often get their worldview, and they grow up to be our local, state, and national leaders. Teacher unions have a pow-erful voice in state and national politics as well.

It has gotten to the point where many educators think they can teach a child better than their parents. I now understand why the book of Proverbs includes advice in teaching children.

- In chapter 1, the king and the queen say to their son, "The fear of the Lord is the beginning of knowledge" (Prov. 1:7 ESV). Parenting is not ultimately about teaching right behaviors; it is about facilitating a right relationship, to respect those in authority.

- The parents in Proverbs say, "For the Lord gives wisdom; from his mouth come knowledge and understanding" (Prov. 2:6 ESV), and "Whoever despises the word brings destruction on himself, but he who reveres the command-ment will be rewarded" (Prov. 13:13 ESV). Worldly knowl-edge is different from many Christian principles.

- "Honor the Lord with your wealth and with the first fruits of all your produce; then your barns will be filled with plenty, and your vats will be bursting with wine" (Prov. 3:9–10 ESV). Teach your kids about generous, faithful, regular giving and being unselfish.
- "My son, do not despise the Lord's discipline or be weary of his reproof, for the Lord reproves him whom he loves, as a father the son in whom he delights" (Prov. 3:11–12 ESV). Now this is a big no-no in public school—corporal punishment. I have seen teachers be fired for even slight touching, such as flicking an ear. So sad.
- "Whoever conceals his transgressions will not prosper, but he who confesses and forsakes them will obtain mercy" (Prov. 28:13 ESV). Kids need to learn not to lie and steal or allow such behavior to be passed off as "kids will be kids."
- "A slack hand causes poverty, but the hand of the diligent makes the rich. He who gathers in summer is a prudent son, but he who sleeps in harvest is a son who brings shame" (Prov. 10:4–5 ESV). Teach your kids to work hard and to make hay while the sun shines! Teach them that work comes before play, and teach them to do something useful. So many kids do to know the value of hard work; they do the minimum to get by and feel entitled.
- "Whoever oppresses a poor man insults his Maker, but he who is generous to the needy honors him" (Prov. 14:31 ESV). Teach your children to treat all human beings with dignity. This is very important in the area of bullying.

Some would say teaching such values are old-fashioned, but clearly, parents should be the *primary* teachers of their children from birth until they move out of the home. I know most good teachers try to work with parents to make sure their students are doing their best. On the extreme side, some parents are so overprotective of their sons and daughters that they develop an attitude that "children are never wrong"; it is the teacher's fault. This is a huge mistake and a terrible challenge to teachers and all school staff and coaches. It drives school administrators crazy!

Since I began my career in health care then moved into grant writing for nonprofits, and finally working in schools, I can see the unique challenges in all three types of organizations. But the education of our youth is so important. It is the core of our country—one nation under God. I was amazed to learn that our Founding Fathers often used the Bible as their primary book for instruction, and many universities were founded by Christian leaders. We have gone so far in the secular direction that real debate on school campuses for most issues is no longer allowed.

I laugh at the argument about "church versus state" as one of no church concepts to be taught in public schools. The intent of our Founding Fathers was to keep the state out of the church, not the opposite. They were fleeing England, where the king was head of both church and state and there was no freedom of religion. I hope and pray students will learn the many sides of many issues and choose for themselves how they want to think. Public education will always have a prominence in our society; let's guard it well but keep our history on church versus state accurate.

Elaine (My Mom)

My mom's name was Elaine Katherine. So what does the name Elaine mean? Elaine as a girl's name is of Greek origin, meaning "sun ray or shining light." It is a French variant of Helen. In the King Arthur myths, Elaine is a character who fell in love with Lancelot (www. thebump). When my parents had children, they named us each after a saint and we had saint plaques on our wall at home. My mom's plaque was Helen. I don't think she ever really lived up to this name— shining light and romantic. Too bad.

My dad died at age fifty-six (heart attack), but my mom lived until age eighty-nine (dementia), so she was a widow for over thirty-three years. My dad had an affair with another woman twelve years before his death, and although he never left my mom, she never really forgave him. Since she had worked in alcohol detox and she thought my dad drank too much, she often nagged him about this issue. Ironically, after his death, she was the one who started secretly drinking. This led to a DUI for her, which resulted in one night in jail, suspension of her driver's license, and loss of her registered nursing credential to work in the field of detox and recovery. This sent her into a downward spiral, a mental health hospitalization, with a diagnosis and treatment for both depression and alcoholism.

She joined AA and was quite faithful to attending daily AA meetings. Even when she came to visit me, we would find AA meetings for her to attend. During this time, she became devoted to following the twelve steps and adhering to the Serenity Prayer. I looked up the full version of this prayer (www.thevoiceoflove.com), written by the American theologian Reinhold Niebuhr.

The Serenity Prayer

God, give me grace to accept with serenity
the things that cannot be changed,
Courage to change the things
which should be changed,
and the Wisdom to distinguish
the one from the other.
Living one day at a time,
Enjoying one moment at a time,
Accepting hardship as a pathway to peace,
Taking, as Jesus did,
This sinful world as it is,
Not as I would have it,
Trusting that You will make all things right,
If I surrender to Your will,
So that I may be reasonably happy in this life,
And supremely happy with You forever in the next.

I am saddened to think she never really embraced this wonderful philosophy for life. Her other favorite poem was "Footprints in the Sand" by Mary Fishback Powers:

> One night I dreamed a dream.
> As I was walking along the beach with my Lord.
> Across the dark sky flashed scenes from my life.
> For each scene, I noticed two sets of footprints in the sand,
> One belonging to me and one to my Lord.
> After the last scene of my life flashed before me,
> I looked back at the footprints in the sand.
> I noticed that at many times along the path of my life,
> especially at the very lowest and saddest times,
> there was only one set of footprints.
> This really troubled me, so I asked the Lord about it.
> "Lord, you said once I decided to follow you,
> You'd walk with me all the way.
> But I noticed that during the saddest and most troublesome times
> of my life,
> there was only one set of footprints.
> I don't understand why, when I needed You the most, you would
> leave me."
> He whispered, "My precious child, I love you and will never leave
> you
> Never, ever, during your trials and testing.
> When you saw only one set of footprints,
> It was then that I carried you."

Once again, I think she knew that Jesus did carry her during the hard times in her life, but I do not believe her Catholic faith was not one of personal relationships with Christ, one that would change her life. How very sad. Both poems still hang in the guest room of our home, where she stayed during her visits. It reminds me that she had the tools but did not submit her life to Jesus and allow Him to change her heart. She did not have the right teacher. But not all was bleak.

My sister Sue told me some wonderful, positive stories about Mom, based on the fourteen years they spent raising their family in northern Minnesota. Mom loved dancing—all dancing! She especially loved tap dancing and was part of a group called the Taporettes. Those were fun times for her. Sue also said she had a memory of Mom and Dad driving away from their first home in Globe, Arizona, and their visit and met their firstborn, Sarah. Mom put her face in her hands and was crying when they drove away. Mom also hosted many grandkids' birthday parties at her home in Pengilly—that was a big group of kids, but everyone had fun. Mom was also a great cook, and she would spend time preparing food so we could all go to the beach as a family. She loved feeding folks and also lake time. Her way of showing love: to feed an army!

She did complete a five-year degree in nursing from the College of Saint Scholastica. She said the nuns who taught her made learning come alive. She loved becoming a nurse. When she did end up in AA, she had a good friend named Loretta who move in with her. She finally had a best friend and a very fun buddy! They could play cribbage for hours. During our growing-up years, the mom of the family down the street (Alice) suddenly died from cancer, and Mom sobbed when she heard the news. She must have been a good friend to her. Alice was a special lady and also was my confirmation sponsor. Her firstborn (Renee) went to school with me. Dear friendships.

During her time in AA, she would retell her story as a "wronged wife," but I guess it was her story to tell. Both she and my dad were responsible for a marriage gone sour, but living with a man with a bad temper and trying to keep seven kids under control and safe from that temper had to be unimaginably hard. Friends from the local Catholic church would tell Sue that Mom was their angel and she helped them on various occasions. My sister-in-law Belinda also told me that she and Paul introduced them to Marriage Encounter. Dad wrote her a love letter. Dad said she read it so much she almost wore it out. Isn't that sweet?

When dementia took over my mom's life and she was moved from one memory unit to another, she always took our saint plaques with her. I guess she treasured her role as a mother but never showed it to us kids. Again, so sad. When she died, I was given all the plaques but only kept the one for my mom, my dad, and myself. I gave the others back to each brother and sister at her funeral. Mom died the weekend a movie named *I Can Only Imagine* was released. So I used that movie and song to write a letter to each of my siblings to place in the envelope with their plaque. Here are my words.

> As we come together for Mom's funeral Mass and memorial, I got to thinking of a very special movie that came out the weekend that she died, *I Can Only Imagine*. It is based on the triple-platinum song recorded by the band Mercy Me. The lead singer wrote it from a broken heart about his childhood and being raised by an abusive father (who drank) and an absent mother (who moved away to escape). If you have not seen it, I highly recommend it. (Lyrics attached.)
>
> I can only imagine what Mom's life was life from early marriage until her death:
>
> - Married at age twenty-three to "the love of her life," planning to have a big family.
> - First year in Monterey, California; second year in Falls Church, Virginia—great adventure on both coasts.
> - Then back to a small house in a small town called Pengilly, with three babies in three years.
> - She must have felt overwhelmed by it all, and alone. I can only imagine.
> - Then maybe scared as the temper of her husband came out and the yelling began.
> - Then the local dentist said she had to have all her teeth pulled due to gum disease.
> - She was fitted for dentures that never really fit, caving in a once-pretty round face.

- I can only imagine how her self-esteem was affected.
- Four more children would come along, and she would not go back to her nursing career until the youngest was in kindergarten, the fall of 1969. (Now eighteen years married and tired out.)
- Then she worked three-to-eleven shift, came home for some sleep, got up to cook and clean and get dinner ready, then off to work again—we did not see her much (getting more tired out).
- I can only imagine how all work and no play wore her down.
- I can only imagine Dad's constant yelling made her withdraw emotionally—such a great contrast to her own mom and dad, who were pretty easygoing.
- I can only imagine being chronically depressed since her thirties but having never diagnosed or treated until after Dad died. She probably did a lot of self-medicating.
- When I heard several of you say you "hated" Dad when you were a teen and couldn't wait to move out of the house, I can only imagine how Mom tried to hold it altogether.
- I can only imagine finding out your husband was having an affair with another woman, knowing you would never leave your marriage or break your wedding vows.
- I can only imagine thirty-two years of being alone after he died at age fifty-six.
- I can only imagine losing your car, your home, and your mind (to dementia), being sent from one facility to another for behavior that was often out of your control.

- I can only imagine being "mad" at God for having you live so long in such terrible health.
- I can only imagine. Can you?

> So let's remember Mom with a lot of grace and forgiveness and understanding. As I said the day she died as we met at a hotel bar, she did the best she could. Let her rest in peace, and now let's imagine she can be dancing with the one she loved, Dad.

This rather sums up my mom's life. How I prayed that she would truly forgive my dad and learn to enjoy her children and grandchildren. It is said in life, when things go wrong, you can get bitter or better. She chose the former. I often wonder how many years of true happiness she enjoyed in her eighty-nine years of life. It was certainly a lesson for all of us children. If only she had known her name meant "shining light," things could have been different. God only knows. She did love animals and worked with stray pets. Let's hope that brought her joy.

The only other Elaine that influenced my life was the assistant at my first job after coming from Arizona back to California in 1990. She was sweet. Kind. Easygoing. It was just the right medicine I needed when I came "back to life." I still share our Christmas letter with her every year. I wonder if I ever told her what a dear friend she was. If not, here's to you, Elaine, for being such a dear friend and colleague to me. You'll never know how much it meant.

Esther (My Friend, His Friend, Biblical Queen)

When I went through my divorce, my best friends were Patrick and Esther. I was with Esther, doing some Christmas shopping in December 1983, and I told her I had finally decided to hire an attorney and file for divorce. She said, "It's about time." Wow. That was a clear confirmation that I was doing the right thing. Ironically, my ex-husband's girlfriend's name at that time was Esther. Yes, God has a sense of humor.

So what does the name Esther mean? The name means "star" in Persian. The book of Esther in the Old Testament tells the story of Queen Esther, the Jewish wife of the king of Persia. The king's adviser, Haman, persuaded the king to exterminate all the Jews in the realm. Warned of this plot by her cousin Mordecai, Esther revealed her Jewish ancestry and convinced the king to execute Haman instead. Her original Hebrew name was *Hadassah* (Behind the Name). It would be years later before I would begin studying the Bible, including the book of Esther.

Mordecai tells her, "For such a time as this, you have been placed upon the throne, to save the Jewish people." After a time of fast and prayer, she decides to follow the advice of her cousin and she says, "If I perish, I perish." "Go, gather together all the Jews who are in Susa, and fast for me. Do not eat or drink for three days, night or day. I and my attendants will fast as you do. When this is done, I will go to the king, even though it is against the law. And if I perish, I perish" (Esther 4:16 NIV). How could you not like Esther? I have come to love this woman, a brave young woman in a Persian world. My friend Esther was placed in my life for such a time as this. Once again, God's protection and provision in my life.

Evelyn (Old And Wise Friend)

I said in my introduction that I met a dear elderly lady at our current church named Evelyn. She just turned one hundred years old in April 2020. Since we were in lockdown for the coronavirus, her big party got canceled, so we had a drive-through celebration for her. She loved it! So what does the name Evelyn mean? The name Evelyn is a girl's name of English origin meaning "wished-for child." Evelyn was originally a surname that derived from the French feminine given name Aveline (www.nameberry.com).

My Evelyn was born in 1920, and I am sure that she was "a wished-for child." That decade was called the Roaring Twenties, but it ended in the Great Depression. Evelyn grew up in the state of Oklahoma, where she met and married the man she fell in love with, named Johnny. They had one son, named Bill, and she now lives with him and his dear wife, as they are all retired. We either pick her up or drop her off from church nearly every Sunday, which has given us time to get to know her. What a joy that has been for us!

Evelyn and I were asked to be deacons at our church during the year she was ninety-six years old. She asked, "Do you think I am too old to be a deacon?" "No," I said. "It is only a three-year commitment, so you will be done by age ninety-nine." She laughed. We served together, and she is now an emeritus deacon beloved in our church. She could have coined the expression "You are never too old to learn." She learned to ski in her fifties and went up the Rocky Mountains with her family to ski for many years. She has a great spirit!

Evelyn is a great woman of faith. A great reader of the Bible. A wonderful woman of prayer. I can recall during one of my many trips to Minnesota, I got a call on my cell phone from Evelyn to ask how my mom was doing. I gave her the update and said she really needed prayer. So we stopped and prayed together at that very moment. I often think how close in "sound" *Evelyn* is to *Elaine*, yet these two women could not be more different. I now think of Evelyn as my "other mom" and thank the Lord He blessed me with our friendship.

While writing her own life story, she told of one experience she called "the empty hands." She had an ectopic pregnancy and lost the baby and nearly died. She had a vision that if she were to meet her Lord that day, she would have to approach the throne of God with empty hands because she had not told anyone about Jesus. She said if she lived, she would spend her life doing just that. And she has. She is an inspiration to me and such a gift from God. Thank you, dear Evelyn, for all you have taught me.

Ethiopia (Mission Pastor, East Africa)

So now I switch gears and will talk about a place that has influenced my life that happens to contain some dear stories about people I know there as well. It all started in 2005, when I met a gal named Sharon who lived in Ventura, California. She was being supported by a local church with a member who was my friend (Angela) who introduced us. Her dad traveled to Ethiopia in 1945 (after WWII) to help treat local people with tropical diseases. Sharon's dad was a surgeon (Dr. Barlow), and he took his whole family with him. He started an organization called the Mossy Foot Project to help locals with a disease that resulted in an elephantiasis of the foot. After he died, Sharon took over the organization. She was seeking financial supporters.

She knew a young man in Ethiopia who was working on his degree at Evangelical Theological College (ETC) in Addis Ababa. He needed someone to support him with his studies, so we became his sponsor. His name is Workineh. He finished his studies in the spring of 2008 and invited us to come for his graduation from ETC. He was also getting married the next day, and we were invited to that celebration as well. Since we had "extended family" in Tanzania, Bill and I decided to make a five-week trip to East Africa, with half our time in Ethiopia and half our time in Tanzania. It was May to June 2008. Gratefully, Bill's brother Jack had a camper and wanted to make a trip to the East Coast, so he took our boys and dogs while we were gone. Thank you, Jack. We could never have traveled with two young boys on this adventure.

We did not know much about Ethiopia when we traveled there. Gratefully, our "adopted son" from Tanzania (Gabriel), who works for the United Nations in Washington, DC, knew that Ethiopian Airlines has a hub in Washington, DC, and they offer direct flights to Addis Ababa, Ethiopia, for a very reasonable cost, so we got our round-trip tickets for about $1,400 each. When we met fellow Christian travelers in the country, they said their average airfare was $2,500. God is so good! We were able to stay with Gabriel the night before our departure, and he helped a lot with the flight plans to/

from Ethiopia to Tanzania. So here is what Britannica Encyclopedia says:

> Ethiopia, country on the Horn of Africa. The country lies completely within the tropical latitudes and is relatively compact, with similar north-south and east-west dimensions. The capital is Addis Ababa ("New Flower"), located almost at the center of the country. Ethiopia is the largest and most populated country in the Horn of Africa. With the 1993 secession of Eritrea, its former province along the Red Sea, Ethiopia became landlocked.

We always thought Denver, the mile-high city, was at a high altitude at 5,280 feet, but we found out that Addis Ababa was 7,726 feet in elevation! The "rooftop" of Africa would come later when we traveled to Mount Kilimanjaro in Tanzania, which has an elevation of 19,341 feet. Let's just say we traveled to high places on this journey!

We primarily stayed at Christian guesthouses during our stay in Ethiopia. It was very affordable, and we got to sit and share stories with other Christian travelers over dinner each night. We discovered that many Americans traveled to Ethiopia to adopt children, and working with the Ethiopian government was anything but simple. Addis Ababa is head of the African Union, so it is a big meeting place in Africa. We were amazed to see how prosperous this capital city seemed compared to the poverty that existed throughout most of the rest of the country. Internet cafés were still pretty rudimentary. Road construction was done by Chinese prison laborers, and we came to find out how the locals greatly disliked these guys. It may have been a good deal for their government, but not for their women, who were often assaulted.

This history really came alive for us during this coronavirus outbreak across the world since the leader of the World Health Organization is from Ethiopia and is very friendly with China. The director-general of the World Health Organization (WHO), Dr. Tedros Adhanom Ghebreyesus, is good friends with President Xi Jinping of the People's Republic of China in Beijing. He gave very positive reviews to the Chinese for their handling of the virus, which was totally inaccurate. Politics! In May 2017, the world health assembly elected Tedros Adhanom Ghebreyesus as its ninth director-general (D-G), the first African to lead the World Health Organization (WHO) since its formation in 1948. Dr. Tedros faced a daunting task, with WHO facing a crisis of confidence after its much-maligned response to the West African Ebola epidemic (US National Library of Medicine, National Institutes of Health). We believe he did not do a good job for the world in helping cover up COVID-19 in its early stages of contagion in China. God sure ties things together in an interesting way, over many years.

So back to Ethiopia in May 2008. After attending the college graduation and wedding of Workineh, we went "down country" (southwest) to Soddo, where the Mossy Foot Project does all its great work. We went to several mossy foot clinics, often held outdoors under trees. The people infected with mossy foot would gather for their treatment, and they would be amazed that people from the USA would come all the way to minister to them. They saw us as coming from a very rich area to one that is very poor. Our interpreters would tell them we were there to be the hands and feet of Jesus. We exchanged many hugs and "holy moments."

At one of these clinics, we met Pastor Zewdie, who served the people with mossy foot; he gave them the good news of the gospel. We got to meet his family in Soddo—a wife and three young children. He invited us to his home one day and asked us if we would like a cold drink. Little did we know that our affirmative response would lead to his son running into the village to get us a cold Coca-Cola. His youngest daughter took a real liking to me. It was very touching. We became very close to Zewdie and his family.

During our time in Soddo, we also met the family of Workineh and his bride. We came to find out that a wedding is not just celebrated for a day but rather for an entire week! During one of those celebrations, Bill and I were given outfits from the local area to be part of a wedding in Soddo. It was such a sweet experience. We had sent Workineh some funds to build a small brick home for him and his new wife, so we visited that house. We also gave them funds for a honeymoon, and we ended up flying to Lake Tana in the north part of the country—the source of the Blue Nile. It was quite an experience that we all enjoyed!

We came to find out that the Nile River originated in Lake Victoria (between Tanzania and Uganda) and it flows north to Egypt and eventually dumps into the Mediterranean Sea. So the Nile River flows through the country of Ethiopia, with dry farmers who depend on rain for their crops to grow. They never use water from the Nile! Apparently, the Egyptians claimed the waters of the Nile as their own, so other countries leave it alone. To that end, drought is common and millions of people die of starvation. It is so common that it never makes the news. The leaders in Addis Ababa seemed to not care about these very poor people in their county. Amazing. Sad. We saw the skinniest cattle we had ever seen.

The people of this country really touched our heart. They are beautiful people, literally, especially the women, both inside and out. While watching the movie *The Ten Commandments*, starring Charleston Heston, I now noticed that when Moses served the pharaoh in Egypt, he would go on journeys to Ethiopia and bring back treasures. These included the beautiful women. It also included coffee. Yes, Ethiopia is the home of the coffee beans. Oh, how Bill loved his macchiatos!

Upon our return to the USA, we made a point to send a box of Christmas gifts to Zewdie and his family. Zewdie told us that his family had never known such a tradition of receiving gifts until they knew the Kramers. One year, we sent a VHS-DVD player and many of our Disney movies that the boys had outgrown. We came to find out that they would have movie time at their home and all the neighborhood children would gather. It was not just a fun event for them but also an experience that helped them improve their English! God works in amazing ways.

We have tried to continue this tradition every year but were saddened to find out that the customs agents in Ethiopia would open our boxes and remove (steal) what they wanted for themselves. So the list of what we sent did not match what they received. One year, we sent money via Western Union instead, but it was not the same. There is so little to buy in Ethiopia or it is so expensive that our actual gifts were a real treasure. So we now keep this tradition alive. A true blessing.

Pastor Zewdie has continued to serve his people by preaching across the country to large gatherings (in the thousands), so one year we helped him buy a Moped to make the journey across the country. His eldest son is now interested in studying for the ministry and may come to the USA to get his degree. We met Zewdie in Pasadena in June 2019 as he was finishing a course in his master's program at Fuller Theological Seminary. We were able to have him with us for four days after the course was completed, and one of the places we got to take him was to the Master's College in Newhall, near where Bill's sister resides.

Here is the description of this Christian College found in Wikipedia: The college was founded in 1927. It was originally named Los Angeles Baptist College and Seminary. In 1961, it moved to Newhall in Santa Clarita, California. In 1985, John MacArthur became the school president; the name was changed to the Master's College, hoping to appeal to a wider evangelical audience. In 2016, the school underwent yet another name change and became the Master's University. In June 2019, John MacArthur stepped down as president and became chancellor, and John Stead, a faculty member since 1970, became the interim president.

Bill has always loved the teaching of John MacArthur, and it appears the pastors in Africa also know of his good work. Would you believe that that man who became the interim president, John Stead, was the good friend of Bill who led Promise Keepers at the church where we met? He was the one who walked and prayed every day, including asking the Lord to send Bill a godly wife. John was born and raised in Rhodesia (now Zimbabwe) and was part of their army. Yes, that is the home of Kathy's boyfriend from high school (Brian). What a small world! We made sure they sat together at our wedding. We even visited John's parents on the east coast of New Zealand, where we spent our honeymoon! God sure connects those He loves in amazing ways!

Bill had planned to travel to Pasadena again in the spring of 2020 until the coronavirus pandemic ended up leading to the canceling of many events and international travel, including Zewdie's trip from Ethiopia. We hope it will be rescheduled in the fall of 2020 so we can rendezvous with Zewdie then. In the meantime, we help buy him books for his studies (mostly Kindle), as well as some for his son's studies. What a privilege it is!

As for Workineh, he came to think of us as "rich Americans," and every time he needed money for something (such as a birthday party for one of his children), we could not support this. It is sad that the leaders of his church encouraged him to reach out to us for money on several occasions and tried to shame us for not supporting all his needs. He did eventually get an American sponsor and now lives on the East Coast of the USA with his family. We suspect he will stay here as long as he can. Our mission's focus is on the indigenous people who stay and humbly serve the people in their country. We do keep in touch with Workineh and always wish him well.

In the summer of 2020, after we put Zewdie on a plane at LAX back to Ethiopia, we traveled north in California to visit some dear friends (Jim and Cindy) at their home on Lake Nacimiento. During our visit, they asked us to join them for several fundraisers for an organization started by a doctor in their church. Ethiopia was one of the places this medical missions group visited. A pastor from there was in the area to get some needed surgery. When we met him at a dinner at the home of one of the mission's teams, we told him of our connections to Ethiopia. He knew Workineh! Yes, it is a small world when you are doing the Lord's work. What a blessed time we all enjoyed.

So Ethiopia has a special place in our hearts—the land and the people and their passion to hear the good news of the gospel of Jesus. We hope to return one of these days, the good Lord willing.

CHAPTER F

Fatherhood (A Godly Man)

So you may say, "Is this a person or a thing?" It is both. When Bill and I got married, he was forty-three years old and I was forty-one. In the world of medicine, any woman who has her first pregnancy after age thirty-five is known as an elderly primigravida. So we tried to start a family, but it did not appear getting pregnant was in the cards for me, so we decided to go the adoption route. (See chapter A.) We became foster parents and decided to adopt children that no one else wanted. Two young boys who had no local family. So we had to go through a "termination of parental rights" for both these single moms in order to adopt our two sons. James was aged three. Josiah was aged four. They came into our life three years apart.

Bill loved his own father very much. I never got to meet him since he died of cancer before we met. As such, Bill always wanted to be a dad to boys and give them what his father had given him. When Bill was diagnosed with polio at age five, he spent one year in a polio rehab hospital. Upon his discharge, his parents wondered how he would do in school. As God would have it, his mom knew the principal of the local elementary school, and he told her to send Bill to his school and he would take care of him, which he did.

At the same time, his dad was determined to raise his son as a normal boy. The family went camping together. This included swimming and water-skiing. They played golf. (His dad was a golf caddie when he first moved to California from Indiana.) They loved all sports, including following the career of the UCLA basketball coach

(John Wooden) who also came from Indiana. They had season tickets to UCLA football and enjoyed time at the Rose Bowl on many weekends every fall.

Bill's polio left him with a right arm three inches shorter than his left arm and very little scapula or normal clavicular joints. Yet his dad taught him to swim and created a device so he could waterski. He also taught him to play golf and used short tee stubs for his shots on the fairway to give his ball a "lift" that his shoulders could not. Bill also joined the high school football team and became the kicker. He spent hours with his dad learning how to kick a football. In essence, his dad normalized his childhood and made him feel like a special son.

Bill's dad was not a believer. He did not attend church with Bill's mom until later in life, when he was retired and struggling with cancer. Bill went to work for the phone company (just like his dad) and did not become a believer until he was in his thirties. He longed to have a wife and raise a family just like he had. If God gave him this gift, He would add in the component of what the Bible has to say about fatherhood (from www.OpenBible.Info). A few examples:

- "As a father shows compassion to his children, so the LORD shows compassion to those who fear him" (Ps. 103:13 ESV).
- "Fathers, do not provoke your children to anger, but bring them up in the discipline and instruction of the Lord" (Eph. 6:4 ESV).
- "Train up a child in the way he should go; even when he is old, he will not depart from it" (Prov. 22:6 ESV).
- "He established a testimony in Jacob and appointed a law in Israel, which he commanded our fathers to teach to their children, that the next generation might know them, the children yet unborn, and arise and tell them to their children, so that they should set their hope in God and not forget the works of God, but keep his commandments; and that they should not be like their fathers, a stubborn and rebellious generation, a generation whose heart was not

steadfast, whose spirit was not faithful to God" (Ps. 78:5–8 ESV).

- "I have no greater joy than to hear that my children are walking in the truth" (3 John 1:4).
- "My son, do not despise the LORD's discipline or be weary of his reproof, for the LORD reproves him whom he loves, as a father the son in whom he delights" (Prov. 3:11–12 ESV).
- "And if it is evil in your eyes to serve the LORD, choose this day whom you will serve, whether the gods your fathers served in the region beyond the River, or the gods of the Amorites in whose land you dwell. But as for me and my house, we will serve the LORD" (Josh. 24:15 ESV).

It is interesting to note that many of these come from the book of Psalms, written primarily by King David or by his son, King Solomon. David was a great king, a man after God's own heart, but he was a lousy dad—he let evil go on in his family and did not stop it. Solomon was one of his sons who must have watched his father as dad versus king, yet God blessed him with great wisdom about all things, including fatherhood. But he went on to have over seven hundred wives and three hundred concubines, so I am not sure "great fatherhood" was even possible!

Bill has always been a great, loving dad. When the boys were young and sometimes defiant, he would not always display great patience, but he always showed great love, and if he got upset, he was quick to ask for forgiveness. He did spank the boys when they were young and needed a good swat, but he did it in a loving way. I think of my own dad and how his temper got the best of him at so many times—I never heard him ever ask for forgiveness. I watched my brothers as they raised children and was, for the most part, amazed and pleased at the love they showed their children, especially as they grew up to be young adults.

At a time when the USA has a culture crisis, the biggest missing element is children being raised in a home with a good father. It is such a key to every civilization. It is my daily prayer that the value of fatherhood return to America. We need God's help in a big way.

Florida (For the Young and Old)

So why pick this state to include in this book? Spring break! Jobs! Family! Beauty! A place with a godly beginning. A place to retire and sail into the sunset of life (for some). When I was a sophomore in college, I did spring break Daytona Beach with a few female friends from my Catholic college and a bunch of guys from the neighboring school, University of Minnesota–Duluth (UMD). We traveled on a bus nonstop for thirty-six hours to reach this sunny destination, and we thought we had died and gone to heaven! And all for $125, including lodging.

Don't worry, these guys were like brothers to us; we had good, clean fun together. My first day on the beach, I met a guy from Toledo named Bob. What a gentleman! He was a few years older, a college graduate, had flown to Florida and rented a car, so we went everywhere together that week. (Again, good, clean fun.) Disneyworld. Glass-bottom boats. Driving through everglades. We had so much fun that I almost missed my bus back to Duluth. Bob said, "Don't worry, I will fly you home." I said, "You don't know my dad!" Needless to say, I made the bus. But I have great memories. Once you return to the tundra of Minnesota and a blizzard hits and your tan fades, you think, *I know there is a God, but He does not live in Minnesota!* Once again, God protected my spring break adventure!

So when I graduated from college, the first place I interviewed for jobs was Florida. I did an interview at a large teaching hospital in Gainesville (home of the University of Florida) and also at a hospital in Fort Meyers. The first location was just too big of an institution. The second was a sleepy retirement city—not a great place for a twenty-two-year-old to live. I also found out that Florida in March (spring break) is far different from Florida in late summer (hot, muggy, buggy!), so I decided the climate might be too much to handle. So I took a job in Atlanta, Georgia, instead.

My dad's youngest brother (Stan) raised his family in Massachusetts but then moved to Florida, from a place of very high taxes to one of no income tax. So I got to go and visit him and his wife on many occasions. He lives in Lakeland, halfway between Tampa and Orlando. Perfect! They are now retired in an adorable three-bedroom home on a small lake with two patios. One of them is a private bed/bath with your own entrance. We love it! They used to play golf and pay no attention when alligators come out (yikes) and enjoy wonderful, warm winters in a land of palm trees and flowers. As it turns out, when folks from Minnesota retire, they more often move to Arizona. But those East Coasters (i.e., New Yorkers) head right to Florida!

We took a twenty-fifth wedding anniversary trip there in the spring of 2020 and got to go and visit Saint Augustine, the oldest city in America! Your Dictionary describes this saint in this way: "The Christian philosopher and theologian Saint Augustine (354–430) is best known for *The Confessions* and *The City of God*. After the authors of the New Testament, he has probably been the most influential Christian writer. The greatest of the Latin fathers of the church, Augustine lived during a period in which the Roman Empire was in deep decline and Christianity was taking root as the official religion. It was a time of great political stress and widespread religious anxiety." My husband loves this man! We have carved wooden plaques by our front doorstep that quotes Saint Augustine: "Our heart is restless until it finds its rest in thee." So why was this old city named after Saint Augustine? It is noted in www.visitaugustine.com, the following reason for naming this old city. Augustine was founded on September 8, 1565, by Spanish admiral Pedro Menéndez de Avilés, Florida's first governor. He named the settlement San Agustín, as his ships bearing settlers, troops, and supplies from Spain had first sighted land in Florida eleven days earlier on August 28, the feast day of Saint Augustine.

Most saints have a feast day, so now we know that the date was very important in the 1500s, when the first Catholic sailors to come to this part of the new world would name the city for this saint. Yes, we know Christopher Columbus sailed the ocean blue in 1492, an earlier time, but his mission was also paid by the queen of Spain. Spanish settlers would have had strong Catholic roots. By the time the Pilgrims arrived in the 1600s, they were the Puritans who were protestors against the Catholic Church. So you might say our Founding Fathers were both Catholics and Protestants—ah, yes, freedom of religion! The First Amendment to our Constitution.

But I digress. Florida is an important state among our fifty states for other reasons. We also have visited Cape Canaveral on the East Coast of the state, the home of the Kennedy Space Center. According to www.spacecoastlaunches.com, the location was chosen because it was relatively undeveloped land. Today, Florida's Space Coast is home to more than 570,000 residents, but when NASA was looking for an optimal spot to build the space program, it was no more than acres and acres of orchards, farmland, and quiet beaches. The second reason that the United States uses Cape Canaveral as its primary launch site is its proximity to the equator. "The west-to-east rotation of the Earth causes all points on Earth (except the poles themselves) to move eastward with some velocity," NASA said. Isn't that cool? So I include Florida in my book as a special place. One final note: I visited Disneyworld in Florida before I ever went to Disneyland in California. They are both located in Orange County. The Florida location will always be my favorite—so much space and beauty (no freeways, smog, and orange trees cut down as in California), and it includes Epcot, my favorite. Sorry, California friends.

Francis (The Saint From Assisi)

My dad was named Richard Francis. I wonder if the name Francis had a special meaning in our family. So what does the name Francis mean? Here is what www.ancestry.com says:

> English: from the personal name Francis (Old
> French from Franceis, Latin Franciscus, Italian
> Francisco). This was originally an ethnic name

meaning "Frank" and hence "Frenchman." The personal name owed much of its popularity during the Middle Ages to the fame of Saint Francis of Assisi (1181–1226), whose baptismal name was actually Giovanni but who was nicknamed Francisco because his father was absent in France at the time of his birth.

My dad's mom was of French Canadian descent, so perhaps a little of that ethnic background was included in my dad's name. We clearly claim our Italian heritage over any French! But this is cool.

As for Saint Francis of Assisi, he was quite an amazing man. I have always loved the Franciscan Order of the Catholic Church. I have heard more books have been written about Saint Francis than any other human being except Jesus Christ. Here is what Wikipedia says about this saint.

Francis of Assisi (Italian: San Francesco Assisi; Latin: Sanctus Franciscus Assisiensis), born Giovanni di Pietro di Bernardone, informally named as Francesco (1181/1182–October 3, 1226), was an Italian Catholic friar, deacon, philosopher, mystic, and preacher. He founded the men's Order of Friars Minor, the women's Order of Saint Clare, the Third Order of Saint Francis, and the Custody of the Holy Land. Francis is one of the most venerated religious figures in Christianity.

Pope Gregory IX canonized Francis on July 16, 1228. Along with Saint Catherine of Siena, he was designated patron saint of Italy. He later became associated with patronage of animals and the natural environment, and it became customary for churches to hold ceremonies blessing animals on or near his feast day of October 4. In 1219, he went to Egypt in an attempt to convert the sultan to put an end to the conflict of the Crusades. By this point, the Franciscan Order had grown to such an extent that its primitive organizational structure was no longer sufficient. He returned to Italy to organize the order.

Once his community was authorized by the pope, he withdrew increasingly from external affairs. Francis is also known for his love of the Eucharist. In 1223, Francis arranged for the first Christmas live nativity scene. According to Christian tradition, in 1224 he received the stigmata during the apparition of seraphic angels in a religious ecstasy, which would make him the second person in Christian tradition after Saint Paul (Gal. 6:17) to bear the wounds of Christ's passion. He died during the evening hours of October 3, 1226, while listening to a reading he had requested of Psalm 142 (141). Wow, he only lived forty-five years!

A lot of Catholic history says, "According to tradition." I am not sure I believe all that was written about this man, but our family does honor many of the traditions started by Saint Francis. We actually have a statue of Saint Francis made by an aunt to Bill. We love all things in nature and animals, including dogs. We have several nativity sets that we display at Christmas, including a very large one on our front lawn, on which we put spotlights. Another is from Bethlehem, made from carved olive wood. Another is from Tanzania carved from African blackwood. I have had the privilege to sit on the board of directors for two Franciscan retreat centers, one in Scottsdale, Arizona, and one in Malibu, California, and I love these humble men of God. I also love "The Prayer of Saint Francis," which is also a song (www.lyricfind.com):

Lord, make me an instrument of your peace
Where there is hatred, let me sow love
Where there is injury, pardon
Where there is doubt, faith
Where there is despair, hope
Where there is darkness, light
And where there is sadness, joy
O Divine Master, grant that I may
Not so much seek to be consoled as to console
To be understood, as to understand
To be loved, as to love
For it is in giving that we receive
And it's in pardoning that we are pardoned
And it's in dying that we are born to Eternal Life

I have read that Francis came from a wealthy family and gave it all up to serve the church. Clearly, if I could meet one saintly man from history, this would be the one. Since my patron saint is Saint Catherine of Sienna and she was canonized the same day as Saint Francis, I rather like this connection. Clearly, both are highly honored in the country of Italy, patron saints of this country. And both names are loved in my family.

Fred (My Dad's Brother)

I feel compelled to put in a short piece about my dear uncle Fred. He is the one younger than my dad but older than Stan (the Florida uncle), the son in between the other two boys. Fred raised two boys and two girls in Minnesota; he also worked for the phone company, just like Bill's dad, both part of the Bell Telephone company that spread from coast to coast. He and his wife (Jan) divorced, and he then married again (Maggie). They built a cabin on a little lake in northern Minnesota, but once she died, Fred decided to sell the land. This led to complete anarchy by his children, who chose to disown him. Thus, our family of seven children became "his kids," and we include him in most everything we do. His older sister (Mary Louise) also named a son Fred. I think she had a special affection for her brother.

Fred had a young son named Charlie who took his own life (see suicide). I knew this was a great blow to Uncle Fred. One should never have to bury one of their own children. He and Maggie did work through the grief together, but I am sure it changed him.

So what does the name Frederick mean? Here is what Wikipedia says. Frederick is a masculine given name meaning "peaceful ruler." It is the English form of the German name Friedrich. Its meaning is derived from the Germanic word elements *frid*, or "peace," and *ric*, meaning "ruler" or "power." How interesting that his name implies the one who rules in peace when he never had much peace in his family. After Maggie died, he became involved in doing ceramics and met another lady named Susie. They lived in her cute home overlooking all of Lake Superior in Duluth, Minnesota. She also died, but her dear family let him stay in this home, where he continued to do his ceramics while he stayed involved in many events in Duluth.

Fred was diagnosed with cancer and then had a stroke, so he is now living with one of Maggie's daughters. He is a dear soul. You might take him for Santa Claus (white beard and cheery face). Nearly every time I went back to Minnesota for a visit, I spent time with Uncle Fred. I just want him to know he is special. You are loved. May you have peace the rest of your days.

One more note on cousin Fred, the son of my aunt Mary Louise. He would join the US Army, get married, raise a family, and be sent to Germany to live. During a drive down the crazy autobahn, he had a car accident and died. It nearly killed my aunt Mary Louise to bury him. I know he had a special place in her heart, among her six children. So both Uncle Fred and Aunt Mary Louise had to bury a son. How sad. I am sure this brought them closer since they spent their final years living in the same city of Duluth. So *Fred* has a special meaning in our family.

Fruit (God Is a Fruit Inspector)

What a strange topic in the middle of interesting people and places! Bear with me. While taking a Bible study in Simi Valley, California, I had a female teacher who described the final scene of our life as we approach the throne of grace (and judgment). We see God wearing an apron that says, "Fruit Inspector." What? Yes, God will want to see what "the fruit of your life is."

According to www.openbible.info, here are some verses to consider:

- "I am the true vine, and my Father is the vinedresser. Every branch in me that does not bear fruit he takes away, and every branch that does bear fruit he prunes, that it may bear more fruit. Already you are clean because of the word that I have spoken to you. Abide in me, and I in you. As the branch cannot bear fruit by itself, unless it abides in the vine, neither can you, unless you abide in me. I am the vine; you are the branches. Whoever abides in me and I in him, he is that bears much fruit, for apart from me you can do nothing" (John 15:1–17 ESV).

- "But the fruit of the Spirit is love, joy, peace, patience, kindness, goodness, faithfulness, gentleness, self-control; against such things there is no law" (Gal. 5:22–23 ESV).

- "Beware of false prophets, who come to you in sheep's clothing but inwardly are ravenous wolves. You will recognize them by their fruits. Are grapes gathered from thorn bushes, or figs from thistles? So, every healthy tree bears good fruit, but the diseased tree bears bad fruit. A healthy tree cannot bear bad fruit, nor can a diseased tree bear good fruit. Every tree that does not bear good fruit is cut down and thrown into the fire" (Matt. 7:15–20 ESV).

- "But the wisdom from above is first pure, then peaceable, gentle, open to reason, full of mercy and good fruits, impartial and sincere" (James 3:17 ESV).

- "For at one time you were darkness, but now you are light in the Lord. Walk as children of light (for the fruit of light is found in all that is good and right and true), and try to discern what is pleasing to the Lord. Take no part in the unfruitful works of darkness, but instead expose them" (Eph. 5:8–11 ESV).

These are just a few, but you get the message that God will "inspect" your life to see if you have borne good fruit for Him. If not, He will turn you away and He will say, "I never knew you." Now that is a scary thought. So we have to look at our lives and ask, "What fruit has come from my life? Have I surrendered my life to Christ and walked in His way, doing His will, and sharing the good news with others?" I think the Sermon on the Mount was the most amazing sermon ever given by Jesus. In it, He turns things upside down by asking for behavior that is uncommon to mankind but the essence of the love of the Lord.

In Matthew chapters 5, 6, and 7, Jesus talks about key aspects of being a "fruit bearer" for the kingdom of God. At the end of the book of Matthew, he talks about the final judgment as being time of separating the "sheep and the goats," those who bore fruit and those who did not (www.Biblegateway.com).

> When the Son of Man comes in his glory, and all the angels with him, then he will sit on his glorious throne. Before him will be gathered all the nations, and he will separate people one from another as a shepherd separates the sheep from the goats. And he will place the sheep on his right, but the goats on the left. Then the King will say to those on his right, "Come, you who are blessed by my Father, inherit the kingdom prepared for you from the foundation of the world. For I was hungry and you gave me food, I was thirsty and you gave me drink, I was a stranger and you welcomed me, I was naked and you clothed me, I was sick and you visited me, I was in prison and you came to me." Then the righteous will answer him, saying, "Lord, when did we see you hungry and feed you, or thirsty and give you drink? And when did we see you a stranger and welcome you, or naked and clothe you? And when did we see you sick or in prison and visit you?" And the King will answer them, "Truly, I say to you, as you did it to one of the least of these my brothers, you did it to me."
>
> Then he will say to those on his left, "Depart from me, you cursed, into the eternal fire prepared for the devil and his angels. For I was hungry and you gave me no food, I was thirsty and you gave me no drink, I was a stranger and you did not welcome me, naked and you did not clothe me, sick and in prison and you did not visit

me." Then they also will answer, saying, "Lord, when did we see you hungry or thirsty or a stranger or naked or sick or in prison, and did not minister to you?" Then he will answer them, saying, "Truly, I say to you, as you did not do it to one of the least of these, you did not do it to me." And these will go away into eternal punishment, but the righteous into eternal life. (Matt. 25:31–46)

This is one of the most severe chapters from the Bible, but it clearly reflects why we must bear fruit in our life in order to be called blessed by God the Father and to inherit his kingdom. It is such a vivid picture of what we are called to do. When our family serves the homeless at the Church of the Open-Door, inner-city Denver, I remember this verse and am reminded to bear fruit in His name. It sure makes fruit take on a whole new meaning!

One fun final comparison about fruit and planting your garden. I found this set of instructions several years back called "How to Plant Your Garden." First, you come to the garden alone, while the dew is still on the roses. For the garden of your daily living, plant three rows of peas.

Planting three rows of peas:

Peace of mind, peace of heart, and peace of soul.

Plant four rows of squash:

Squash gossip, squash indifference, squash grumbling, and squash selfishness.

Plant four rows of lettuce:

Lettuce be faithful, lettuce be kind, lettuce be patient, and lettuce really love one another.

No garden is without turnips:

Turnip for meetings, turnip for service, and turnip to help one another.

To conclude our garden, we need thyme:

Thyme for each other, thyme for family, and thyme for friends.

So I guess the Lord likes both fruits and vegetables!

CHAPTER G

Gabriel (Adopted Son and Special Angel)

In January 1997, while participating in a church ministry to international students, we were assigned a young man from Tanzania in his first year of college at Cal Lutheran University (CLU). His name is Gabriel. He lived full-time on the campus but would come to our home for holidays and school breaks, when it was too expensive for him to travel all the way back to his home country in East Africa.

So what does the name Gabriel mean? Here is what Wikipedia says. Gabriel is a given name derived from the Hebrew name Gabriel, meaning "God is my strength" or "God is my strong man." The name was popularized by the association with the archangel Gabriel. Wow, what an honor to have the same name as the archangel Gabriel. He was the one who appeared to Daniel and explained his visions. He also appeared to Mary to tell her she would have a child who was the son of God. So he was quite the messenger from God!

During his senior year, Gabriel became the student body president at his college—yes, he was quite a leader on his campus. Sadly, within a few months of his taking this role, a young man died on campus of an alcohol overdose. This was a time he rose to the occasion. Upon his graduation later that year, he gave the commencement address to 648 graduates. We were honored that his mom (Flora) came from Tanzania for the occasion. His American mom (Ruth), who brought him to the USA for high school, also came from the state of Washington. They both stayed with us. What a great time we had together! That was Mother's Day weekend, and Gabriel had three "moms" present to celebrate.

Gabriel spoke at his CLU graduation about his plans to pursue a career in diplomacy. (He told us he plans to be the president of Tanzania someday!) Here is part of the article in the *LA Times* from May 14, 2000:

> He joked with his peers from the stage. "This class has endured Y2K, El Nino, Monica Lewinsky...and the school cafeteria!" He was raised with six siblings in Tanzania. His American missionary teacher, Ruth Klavano, sponsored him to come to Washington in 1994. Two years later, he enrolled at Cal Lutheran. After he crossed the stage, Laizer's mom who wore a brightly colored African dress, squeezed his hands and beamed with pride.

Gabriel may be saying, "How did you remember all this?" I kept a clipping from that amazing article that made us so proud! Yes, a bright and beautiful mom in a bright orange dress was on the front page!

Gabriel lived with us the summer of 2000, until he left for graduate school at American University in Washington, DC. That summer we began the adoption of our second son from foster care, Josiah. One of my sweetest memories are the photos that we had taken that summer of our expanded family—Gabriel, James, Josiah, and our two dogs. "Kathy and her crew." Our guys really enjoyed their time with Gabriel. We all traveled to Washington, DC, two years later (2002), when Gabe received his master's degree in international development. Gratefully, Bill had a cousin who lived in Washington, DC, and we stayed with Michael and his family during our week in DC. Gabriel's mom and dad both flew in from Tanzania, and Ruth flew in from the state of Washington. We had a great time together! We promised Gabriel Sr. and Flora that we could come to Tanzania to visit them one day.

That opportunity came six years later (2008), when Bill and I traveled to East Africa for five weeks with half our time in Ethiopia and half our time in Tanzania. During our time in Tanzania, we got a call from the state of Washington that Ruth had been admitted to the hospital and died suddenly. Gabriel Sr. had a gathering of friends and neighbors to "anoint us" as Gabriel's American family. We were so honored.

Six years later (2014), we would meet again in Washington, DC, for the wedding of Gabriel to Bridget at Georgetown University, where she worked. It was fun to see Gabriel Sr. and Flora, so we wore our African clothes they had given to us in 2008. They were so honored. Just like our marriage, a Lutheran guy married a Catholic girl. This time we made a toast to Ruth, who was no longer with us. We would return to Washington, DC, in the fall of 2017 to visit Gabriel and his expanded family—a daughter born in January 2017—the purchase of a home and a car, and now family life in the DC suburbs. Gabriel now works for the United Nations (like an aunt before him), and we fully expect that one of these days they will all move back to Tanzania, where he will become the president of the land of this birth.

So we have a special place in our heart for our third "adopted" son, Gabriel. He lives in the liberal bubble of Washington, DC, while we live in a republican county in Colorado as Christian conservatives. Yes, our politics and worldview are quite different, but love crosses all those boundaries. During our 2017 visit to see Gabriel and Bridget, we attended church at Luther's Place, one of the oldest churches in the city. Wikipedia describes it this way: Luther Place Memorial Church is a congregation belonging to the Evangelical Lutheran Church in America. The neo-Gothic church in Washington, DC, was designed by architects Judson York, J. C. Harkness, and Henry Davis and constructed in 1873 as a memorial to peace and reconciliation following the American Civil War. The pulpit had a banner on it that said "Black Lives Matter," while a stained glass window with Martin Luther was located just above. Such contrasts. We do pray that peace and reconciliation will someday happen in this city.

135

Just a quick mention of one other Gabriel in my life. I did some grant writing for an African American named Gabriel who belonged to the Church of God in Christ. Gabriel taught me a lot about the African American culture and his desire to provide housing, programs, and services for the poor of his community.

We traveled to Muskegon, Michigan (north of Chicago on the shores of Lake Michigan), where I got to meet a senior church leader who was setting up services for needy folks in town, including a food bank for poor families, an early childhood center day care for working moms, low-income housing, and even job creation for inmates who had just been released from the local prison. He knew how to combine his nonprofit status with government grant funds to create viable programs. It was an interesting learning experience.

Years later, when Barack Obama rose from being a Chicago community organizer to US senator and then president of the USA, I remembered the things I had learned during my trip to Muskegon. The black pastors I met were quite unique in their community-organizing skills and pulling together funds from so many sources. Very resourceful.

I guess the name Gabriel comes with high expectations! It seemed to hold true for the two guys I know named Gabriel. May God bless their work to help those in need.

Gary (My First Husband)

It was the summer of 1977 when I moved to beautiful Santa Barbara, California. In the ordinary course of my job as director of medical records at the county hospital, I was the official custodian of medical records and routinely accepted subpoenas for hospital records. While being served with one such subpoena, I met Gary, and he asked me to dinner. He was an attractive and bright fellow. We dated for one year, then got engaged one year and married in the summer of 1979. His friends became my friends, and we had good fun together. I still remember steak and eggs on the deck of his apartment, listening to George Benson music. It seemed quite perfect.

So what does the name Gary mean? According to www.sheknows.com, here is what it means.

The name Gary is an English baby name. In English baby names, the meaning of the name Gary is "hard or bold spear." Yes, I think that name fits his personality. Hard. Bold. Bright. Driven. Fiercely competitive. He was born to older parents (perhaps an "oops" baby) during a time they had a teenage daughter who was born with one kidney and died in a hospital. As such, he was mostly raised as an only child in Torrance, California, referred to as the South Bay.

He had attended University of California–Santa Barbara (UCSB) and loved the area so much he took a job at the office of the Santa Barbara District Attorney as the victim-witness coordinator. All his friends were attorneys and judges, and these people would become my friends as we lived, worked, and played in beautiful Santa Barbara. I was twenty-three, and he was twenty-five when we met. I had reached a point in my life where I was ready to settle down and get married. We met each other's parents, and our lives became intertwined, so it was natural to get married and officially join our lives. Unfortunately, It was a logical choice for me and not one of being madly in love. Gary wanted and needed someone who put him up on a pedestal and loved him desperately. On the outside, we appeared to be the perfect couple living in a perfect place. Not inside.

I came to find out that his dad had a desperate fear of dying in a hospital. He suffered from diabetes and Parkinson's disease and then got diagnosed with heart problems and had a pacemaker inserted in 1982. I remember sitting at his bedside and talking about the Dodgers baseball team. His blood pressure and pulse came down, so the nurses told me to keep it up. Yet in his fearfulness that he would end up dying in a hospital and not wanting to be a burden on anyone, he took his life in the spring of 1982. Gary and I had traveled to Arizona for the weekend to visit my sister and her husband, who had moved there. Upon our return to Los Angeles, his mom picked us up at the airport, and when we drove back to their home, it was locked, with the dogs barking loudly in the backyard. That was where we found him, where he had shot himself in the head. A bloody mess. Shocking to all of us.

I called my mom and dad, and they immediately flew to Los Angeles to help me manage the tragedy and help with the graveside service. I know Gary and his mom really appreciated their time with us. This tied our families together even closer. By the following year, they came and visited us at our new home in Ventura, and Gary had become distant, staying late for work all the time despite having my parents at our home. I shared my concerns with a friend at work, and she said, "He is having an affair." What? Was I blind? Yes. This friend happened to live in Santa Barbara, so she dropped me off at his office one day after work while I waited to surprise him. He did not show up for several hours. When he did, we rode back to our home together. Let's just say the ride home was pretty icy.

He admitted to having an affair with someone he was working with, yet he was in conflict because he loved me as well. We ended up being separated and tried to reconcile through a marriage counselor, but Gary had his own ground rules. "She has to accept 50 percent of the responsibility for my affair." The counselor explained the trust in our relationship had been broken and he bore 100 percent of the challenge to win back my love and trust. He left that first session and never came back. I continued in counseling in 1983 and 1984, a time when I suffered from a situational depression. It was a very low spot in my life. Thank goodness for that counselor. So much God. So much manna.

I did retain an attorney at the end of 1983 and filed for divorce in 1984. I continued to live in our house until it sold late in 1984. We split everything fifty-fifty and both started a new life in 1985. I also filed for an annulment within the Catholic Church, so if I did decide to get remarried, I could marry in the church. I needed to have three witnesses to create lengthy written testimonies, so I chose his best three friends who had been in our wedding. They all completed these forms, and when I went to the marriage tribunal, the defender of the bond (a local well-known defense attorney) said he had never seen such a clear case of "failure to make a commitment" on behalf of one of the marriage parties. The annulment was granted in less than twelve months. Gary would remarry in 1985, but it would be ten years before I chose to remarry.

I am so happy to know that his marriage is still intact thirty-five years later. He and his wife raised twin girls while I was raising two boys with my new husband, Bill. When my dad died in 1986, I never thought to call and tell him (our lives were completely separate), but I heard from a second party that he was sad he had not been notified. How interesting. I do think my family had become his family, and he did miss that part of our relationship. My grandmother had become good friends with his mother, and they stayed in touch. Sadly, Grandma died the same year as my dad. So many losses. For all of us.

So what did I learn from this failed first marriage? First, that there was such a thing as being "unequally yoked" (a biblical term to one who never knew the Bible). Gary's mom played the organ at a small church in Torrance, and we did attend this church during our time together. It was sweet. He did not, however, ever attend the Catholic church with me, so we lived "married single lives" in our five years of marriage. He never had any professed faith except in himself. He was bright. Handsome. Had a good job. And he loved me. Wasn't that enough? No. Here is what the Bible says:

> Do not be bound together with unbelievers; for
> what partnership has righteousness and lawless-
> ness, or what fellowship has light with darkness?
> (2 Cor. 6:14 NASB)

Here is what www.GotQuestions.org says about this term. A *yoke* is a wooden bar that joins two oxen to each other and to the burden they pull. An "unequally yoked" team has one stronger ox and one weaker, or one taller and one shorter. The weaker or shorter ox would walk more slowly than the taller, stronger one, causing the load to go around in circles. When oxen are unequally yoked, they cannot perform the task set before them. Instead of working together, they are at odds with each other. Wow. This explained a lot to me.

During our premarital preparation (a weekend retreat held by the Catholic Church), I had a gut feeling I was not getting into a good marriage, but the plans had been made and we were too far along to turn back. I thought about breaking it off, but he pleaded with me to not leave him during one episode where he ended up in an ER with an infection. So I stayed in the relationship. This was a mistake. Always trust your gut.

In some final soul-searching conversations that we had before our final split, he admitted he had been with many women in his life before and during our marriage. Many years later, I had to laugh at how much like Bill Clinton he was! He even said to me that my problem was that I saw life in black-and-white terms while he saw it in fifty shades of gray. (That book came out many years later—ha!) Yes, our moral compass was completely different. Ours was never a "till death do us part" union. God had other plans for both of us. So much for "my will" versus "His will be done." But I do want to thank Gary for teaching me a lot about myself and the mistakes that I made. It led to many years of being single before I would find a person who shared my same values and wanted to marry me. That was a long time of yearning for a real soul mate.

PS: Thank you to the marriage counselor that I continued to see during my separation and divorce. He helped put the whole mess into perspective for me. I had to learn the meaning of the word *narcissist* and be able to stop beating myself up for my first real "failure" in life. Our weekly sessions were so helpful to me—so many wild stories to share, but not here. Some things are not meant to be. Our ability to let go and keep going is so important. God carried me through all this, with much protection and manna.

Great Britain (England, America, the Bible)

As I explained in chapter B with my first love, Brian, I have long had an affection for all things British. It is interesting to note that many of our Founding Fathers remained loyal to the king of England even after they moved to America. Today our countries are great allies; after all, we saved them during WWII! They never rebuilt a strong military or Navy (investing instead in social medicine), so they have also come to depend on the USA as a very important military ally in the world. So where do these two countries stand in the area of biblical prophecy?

The Bible talks a lot about the twelve tribes of Israel, descendants of Jacob (his father was Isaac, who was born to Abraham). God promised Abraham that he was blessed to be a blessing and the father of many nations. This blessing carried onto Jacob, who God renamed Israel. When he was about to die, he gathered together his twelve sons and gave each of them a blessing. The firstborn son, Rueben, did not get a blessing since he slept with his father's wife (Gen. 48:3–4). According to www.freebiblestudyguides.com, Jacob went on to give a double blessing to his favorite son, Joseph. In Genesis 48:15–16, 19–20, Jacob pronounced special birthright blessings on Joseph's two sons. In essence, Jacob was adopting his grandsons as his own sons (v. 5). In Genesis 48:17–20, we learn God put Jacob's second son ahead of his first son:

> When Joseph saw his father placing his right hand on Ephraim's head he was displeased; so he took hold of his father's hand to move it from Ephraim's head to Manasseh's head. Joseph said to him, "No, my father, this one is the firstborn; put your right hand on his head."
>
> But his father refused and said, "I know, my son, I know. He too will become a people, and he too will become great. Nevertheless, his younger brother will be greater than he, and his descendants will become a group of nations." He blessed them that day and said, "In your name will Israel pronounce this blessing:
>
> 'May God make you like Ephraim and Manasseh.'"
>
> So he put Ephraim ahead of Manasseh.

He said, "Let my name (Israel) be named upon them" (v. 16). Many believe that since England came first, it was the tribe of

Manasseh. America came second, so it was the tribe of Ephraim and would be the greater power and be one nation "of many nationalities"—we are a melting pot. No wonder the British and American people have felt like brothers—they descended from brothers! The key is that Israel is a group of nations (not the physical country of Israel). It is the tribe of Judah that is the chosen people, the Jews.

God inspired many descendants of Manasseh to relocate from Britain and other European countries to colonies in America. As a result of the American Revolution, the two brothers became separate politically. Sometimes you will hear the phrase "Thirteen tribes of Israel." That is when someone is counting the descendants of Ephraim and Manasseh as two different tribes. The Bible's many end-time prophecies of Israel are often referring to the USA, Britain, and other related people whose native language is English. End-time prophecies of Judah refer to the modern state of Israel (home of the Jews). Many prophecies warn of God's judgment and punishment to come on both Israel and Judah for their disobedience, but others show how both will be later restored to greatness and roles of leadership. That is why America must always stay a friend to Israel. So Great Britain, America, and Israel are all tied together. Cool. Some ask why the USA is not mentioned in the Bible. It appears that it is, just under the tribe of Ephraim.

I find this linkage of the United States and Britain to be very interesting. In England, the king is also the head of the Church of England (Anglican Church), but in America, citizens enjoy a freedom of religion as "one nation under God." This is promised in the First Amendment to our Constitution. In my own life, it is quite interesting that my British boyfriend was Catholic, the very religious group that fought against the protestors. The Church of England and the Church of Rome never got along. I am now part of the "protestors" (Protestant) who follow the Bible and owe no allegiance to a higher organization like the papacy. My story is embedded in one bigger story. And it all comes together at the end of the age. Amazing.

CHAPTER H

Hawaii (Pearl Harbor to Island Vacation)

Since my book is chapters A–Z, I had to come up with at least one person, place, or thing for each letter of the alphabet. When I got to *H*, my mind could only think of Hawaii. So let me describe how this beautiful place also has a person component for our family. I discovered this beautiful place on my first honeymoon to Maui, Kawai, and the big island of Hawaii. It was quite extraordinary! So what is the history of this fiftieth state? Here is what Wikipedia says.

The history of Hawaii describes the era of human settlements in the Hawaiian Islands. That history begins sometime between AD 124 and AD 1120, when the islands were first settled by Polynesians. Hawaiian civilization was isolated from the rest of the world for at least five hundred years. Europeans, led by British explorer James Cook, arrived in the Hawaiian Islands in 1778. However, some researchers state the Spanish captain Ruy López de Villalobos was the first European to see the islands in 1542. Within five years after Cook's arrival, European military technology helped Kamehameha I conquer and unify the islands for the first time, establishing the kingdom of Hawaii. The kingdom was prosperous and important for its agriculture and strategic location in the Pacific. (Yes, King Kamehameha statues are everywhere in Hawaii!)

American immigration began almost immediately after Cook's arrival, led by Protestant missionaries. Americans set up plantations to grow sugar. Their methods of plantation farming required substantial labor. Waves of permanent immigrants came from Japan,

China, and the Philippines to work in the fields. The government of Japan organized and gave special protection to its people, who comprised about 25 percent of the Hawaiian population by 1896.

The native population succumbed to disease brought by the Europeans (particularly smallpox), declining from three hundred thousand in the 1770s to over sixty thousand in the 1850s to twenty-four thousand in 1920. Americans within the kingdom government rewrote the Constitution, severely curtailing the power of King David Kalākaua and disenfranchising the rights of most Native Hawaiians and Asian citizens to vote, through excessively high property and income requirements. This gave a sizable advantage to plantation owners. Queen Liliuokalani attempted to restore royal powers in 1893 but was placed under house arrest by businessmen with help from the US military. Against the queen's wishes, the Republic of Hawaii was formed for a short time. This government agreed on behalf of Hawaii to join the US in 1898 as the territory of Hawaii. In 1959, the islands became the state of Hawaii of the United States. It is surely a land of amazing history! Of course, Wikipedia may have its own emphasis.

When I met my current husband, Bill, I found out that his mom's family had a direct connection to Pearl Harbor. When his mom was just a teen (before being married or having her own children), she had an older brother who was killed on the battleship *Arizona* in Pearl Harbor on December 7, 1941—yes, that day of infamy that brought the USA into WWII. When his mom died in 2006, her sons took down boxes from her attic and found remnants from that time that included such things as an embroidered pillowcase that said "USS *Arizona*" that was sent to the sailors' moms on Mother's Day 1941. The family decided to donate this to the USS *Arizona* Memorial Museum that was rebuilt and opened in December 2010.

Bill and I took our two sons and joined his sister, brother, and cousin for a week in Honolulu for the occasion as invited guests. This cousin (Judy) had lived on Ford Island in Hawaii when her husband was stationed there, so we got a private tour and special access to commissary prices at a special hotel for such families. It was great fun! The boys got to understand a real, personal family connection to Pearl Harbor, and I know it made history come alive for them.

Bill and I had traveled to Oahu on a business trip with his company in 1994 and enjoyed the best of everything from his generous boss with a great expense account. We took our boys to the island of Maui when they were younger—we won one week at a condo there during a live auction for charity, so our boys have been there twice. We have another friend who was born in Hawaii, and as a native, he is given a plot of land there where he someday hopes to build a home. We will be ready to visit, for sure! We love this beautiful place. I now appreciate that some of its history was about Christian missionaries. Our fiftieth state is very special indeed. Bill even loves the Hawaiian Christmas songs!

CHAPTER I

International Baccalaureate (World School Learning)

Since I have spent the last two years of my life as the administrative person in an international baccalaureate (IB) school in our district, I had to include a section on this "thing" that I never knew much about until I jumped in with both feet. So what the heck is an IB school? According to www.ibo.org, the IB offers an education for students from age three to nineteen, comprising of four programs that focus on teaching students to think critically and independently and how to inquire with care and logic. The IB prepares students to succeed in a world where facts and fiction merge in the news, and where asking the right questions is a crucial skill that will allow them to flourish long after they've left their programs. They are supported by IB teachers and coordinators who develop and promote the IB's curriculums in over five thousand schools globally every day, in over 150 countries around the world.

So the IB program where I worked was "a school within a school," one of international distinction that is free to the students who attend while part of a public school in America. The only fees that are assessed are for the final IB exams in the last month of the high school senior year. In many countries, IB schools are private and require tuition to be paid by the parents. As such, when foreign families move to the USA (i.e., from a country like India), they are delighted to be able to enroll their student at no cost. Grades K-6 are the primary years program (PYP); grades 7, 8, 9, and 10 are considered the middle years program (MYP); and grades 11 and 12 are the diploma program (DP). There is also a career program (CP) at some schools.

If I had had the chance to be part of an IB program in high school, I would have taken it! In many ways, my "learning" over the years is very much IB in nature since it includes an IB profile of learning traits. Here is what www.IBO.org says:

> Inquirers. They develop their natural curiosity. They acquire the skills necessary to conduct inquiry and research and show independence in learning. They actively enjoy learning and this love of learning will be sustained throughout their lives
>
> Knowledgeable. They explore concepts, ideas and issues that have local and global significance. In doing so, they acquire in-depth knowledge and develop understanding across a broad and balanced range of disciplines.
>
> Thinkers. They exercise initiative in applying thinking skills critically and creatively to recognize and approach complex problems, and make reasoned, ethical decisions.
>
> Communicators. They understand and express ideas and information confidently and creatively in more than one language and in a variety of modes of communication. They work effectively and willingly in collaboration with others.
>
> Principled. They act with integrity and honesty, with a strong sense of fairness, justice and respect for the dignity of the individual, groups and communities. They take responsibility for their own actions and the consequences that accompany them.
>
> Open-minded. They understand and appreciate their own cultures and personal histories,

and are open to the perspectives, values and traditions of other individuals and communities. They are accustomed to seeking and evaluating a range of points of view, and are willing to grow from the experience.

Caring. They show empathy, compassion and respect towards the needs and feelings of others. They have a personal commitment to service, and act to make a positive difference to the lives of others and to the environment.

Risk-takers. They approach unfamiliar situations and uncertainty with courage and forethought, and have the independence of spirit to explore new roles, ideas and strategies. They are brave and articulate in defending their beliefs.

Balanced. They understand the importance of intellectual, physical and emotional balance to achieve personal well-being for themselves and others.

Reflective. They give thoughtful consideration to their own learning and experience. They are able to assess and understand their strengths and limitations in order to support their learning and personal development.

The IBDP program has such great academic rigor that grades are "weighted." For example, a B has a weight of 4, and an A has a weight of 5. These student GPAs often put them at the top of their class and make universities put their applications at the top of their stacks. Students must also do an extended essay, be part of creativity activity service, and take an evening class in how to learn the so-called the Theory of Knowledge. They do lots of journaling and writing and develop a great skill set to do well in a university setting.

I learned that this program, just over fifty years old, was started by a group of diplomats who had to move a lot, and as such, their children faced varying kinds of curriculum, especially in high school.

By creating a standard, rigorous curriculum in English, world languages, history, science, math, and theater and arts, they could move from one area to another and not miss a beat. This curriculum was international in its rigor and consistency. The headquarters are in the Hague (Netherlands), with information systems based in Wales. It was fun to hear that British accent and manners come across on my inquiry calls. My love for all things British—again!

I have to dedicate some space to the course called the Theory of Knowledge, TOK. According to www.IBO.org, this class provides an opportunity for students to reflect on the nature of knowledge and on how we know what we claim to know. As a thoughtful and purposeful inquiry into different ways of knowing and into different kinds of knowledge, TOK is composed almost entirely of questions.

The most central of these is, "How do we know?" while other questions include thus:

- What counts as evidence for X?
- How do we judge which is the best model of Y?
- What does theory Z mean in the real world?

Through discussions of these and other questions, students gain greater awareness of their personal and ideological assumptions, as well as developing an appreciation of the diversity and richness of cultural perspectives.

TOK aims to make students aware of the interpretative nature of knowledge, including personal ideological biases—whether these biases are retained, revised, or rejected.

It offers students and their teachers the opportunity to

- reflect critically on diverse ways of knowing and on areas of knowledge, and
- consider the role and nature of knowledge in their own culture, in the cultures of others, and in the wider world.

In addition, TOK prompts students to

- be aware of themselves as thinkers, encouraging them to become more acquainted with the complexity of knowledge, and
- recognize the need to act responsibly in an increasingly interconnected but uncertain world.

At our high school, this required course is offered on Wednesday nights from 5:00–8:00 p.m., so I asked my boss if I could audit the class, and he approved. So I spent a few weeks at the beginning of January 2019 to attend this evening class. As part of the experience, I did my own TOK journal (required for TOK students) along the way. I also discovered that our school had hosted a TOK symposium each year for IB students across the region. The first such event occurred in February of 2018, with a theme of truth; the following year it was identity, and in 2020 it was power. So I helped prepare for the last two events. A videotape of each event was created, so I started my learning about this event by watching the TOK video on truth.

What is truth? Speakers from various areas of life gave breakout presentations, including such fields as law, news/media, performing arts, politics, religion, science, and visual arts. I was shocked to hear students say, "There is no such thing as absolute truth. It is all relative. Your truth may be different from mine." Wow. No wonder young people are so confused—they have no compass to follow. My mind went back to a course we took at our first Colorado church, called the Truth Project. According to www.FocusOnTheFamily.com, this course is defined as a ground-breaking small-group curriculum on the biblical worldview. This video-based home Bible study is the starting point for looking at life from a biblical perspective. Join Dr. Del Tackett as he takes you through thirteen engaging video lessons on the relevance and importance of living the biblical worldview in daily life, featuring insights from biblical experts like Ravi Zacharias, R. C. Sproul, Os Guinness, and Gordon Pennington. I have since learned that Del is a history teacher—what a joy to learn from him. It also showed me the importance of our worldview, where the biblical worldview is so different from the secular environment in which we live.

When the focus was identity, I was very curious what the Methodist pastor would say during his presentation. He shared the stage with a female leader from the Muslim faith. Once again, I was shocked. As he was a Christian pastor, I expected him to find his identity in Christ and his Word, the Bible. He never mentioned either one. Instead, he talked about finding God in nature and that it was all about a good god who made a beautiful creation. He said his faith was not much different from his Muslim sister's—they both believed in a god of peace and love.

During breakout sessions, I listened to students express their complete disinterest in the faith of their parents since it never had any impact on their life—they were forced to attend by their parents until their teen years. Many had an empty sense about what life is all about. Again, I was very sad that there had not been a bold defense of the Christian faith that is all about your identity in the Lord God, who created the heaven and the earth. Jesus said, "I Am the way, the truth, and the life" (John 14:6). "No one comes to the Father except through me." There are not many roads to God. It made me sad to think of what a lost generation we have—they do know this truth or have a rock-solid identity for their lives.

The next symposium was on power. My boss used this quote from Toni Morrison as the anchor for the day: "I tell my students, 'When you get these jobs that you have been so brilliantly trained for, just remember that your real job is that if you are free, you need to free somebody else. If you have some power, then your job is to empower somebody else. This is not just a grab-bag candy game." This was an interesting perspective from a doctor of philosophy.

He also has a quote from Tao Te Ching:

What makes the rivers so noble and respected
Is that they skillfully adopt the lower position
This is why the fertile valleys all flourish around them.
In the same way, he who wants to rule the people,

Must act with humility.
He who intends to be the face of the populace,
Must be utterly self-effacing.
To lead, he must place his ego behind.
In this way,
Though the sage actually sits above them,
The people do not feel his weight.
Though he stands out front,
He does not block the way.
The world never tires of exalting him-
It is because his needs do not contend with theirs
That they will never find any reason to contend
with him.

I could not help but think about Jesus as the ultimate "servant leader." I hope that this was the overall message that came across. I could not attend the event (I was ill), but I did pray that minds would be opened to the only one who had the real power in our universe, God.

If an IB education really included a way to think of the world from many perspectives, they would welcome open discussions that included the Christian worldview. Sadly, I did not hear this voice as being accepted in the liberal education system. As these IB students attend colleges and universities, they will likely find that most professors only teach one perspective, and if you challenge their teaching, your grade will suffer. So sad. I had hoped IB would be different. I pray that those who do have Christian worldview will have the courage to speak up. Even in IB.

I have to include one final perspective, that TOK journal that I created during my time in the class. Here are some excerpts from my journal entries. I was pleased that my boss saw it as a great reflection. Please excuse the length and detail of my entries. Believe me, it was heartfelt.

Theory of Knowledge (TOK) Reflections
By Kathy Kramer, January–May 2019
Class January 23, 2019

This was my first TOK class, so I tried to listen, learn, observe, then reflect. The way to learn was related to senses tonight, starting with the sense of taste. The hands-on presentation and exercise led by Lisa was excellent—great small-group exercise with very interesting Q&A afterward. In a later small group, a way of knowing the question raised by a student was about someone with a hearing impairment. How do the deaf learn? What other senses do they rely on? I suggested watching the movie *Mr. Holland's Opus*, where a music teacher has a deaf son and can't believe he could know/appreciate the music of John Lennon.

After the class, I got to thinking of the old days of studying current events in school. On this week, this date, there was such a missed opportunity for learning from two other senses, seeing and hearing. The news was about a Right to Life March in Washington, DC, by Catholic students. They were confronted by a Native American pounding a drum, and the whole news report was reported almost entirely inaccurately. The entire event was on a videotape that lasted almost an hour. It became a political issue of right versus left, with a liberal bias toward pro-abortion. If you don't agree, you are wrong/bad.

January 22, 1973, was the landmark Supreme Court ruling on *Roe v. Wade*, allowing Americans to have abortions. Therefore, every third week of January, there is a Right to Life March held in our nation's capital to those defending the life of the unborn. This is often a gathering of Christian folks, students and adults, all ages and sizes, peaceful gathering. Forty-six years after *Roe v. Wade*, this is still a hot topic in political circles. I can relate because I attended a Catholic college and my major math professor (with a PhD in math) gave up his career as a college instructor to go work for the Right to Life Movement.

This week the current event story is, New York governor Cuomo passes pro-abortion legislation up to time of baby's birth. Cuomo is a Catholic. This is in direct contrast to his professed faith. As such, the Catholic bishops strongly denounced his passage/support of this new law. Some Catholic leaders are calling for him to be excommunicated. Again, a hot topic in the news that is primarily political, right versus left, with a wide array of news coverage. My thought is, *What do you hear and see, and what do you know based on your own perceptions and background versus the news?* I bet most students don't even know what *excommunicated* means. Heck, most Catholics get it wrong.

What a great opportunity to talk about how we know. Where is our identity, based upon our upbringing versus the news versus what is taught in school versus personal research? When a new Supreme Court justice nominee is brought before Congress, the *Roe v. Wade* issue is the number 1 topic of questions (direct and indirect) offered by primarily Democratic politicians. It is a core principle/value of the Democratic Party. It is now the number 1 cause of death in the United States. With all the other hot topics that affect daily lives, why is abortion the one that causes the greatest division/upheaval? Why have there become three choices?

Right: I believe the unborn is a live baby and an abortion is killing a child.

Left: I believe the unborn is only "tissue" and a woman and her doctor should have the right to choose if/when they will terminate the pregnancy.

Center: I don't personally believe in abortion, but I respect the right for someone else to choose what they want. Who am I to decide? (Clearly, politicians love this one!)

The other issue is, Who pays for abortion? The real issue for politicians is, Will government pay for these abortion procedures? Many states are passing legislation to say they will not pay for such procedures. This includes anyone on federal Medicaid benefits. It also begs the question of the choice of the hospital, such as Catholic hospital not wanting to have abortions done in their facilities since it is contrary to their core Catholic beliefs.

We need to look at the TOK ways of knowing and areas of knowledge.

TOK Ways of Knowing	TOK Areas of Knowledge
Language	Mathematics
Sense Perception	Natural Science
Emotion	History
Reason	The Arts
Imagination	Ethics
Faith	Religious Knowledge
Intuition	Indigenous Knowledge
Memory	

I don't sit on the TOK planning team to develop curriculum for each session, so I know there is far more to come. Perhaps each week is to focus only on one area of knowledge? Or one way of knowing? It just seems richer to cover many of these in class. In this case, there is plenty of natural science about the fetus—ultrasounds show a lot of detail. Religious beliefs are also pretty clear-cut; just look at church doctrine for each faith. Your emotions, reason, and faith certainly play key roles in any discussion of abortion. My reflection is, don't pass a great opportunity of something happening real time in our culture; open dialogue is needed.

Class January 30, 2019

Tonight the way of learning was sight, beginning with an exercise to draw the stuffed giraffe that Kelse had brought to class, with partial knowledge/sight of the object. (I came in late, so I missed the introduction—just heard the discussion.) How do you know what you see versus what is it supposed to be? I am amazed at some of the "deep" answers offered by students:

- Fear and self-preservation force us to be curious.
- Nature abhors a void, so imagination fills in the blanks.

- Ways of knowing include memory, imagination, reason, emotion.

The second session was about the upcoming TOK symposium at DU on February 9, with a focus on identity. Only two students have signed up so far. The TOK video of last year's seminar was shown. It is always good to hear the connection/laughter when students see someone they know in the video. This just underscored one of the best ways to engage students is by other students who have gone before them.

The next session was on the CAS trip during fall break 2019 to Prague and Krakow. Kelse did a nice job of differentiating the trip as not "a normal tourist trip" but rather a hands-on creativity activity service (CAS) experience. The Prague piece will include the homeless, urban farming, urban cooking, treasure hunt, and street art. What a way to see the Czech Republic! It was called Czechoslovakia when I visited many years ago. The Czech Republic is a unitary parliamentary constitutional republic in which the president is the head of state and the prime minister is the head of government. I cannot recall if it was ever Communist but glad to see it is not today.

The Krakow piece will be about the Holocaust, Auschwitz, meeting survivors, players acting workshop. This year is the twenty-fifth anniversary of the film *Schindler's List* (the production director for our church Christmas concert chose one of the songs from the film, so we learned). It might be a great exercise before the trip to have the class attend this movie as a group and then have a discussion afterward. The Holocaust is such a heavy topic. What is so sweet about this movie is that it begins and ends with survivors coming together in Israel to honor those who helped them during the reign of Hitler. Oscar Schindler's family was included since this is a true story. I have visited both these areas—the trip should be very eye-opening.

Two pieces of art—the same? Dr. Fleet showed two pieces of art by two different artists, and students had to present an argument on why they were the same. Such interesting discussion based on so many areas of knowledge:

- Art: In the eyes of the beholder, same color and style.
- Math: Angles, photography, quadrants had same pictures.
- History: Names/times of artists and the work that they did.
- Science: Cannibalism, both death, devouring each other.

When I heard one was a very large painting on display in the Louvre, it gave me a different appreciation for the work. I may need to look more closely at art in the future.

The final exercise in which I participated was in honor of the Wish Week Harry Potter Theme. Kelse led an exercise in the computer lab to go to the Pottermore.com website and take the personality test to see which house you are most likely to belong. Talk about identity! Since I know very little about Harry Potter, here is what I learned from listening to the discussion. As bad luck would have it, my computer would not access the internet, so I just had to watch and see what others said.

- Hufflepuffs (yellow color; animal, badger): Most inclusive, kindest of all the houses, with key traits such as fair, loyal, tolerant, patient, and dedicated. Wow, that is my hall, the freshman team I am supporting this week. I like it.
- Gryffindor (red color; animal, lion): This was *the* house for Harry Potter and appears to be the favorite since it includes the traits of bravery, chivalry, strength, determination, and courage. I love red. I would like to be a member of this house.
- Ravenclaw (blue color; animal, raven): This appears to be the house of intelligence and ready minds, with traits that include creativity, uniqueness, wisdom, originality, and intuition. Hmmm, sounds good to me, but really, a big bird with big claws? Also sounds kind of scary. Blue is usually such a cool color.

- Slytherin (green color; animal, snake). I hate snakes! And I thought green was such a fresh spring color! The traits include preservation, resourcefulness, cleverness, and ambition. Sounds like Satan himself. I can see why this might be perceived as the "bad guy" among all the houses. I guess the Harry Potter bad guy was from here.

What amazed me most is that despite what Kelse said about all this being purely imaginary, I can see how it could affect a person who took it seriously as relating to their identity. It is clear people do sometimes draw their identity from fictional characters. This seems pretty sad to me, but something to be aware of, especially with something as popular as Harry Potter—so many books, movies, and its own Universal Studios land. It also has a language all its own. As I walked down the halls to leave the building, I took a closer look at the many decorations. I guess I need to read the book(s).

Kelse stressed there are *negative* words and *positive* words, so we often tend to see ourselves in a more positive light. Do we really see/ know our negative traits? Can they be changed? Several students claimed their negative-type traits and explained how they could be used in a positive way (realism). It certainly was a lively topic for Wish Week.

Finally, a handout called Windows was copied for distribution. It talks about looking from outside into an open window versus a closed window, including one that just has candlelight inside. I did not hear any presentation/discussion. For me it roused a memory of the painter of light, Thomas Kinkade, since I love his work. I read when he was a child (Placerville, California), he had one brother and a single mother who had to work two jobs. His job was delivering newspapers, and he was intrigued with all the beautiful homes with lights beaming out. Their home was always a dark place to return— no one home. How precious he bent to the light and not the dark, and as a result, we have many beautiful paintings!

TOK at DU

Leadership and identity (Mike Coffman and Dr. Thomas Tucker). It was quite interesting to hear from both our retired US congressman (Coffman) and current school superintendent (Tucker) since their backgrounds and perspectives were quite different.

Mike Coffman said his identity started with his high school experience. He was a poor student who dropped out to join the US Army. He used the GI Bill to further his education and went on to join the Marines. After military service, he started his own business (property management) and went on to serve in the State House and Senate and then the US Congress for ten years. He now plans to run for another local political role. His identity early in life was a military one; his dad was in the military, and he lived on bases. At age thirteen, his first time off base, he saw the public response to the Vietnam War. His worldview became broadened at that time. He believes 2019 is an "urgent time" for our country to talk about identity, with "nationalism" seeming to be popular among leaders rather than a more global perspective. He also noted that social media is having a huge impact on how we see the world, affecting our identity, and the media is pushing us more in a liberal direction.

Thomas Tucker said his identity was deeply rooted in faith and family and self and education. He talked about our unique DNA and all being part of the human race—ethnicity is a better descriptor. He was born in 1964, during the Civil Rights era, the youngest of eleven children born in Arkansas, but the first born in a hospital. He had to be "rushed" home within twenty-four hours since white women didn't want their babies in the same nursery as a black baby. He noted legislation that he believes changed our national identity, the 1954 *Brown v. Board of Education* (school integration) and 1965 Voting Rights Act (giving blacks the right to vote). He said he was part of a family with three generations as Baptist pastors, so if his style sounded that way, he came by it naturally.

He went on to say his leadership was based upon faith, tough skin, truth, courage, intellect, persistence, growth, and an ability to "read the tea leaves" (be still and listen to what others say). He warned the young generation in attendance to not fall into "groupthink" promoted on social media but be true to yourself and your values. During the Q and A, it was asked, What common unifying factor did America now have? (Compared to being against Communism during the Cold War.) He said we need to focus on our common factors and not our differences. He believes that parents in our school district are the same way—they want what is best for their children (not right versus left), and we all need to rally around the fifty-one million public school students in the USA.

He had an exercise for students to write down four things that define them. When answers were shared, the biggest common areas were family, faith, education, and values, but *not* one mention of money. Seeking wealth does not drive our identity, but being true to things like civility, compassion, and kindness.

Religion (Paul, a Methodist pastor; Iman Jodeh, Islamic leader). It was interesting to listen to the afternoon session on identity in religion, where twenty-one students sat in a circle on the floor during the discussion. They were asked to identify their name, school, religious background, and gender pronoun. (This perplexed many, especially boys. He/she—what?)

Paul described his role as a Methodist pastor over fifty-plus other Methodist pastors in the greater Denver area. He grew up in the western part of the state, near four corners, and came to love nature. He described his identity with God found in nature (such as backpacking) and finding the deeper meaning of life in nature. He went on to describe Christianity as a religion to follow Jesus, who Himself was a Jewish rabbi who taught by asking a lot of questions. He often answered questions with more questions. He noted that much of what Jesus said was not written down until many years later. It was not until AD 230, with the Council of Nicaea (Roman Emperor Constantine), that an "empire religion" (the papacy) was established. The Reformation of this church by Martin Luther in the 1500s was more about politics than faith. It happened at the same time as the Renaissance, which questioned many things in science and art. He believes we are now in a Great Reformation, where the religion most noted on forms is none. He believes an interfaith movement is happening where all are the same.

Netta was sitting in for Iman Jodeh, and she said Islam is a faith that follows the Koran, which often begins many sentences with "Don't you think…?" Also a book of questions, such as in Jesus's words. She said she had read and searched about her religion and believed it to be a continuation of Jewish and Christian religions, with a major theme of "Don't judge." Fast and pray and then choose what is right for you. Prophets are just messengers from God, but faith is a one-on-one relationship we each have with God. We get to pick our own path.

Iman Jodeh did come and said her Muslim upbringing "ways of knowing" was based a lot upon language. She had to do religious studies to understand. The students were split into seven groups of three to discuss and "share your identity based upon your upbringing in any faith." Most students said they based their religious identity on emotion, intuition, memory, what they were taught, with many not knowing what their current religious identity was. A handout, Meet the Middle East, was then distributed, with an invitation to become a youth ambassador, including a full immersion trip to Israel to learn more about the Middle East. The program is designed to educate high school teens to listen and dialogue, conflict resolution, negotiation, Judaism, Christianity, Islam, and the Israel-Palestine conflict. The seven-month class is Tuesday evenings during March, April, May, with the trip on June 10–19. It would be exciting if a few of our IB students took advantage of this learning opportunity.

My final reflection on this day was one of "very interesting" but, again, several missed opportunities. I was disappointed that a Christian pastor would not discuss "Identity in Christ" as reading and understanding the Bible and following what it says. The Bible was never mentioned. To say this book is the same as the Koran or the Mormon Bible is simply not true. An opportunity for students to become biblically literate should have been offered. Students in the small groups seemed to have lost any identity based on religion except to reject most of what their parents had taught them or forced them to do—they wanted to find their own identity. This requires "digging deeper" into each choice and coming to understand what each means. This seems to be the essence of an IB education. You can't make an informed choice if you don't first know what each one offers. (See next page, my epilogue.)

Religion versus Identity: An Epilogue by Kathy Kramer

This issue is dear to my heart. I was raised in a large Catholic family in the upper Midwest. I went to a Catholic Benedictine College. I was true to my faith until I was thirty-six years old—it is all I knew, and I was always a "dutiful daughter and student." I can remember when I graduated from college and went on a trip to Europe through an international student exchange with the University of Illinois–Urbana, twelve countries in twelve weeks for only $1,200. What an amazing life adventure! (Being a good Catholic, I found a Catholic church every Sunday during the trip to go to Mass.) At the end of our trip, we had a final party, and I was on the planning committee. We wrote limericks for each member of our group. I don't know why, but I do remember the one written for me:

> *There once was a gal named Kathy S. As talkers she*
> *is one of the best.*
> *She was top of her class and used to go to Mass,*
> *but now she's gone down with the rest!*

Just to clarify, I did nothing illegal or immoral on the trip—just a whole lot of fun! There were European men who took a liking to me, such as the gondolier in Venice, Italy, and the son of the restaurant owner with a motorcycle in Athens, Greece, but my guy friends were always there to rescue me! I even spent time at the beginning and end of my trip in London with my high school boyfriend, who was in medical school there. Yes, I was pretty innocent and naïve—a real Goody Two-Shoes. But this trip expanded my world. Thank goodness God protected me from harm.

I digress. What happened when I was thirty-six years old? I was invited by a friend (who also grew up Catholic) to a nondenominational Christian church Bible study. I had never studied the Bible, so I jumped in. Our pastor said he was the shepherd of the second biggest Catholic church in the area since so many of us "wondering Catholics" came to hear him preach. We stayed. I was even married in this church. I did have a Catholic priest come to do a prayer and a blessing at our wedding (I have lots of Franciscan priests who are friends), and my family really appreciated that! Years later, my sister Sue asked, Why did I abandon my faith? If anything, I was the most likely one to become a nun—ha!

I told her I did not leave something but rather expanded my faith and grew to know more about one true faith in Jesus by reading and studying the Bible. We *never* studied the Bible during my Catholic upbringing. There was no college class in "Study of the Bible," although I am sure there was a department of theology (the study of God, Catholic version). This book (the Bible) is quite complicated and can take a lifetime to study, but the more I studied, the more Bible studies I took, the more I wanted to learn even more, to go deeper. I have longed to tell my Catholic family members about some of the things "added" by the Church of Rome, not biblical, so they could know/understand the one true faith.

I first saw the Vatican in the summer of 1976. I would go back in the summer of 1996, now married and traveling with my new Bible-based pastor. When we got to Saint Peter's Basilica in Rome, he pointed out some things I never would have known about twenty years earlier. There is a statue of Saint Peter just outside the basilica with his name, where he is standing, holding some keys. Our pastor explained a verse from Scripture that said something like, "On this rock I build my church, and I give you the keys to the kingdom." The early church took that one verse literally and said Peter was the first pope, a vicar of Christ on earth. Catholics must go through their local priest, bishop, cardinal to obey the pope and take part in the sacraments to get to heaven. It is a faith based on works. You can work your way to heaven with good works. (I even recall many jokes about when you get to heaven's gate, Saint Peter will be there to ask you some questions you must get right to enter in. Really?)

This was the very issue that Martin Luther (a Catholic priest) challenged in the 1500s when he nailed his thesis to the doors of a large German church. Faith in Christ alone is what brings salvation. The papacy was corrupt. They added many rules and "financial obligations" to church members to keep control of their large political power. This included having people buy indulgences so they can "pay their deceased loved ones into heaven," from purgatory, something else made up by the church. Martin Luther wanted to reform the church (hence the name Reformation), but he was so feared by the papacy he was kicked out and a bounty was put on his head! Today, two of the holy days of obligation include All Saints Day (November 1) and All Souls Day (November 2), so Catholics still pray for dead people all the time! My new faith says you make your choice on earth and live according to His will; you turn your life over to Jesus. Once you die, you die. No one can pray for you beyond the grave. Your relationship with Jesus is personal, not something you "inherit" or something your children inherit from you. God has no grandchildren.

When we adopted our two sons from foster care, one of them had a birth brother whose adoptive family moved from California to Salt Lake City, Utah. They were/are surrounded by members of the Church of Christ of the Latter-Day Saints (Mormons). On tours of the great Mormon Temple, we were told when you die, if you had lived a good life, you will get your own planet to rule. Somehow, the prophet Joseph Smith heard from an angel named Moroni that Jesus and Satan were brothers. They had a fight. Jesus won. Really? I came to now wonder what all the other faiths/religions taught. Back to my sheltered Catholic upbringing. I am a lifelong learner, and this challenged me to learn more about other world religions. I took a class called Perspectives, which teaches about faith traditions across the world. You *must* understand the traditions of a faith before you can become an effective missionary to a certain people group. Makes sense to me. To know, to understand, you have to study.

So my identity based on my faith has gone from believing what I was told (without question) to making choices based upon a thorough study of what different religions have to offer, what they teach or do *not* teach. Jesus said, "I am the way, the truth, and the life. No one comes to the Father except through me." Yes, that's a pretty "exclusive" sentence, and we are in a very "inclusive" world, so it does not ring true to a lot of people. Hence, we have to "tread lightly" when we discuss religion with others; like politics, it can turn into a big fight! (My dad became a Reagan Democrat; he became conservative as he grew older.) What I do know is that, like Dr. Tucker, my identity is based upon faith and family for me, my new faith and the family of believers to which I belong. The joy of the Lord is my strength, and I hope people see Jesus through me. He was a good God man who cared deeply about people and died to save them.

His Word is amazing! All sixty-six books of the Bible, from Genesis to Revelation, are linked by the "thread" of Jesus. He was there all along. In the Old Testament, prophecies were written about the Savior. In the New Testament, the prophecies were fulfilled in Jesus. Beyond Revelation, we are told He will come again to rule and reign. Genesis alone is so rich in history that affects our world today. God made a covenant with Abraham; he would have a child in old age (Isaac) who would be the son of the promise, over his chosen people. Abraham's wife (nearly ninety years old) couldn't wait, so she had her maidservant (Hagar) jump in and have a child with Abram (Ishmael). God told Hagar he would be a "wild donkey of a man and against everyone." He would have twelve tribes. This was the beginning of the Arab race. Wow. Modern-day Iraq may even be the site of the original garden of Eden. Amazing!

Isaac went on to have twin sons (Esau and Jacob), and before they were born, God told the mom (Rebecca) that "the younger [Jacob] will rule over the older one." She helped Jacob steal his birthright from Esau (not really necessary since God had already chosen him). God changed Jacob's name to Israel. He had twelve sons, who are known as the twelve tribes of Israel. They are the ancestors of the modern-day Jewish faith. Jesus came to earth to save His chosen people, but they rejected Him, so He included all the Gentiles (non-

Jews) who believed in Him. They, too, could be saved. He chose a man named Saul (later called Paul), who went from being a persecutor of the followers of Jesus to the man who brought the gospel to the Gentiles. He wrote over one-third of the New Testament. His letters (epistles) are amazing. He had to be "knocked off his horse" to see/meet Jesus personally.

So the modern-day Arab-Israeli conflict can be traced to these two *true* stories found in the first book of the Bible, Genesis. Wow. I grew up in a home with no books and no Bible. How I envy those who grew up with a love of reading any/all books and especially the Bible. I only started learning about these rich facts when I was in my late thirties. In fact, when I went to see the play *Joseph and the Amazing Technicolor Dreamcoat*, I heard someone say, "That was always a favorite Bible story of mine." What? This is from a Bible story? Yes, the last third of the book of Genesis is about the favorite son of Jacob, called Joseph. He was so favored that his siblings grew to hate him and sold him into slavery.

He had dreams about how his brothers and father would bow down to him. Not a good thing to share with those who already hate you! He went on to live in Egypt, be imprisoned twice, but came to work in the palace of the pharaoh, who made him prime minister in a time of seven years of good harvest followed by seven years of famine. (Joseph had that dream too.) He had the people store up grain for the coming time of famine, and that grain was what ended up saving Joseph's brothers, who came to Egypt seeking food to eat. They ended up finding out he was the lost brother, the one they told Jacob had been killed by a wild animal, and they feared retribution would happen. It did not. "What you intended for evil, God meant for good." Wow. I was my dad's favorite child, loved by all teachers and adults, and my siblings hated me for it. I could really relate to this true story! I wish I had known about it sooner. So many other true stories from the Bible have such rich meaning to our individual lives.

So you might say I have a strong longing for everyone to gain biblical literacy. If they only knew. When I go visit my sister who asked, "Why did you abandon your faith?" I still attended Catholic

Mass with her. I honor her faith. But I *long* to tell her more about my new identity in the Jesus of the Bible. They say one cannot be a prophet in his own home. Family/people don't want to listen. They have their preconceived notions about you, and nothing you can say will change that. Even Jesus was rejected by those who lived in His hometown of Nazareth. What to do? Brush off your sandals and move on. That was what Jesus told his followers. And pray. My favorite part of the last book of the Bible (Revelation) is knowing that when the first heaven and earth pass away, God will keep one thing, the prayers of His saints. He considers them so precious. Wow. What an honor to climb on His lap and talk to Abba Father God, knowing all I share is so special to Him! So I live. I pray. I try to be like Jesus. But if I get the chance, I *love* to share where my identity comes from and how it has evolved. Isn't that what IB is all about? An open-mindedness to learning and growing? May I never stop.

So religion and identity are central in my life, something I love to share. Biblical literacy would be such an excellent course to be taught in schools. It brings much understanding to modern-day world conflicts and the end of time.

Seeking Allah, Finding Jesus: A Book by Nabeel Qureshi

I discovered this book through a Sunday school class at my church. We also watched videos narrated by the author, Nabeel Qureshi, an American Muslim who became a trained doctor. He had a best friend through high school and college (David), and they shared many discussions about the origins of each of their faiths. For Nabeel, that was the Koran and Muhammad; for David, it was the Bible and Jesus. Both wanted to do a "deep dive" into why they believed what they believed. One chapter even states, "TOK was our favorite subject since it taught us how to think." So I shared the book with my boss, the head of the TOK class at DCHS, Steven Fleet.

When he recently returned the book, I asked if he liked it, and he responded, "Yes, it was interesting. I enjoyed the dialogue between the two boys." Oh, dear, not much enthusiasm. I think the book has two things against it. First, the title ends in *Finding Jesus.* Gulp. Sounds like proselytizing? I would have preferred *Seeking Allah: What Is the Koran About?* Also, the conclusion to the book. Perhaps one of "I am not sure what to think"—more questions than I ever expected would have been easier for many to accept, a "continuing personal search" for all of us. For me, the book was well written and told me a story of the faith of an American Muslim, their family traditions and beliefs, in a personal way. I liked that. I guess for someone who is trying to remain "neutral," it ends with one final truth that many folks would not accept.

The book cover even states it was an "unexpected journey" from Islam to Christianity. The book is complete with friendships, investigations, and even supernatural dreams along the way. Nabeel is a nice guy. He loves his family. He loves his faith and traditions. He was unable to deny the arguments for the deity of Jesus, and not wanting to deny his family, he struggles with an inner turmoil that can challenge Christians, Muslims, and all those who are interested in the world's great religions. Since our IB year has a theme of identity and one of the TOK symposium presentations was on identity and religion, I thought it would provide some useful things to discuss. I guess it was "too conclusive."

It did learn a lot about language and how words affect what people hear and believe despite hearing it from an author with amazing educational credentials. Here is a man with a medical degree from Eastern Virginia Medical School. An MA in Christian apologetics (defense of the faith) from Biola University. An MA in religion from Duke University. And he was pursuing a PhD in the New Testament at Oxford University until he died in 2017 of cancer while just in his thirties. Most highly intelligent people love to learn from others who are also very well studied about their lecture topics. Perhaps if you could "meet the man in person," it would be different. I met him through his videotape series. He was a very kind and caring soul, not a right-wing religious zealot. How to get past the language?

How does one start the debate about this hot topic in an educational setting? Perhaps by looking at the ten contributions by scholars and experts, one for each section of the book:

1. *Called to Prayer*, by Abdu Murray, lawyer, former Shia Muslim, Author of two published books on Islam, current president of Embrace the Truth International.
2. *An Ambassador for Islam*, by Mark Mittelberg, author of *Becoming a Contagious Christian*; evangelism director, Willow Creek Association.
3. *Testing the New Testament*, by Daniel B. Wallace, professor, New Testament studies, Dallas Theological Seminary; author of *NET Bible: Biblical Greek Grammar*.
4. *Coming to the Crux (Crucifixion)*, by Michael Licona, associate professor, Houston Baptist University; author of *The Resurrection of Jesus*; speaker at many college campuses.
5. *Jesus: Mortal, Messiah, or Divine Son of God?* by J. Ed Komoszewski, professor of biblical and theological studies at Northwestern College.
6. *The Case for the Gospel (So Many Witnesses)*, by Robert M. Bowman Jr., director of research, Institute for Religious Research, Grand Rapids, Michigan; author of thirteen books.
7. *The Truth about Muhammad*, by David Wood, director of Acts 17 Apologetics; PhD in philosophy from Fordham University.
8. *The Holiness of the Quran*, by Reverend Dr. Keith Small, Quranic manuscript consultant to the Bodleian Library at Oxford University; associate fellow, London School of Theology.
9. *Faith in Doubt*, by Gary Habermas, distinguished research professor and chair of the department of philosophy at Liberty University; author of thirty-six books.
10. *Guided by the Hand of God*, by Josh McDowell, internationally recognized evangelist and apologist for over fifty

years; coauthored more than 130 books, including *More Than a Carpenter.*

Since I work for a doctor of philosophy, I thought I would read what the three philosophy experts had discovered and shared in their contribution to the book. The focus is around Muhammad, the Koran, and Muslim faith in doubt. Here are some excerpts directly from the book.

David Wood originally had bitter fights with Nabel, who was trying to defend his beloved prophet, Muhammad. David examined many Muslim sources about Muhammad's life and found several disturbing facts that bring into question his being a "good prophet" who was visited by the angel Gabriel, but rather one who had a demonic spell cast on him during his time "in the cave," where he had his revelation. I prefer to look at facts instead of opinions when reviewing any matter.

Historical Problem. Islam's earliest source is the Koran. Claimed to be the eternal word of Allah, it only mentions Muhammad four times, so you must go to other texts to find out about his life. The earliest biography was written over one hundred years after he died. The favorite biography was written over two hundred years after his death. This amount of time allows for a lot of "fabrication" by the authors. By contrast, much of the life of Jesus, written in the Bible, are from firsthand witnesses.

Brief History. Muhammad was born in AD 570 in Mecca and began work in the Meccan caravan trade, which put him in touch with many religious traditions. At age twenty-five, he married a widow fifteen years older than him and, like many Muslims, would retreat to a cave for times of prayer and reflection. At age forty, he had a mystical experience in the cave and began making inflammatory remarks about polytheists (those who worship many gods). He was persecuted and had to flee to Medina, where he formed an army to fight against the Muslims in Mecca. He was able to finally subdue all of Arabia by violence.

Many Muslims claim he only used violence in self-defense, but this is simply not true. He ordered the murder of those who wrote poems to oppose him. He ordered, "Whoever opposes our religion, kill him." He promoted peace while his sect was in the minority, but once in the majority, he changed, as did his revelations. "Fight those who believe not in Allah or the last day." "Strive hard against unbelievers."

Muhammad and Women. The Koran allows a man to have up to four wives—Muhammad had at least nine wives at one time. He said he had been given a special revelation to be able to ignore the four-wife limit. One wife was only nine years old, and one was married to the wife of his adopted son. He struck wives for lying to him. He said Allah allows men to rule over women, to obey their husbands or be admonished and even banished; he allowed his followers to have unlimited number of sex slaves. They could also pay a woman for sex, marry her for a few hours, then divorce her.

Spiritual Concerns. Muhammad's first impression of his revelation were that they were demonic; he became suicidal and tried to kill himself, until his older wife convinced him he was not possessed but rather a prophet of god. He also included Satanic verses in his revelation. Many Muslim sources note that he was the victim of black magic. This gave him delusional thoughts. All this points to a man that was hardly an exalted, holy man to be followed and believed.

Many Muslims sort through all that was written about Muhammad and only report the positive and dismiss any unfavorable stories (as did Nabel). This method can be used to make any historical figure appear trustworthy, so Nabel had to admit this tendency and look at *all* the truth about the prophet. He was not the man Nabel had been taught about as a child.

Keith Small from the London School of Theology and a manuscript consultant at Oxford talked about the New Testament and the Koran, the book with inviolability that is a life-and-death issue for Muslims.

The appendixes also include a topical table of contents (easy reference guide). There is also an appendix to respond to Ahmadis Muslim (his sect of Islam). The final appendix is called a "sneak peek," no God but one—Allah or Jesus? It was an excerpt from his coming book, *No God but One: Allah or Jesus.* He also wrote a book called *Answering Jihad: A Better Way Forward.* Isn't that what the world needs, a better way to go? I think I will have to find and read this last book and see what it says. "If you are not with us, you are against us. Kill the infidels"—a quote from Muhammad used by jihadists. It would be good to know if they have taken his words out of context. Jesus said just the opposite: if they are not against us, they are for us.

Gary Habermas is a distinguished research professor and chair of the department of philosophy at Liberty University. His chief areas of research are related to Jesus's resurrection, but he also published works on belief versus doubt. Has authored and coauthored more than thirty-six book and written more than one hundred articles and reviews for journals and other publications.

His focus here was on two religious doubters—one began his search as a Christian, but the other did not. They came from diverse educational, religious, and ethnic perspectives, and in both cases, their doubt was resolved after years of research. He personally met Nabeel Qureshi during a yearly family visit to Virginia Beach—he was part of a group of "searchers" who met regularly to discuss scientific, philosophical, and theological issues at his friend's home. He also met a former rather-militant atheist and philosophy student, David Wood. (His contribution already noted.) Another was an agnostic Buddhist named Zach. What a group!

Gary's personal study centered on the resurrection of Jesus since he concluded that if it had occurred, it could bear the weight of the Christian message. After years of study, he reached an impasse and determined it could not be shown. Then he wrote his PhD dissertation and broke through the stalemate. He still had a lot of anxiety and found that during these periods of being downcast, you have to work through your anxieties and fears. He found the strongest cognitive passage in Scripture was where Paul instructs his readers to exchange their anxiety for God-honoring truths instead of ruminations.

He used a cognitive method outlined in the book *Telling Yourself the Truth* by William Backus and Marie Chapian. Although often very painful, the effects of emotional doubt may be eliminated or at least severely reduced using cognitive methods to answer the haunting questions that come your way. He found the remedy was the habitual and forceful application of techniques that correct our mistake, thinking, and behavior.

This struck such a chord with me since I went through a "desert experience" in my life, one of major depression that had me doubt myself completely, whether I had any hope for a future. I was rescued out of this desert in Arizona to return to California, where I slowly healed from a time of extreme emotional and spiritual distress. I also began to understand the concept of spiritual attack since I had become an unknowing victim of a group of witches (demons), all before I ever owned my first Bible. I was literally fighting a battle with no armor. I now know more about the "armor of God" and fighting the evil forces we cannot see but come against us to destroy us, if we let them.

In conclusion, I keep an open mind about the Islam faith. Like my own Catholic faith, I know it is the faith of my father's, and it was all I knew until I was thirty-six years old. But once you start the deep dive into why I believe what I believe, it is hard to go back. I hope others have such open minds on this very important aspect of identity. It would have been of tremendous help in my time of greatest distress, and I hope that others will find it before any such episodes occur. The peace that passes all understanding is difficult to understand but amazing to experience. It is all worth a rigorous debate.

So my TOK journal experience was very interesting and insightful. That's real learning.

Israel and Italy (So Much Bible Learning!)

Bill and I were fortunate to have a pastor at our first church who had lived in Israel for a couple of years. As such, he knew how the Bible comes alive when you can study it in the land of Jesus's birth, death, and ministry. He took a group from our church to the Holy Land every few years, and we were able to join this pilgrimage one year into our marriage, the summer of 1996. Prior to our departure, we spent time every week studying the history, geography, and biblical significance of every place we would be visiting—that was an awesome preparation for us!

Our trip was via Italy, with a couple days at the beginning and end of our journey in the country visited by the apostle Paul and the place where he died—yes, Rome. We got to visit the home of the Roman Catholic Church (Vatican City) as well as the catacombs. We also had a free day in which we traveled up to Assisi to see the home of Saint Francis in the wine country of Italy. I had been to Italy twenty years earlier as a new graduate from a Catholic college and now saw the Basilica of Saint Peter in an all-new light, literally and figuratively.

During my 1976 visit, the ceiling of the Sistine Chapel (Michelangelo's great masterpiece) was covered in soot from the candles that burned there for hours on end. It has now been meticulously cleaned, and the colors on the painted ceiling were bright and beautiful! In 1976, I saw a place of beautiful art that happened to be the home of the Roman Catholic Church. This included a large statue of Saint Peter holding the keys to the kingdom in his hand. After all, he was the first pope, right? The vicar of Christ on earth? The one for whom so many jokes, stories had been told. When you get to heaven and Saint Peter is at the gates, what must you say to get in? I even asked our tour guide if she liked the current/new pope. She said, "Of course. He is our holy Father!"

Now, twenty years later, I knew more about the passage from Matthew 16:19, where Jesus speaks to Peter, saying he would give him the keys to the kingdom. According to the NIV Study Bible, the meaning of this verse has been a subject of debate for centuries. Some say the keys represent the authority to carry out church discipline, legislation, and administration, while others say the keys give the authority to announce the forgiveness of sins. Still, others say the keys may be the opportunity to bring people to the kingdom of heaven, by presenting them with the message of salvation found in Scripture. The religious leaders thought they held the keys of the kingdom, and they tried to shut some people out. (Jesus severely chastised church leaders of His day.) We cannot decide to open or close the kingdom of heaven for others, but God uses us to help others find the way inside. To all who believe in Christ and obey His words, the kingdom doors are swung wide open. I believe this last explanation.

But I digress. We were just in Italy as a stop going to and from the Holy Land, right? I think that our pastor wanted us to see where the first church started by a bunch of Jewish guys who were called the Way, led by a guy named Peter. All but one apostle was martyred for his faith. Only John lived to be an old man who was banned to the island of Patmos, where he was given the words of the book of Revelation by God. Many martyrs are buried in the catacombs of Rome, another fascinating place to visit. I even found the tomb of the patron saint of music, Saint Cecilia! That was the name of the Catholic church in which my dad was raised and where my mom had her funeral. Our choir director is named Cecil, so I was sure to let him know!

Did you know most Europeans buried their dead underground, while the Romans preferred cremation? Christians preferred burial to cremation because of their belief in bodily resurrection at the second coming. In any case, more than forty bodies have been found in the catacombs, and the artwork found there is amazing. Dust to dust, ashes to ashes. Both are okay to me for burial.

Bill was amazed how the teenagers of Rome hung out in grand historical places like the Trevi Fountain, while our teens just went to the mall! We got to see the Coliseum, where Christians were killed for sport. (Architecturally like the Los Angeles Coliseum.) In California, it was the place where Los Angeles hosted the Olympic Games in 1932 and 1984 and will host again in 2028—the torch is always lit at the Coliseum. It is also the home to my USC Bruins football team and formerly the home of the LA Rams. It was the place where Billy Graham held his last California Crusade in 1985 (started there in 1949), as well as the place where Pope John Paul II visited in 1987. I was blessed to enjoy *all* these recent events, so I found being in the original Coliseum to be quite touching. You have to love history! We also got to go to the wine country of Assisi, home of Saint Francis (see Francis). So we had a lovely time exploring this amazing country. It is also the place where I had my first cappuccino and gelato—both so yummy!

So what is it like to visit the Holy Land of Israel? It is not just a cool vacation but an amazing pilgrimage that every Christian should make in order to better understand the Bible. The country is quite small, and much of the land is pure desert. It reminded me of the first time I visited California, driving in from the east, where you had to cross ugly desert before you reached the beauty of the coast. For our visit to Israel, we did just the opposite and flew in by the coast of the Mediterranean and headed north; we crossed over to the Sea of Galilee, went farther north to the area of Caesarea Philippi, and then traveled south down the Jordan River before reaching Jericho, the oldest and lowest place on earth! We went up to Jerusalem (west) from there.

I always thought, if you went up to any place of travel, that meant north. (Such as in Minnesota, where folks from the Twin Cities head north to enjoy the lakes.) Not so with Jerusalem. Everyone who goes there goes up because it is a city on a hill. The Holy City. The place of the most famous Jewish temple in the world, first built by the son of King David (Solomon), then destroyed, rebuilt by King Harrod, then destroyed. Today it is in partial ruin, and at the top is the Dome of the Rock, which is actually a Muslim mosque. Now that was a shocking surprise! The Muslims consider it the second most holy place in the world, after Mecca (Saudi Arabia). The Jewish people plan to rebuild it someday. Soon?

Our pastor taught us that the hill on which Jerusalem is built is the same mountain on which Abraham was asked to sacrifice his son Isaac, Mount Moriah. That request to sacrifice one's only son was fulfilled in Jesus. Since Muslims are also descendants from Abraham (through his first son, Ishmael), they also consider this their holy place. President Trump declared the city to be the capital of Israel, which pleased our Jewish friends, but not the regional Muslims. There is so much importance to this city!

At the time of our visit, we were able to visit Bethlehem, the place of Jesus's birth, but it was heavily guarded by armed soldiers. Not all groups get to enter this special place. We were able to buy a nativity set there made of olive wood, and it sits on our mantel every Christmas. Very special. I just went back to the photo album I created from the entire trip, and here are some of the captions from my favorite places:

- Mamertine Prison, where Paul wrote several books of the Bible—a stone's throw from the emperor, in his dungeon, where he wrote about joy!
- Constantine's Arch—the emperor who proclaimed Christianity would be the religion of the people. His mom went to Israel and bought all the land where Jesus had lived and walked and talked, born and died, to preserve as sacred places.
- A walk through the old streets of Joppa, where we bought a painting/print of the *Fiddler on the Roof*, with the complete book of Ecclesiastes and Song of Solomon written in Hebrew (we have this poster in our current powder room with a dedication to my dad, who loved *Fiddler on the Roof*).
- Caesarea, the crusader city, on the Mediterranean—an important port to the Romans and Crusaders with an amazing aqueduct system.
- The theater at Caesarea, where Paul defended his faith to Agrippa—perfect acoustics.
- Megiddo, the valley of Armageddon, the place of the final battle described in Revelation.
- Mary's well at Nazareth, now the site of a Catholic church, a view from the ridge above where Jesus was threatened by local people to throw him over (a prophet in his own home is seldom welcome).
- Cana, the site of the first miracle at a wedding. We were the newlyweds in the group, so we got to do the reading (we have Cana wine cups on our mantel now).
- The area of the Sea of Galilee and the Sermon on the Mount and the feeding of five thousand—a mosaic of the loaves and fishes (we have this plate on our mantel as well).

- The Church of the Beatitudes and beautiful gardens kept by the Franciscan friars, Catholic churches everywhere run by Franciscans.
- Kathy's baptism in the Jordan River, same place where Jesus was baptized. I have that certificate framed on our wall at home. (We did kayaking on this river as well!)
- The Jesus boat across the Sea of Galilee, including throwing out the fishing nets.
- Capernaum, home of Peter's mom, where Jesus likely lived when he visited. The synagogue where he taught, now a very large modern Catholic church.
- A trip north, where the tribe of Dan settled. Caesarea Phillipi, where Jesus asked, "Who do you say I am?" A beautiful, lush green area.
- Many altars of worship carved into the cliffs to honor gods, such as Pan, the god of shepherds; the gates of hell.
- Excavations at Bet Shaan, where King Saul died, only executed since 1986; the Disneyland of archeology.
- Onto Jericho (oldest and lowest city on earth) and up to Jerusalem, including camel rides—they loved our watermelon rinds.
- Bedouin boys who would let you take his picture for one American dollar—we got our Bedouin head scarves.
- First view of Jerusalem from the Mount of Olives, onto the Western Wall, and tour of the tunnels below—the fourth largest hewn stone in the world!
- What? Only men and boys allowed at the Western Wall? No women? Not even for the bar mitzvah or bat mitzvah of their children?
- Entering the Dome of the Rock (a Muslim temple), where we had to remove our shoes, our crosses, our Bibles—very creepy.
- Saint Anne's Chapel just below the temple where we sang "How Great Thou Art" with a choir from South Africa—a wonderful spiritual contrast to the dome!

- The Pool of Bethesda, where many people came to be healed.
- Roman lunch in togas in the heart of Jerusalem!
- Bethlehem Church of the Nativity (place of Jesus's birth), down to a cave where shepherds came—we sang Christmas carols!
- The Upper Room, the beginning of the "passion," where Jesus shared the last supper with His disciples. (We have our wooden cups from our communion time.)
- The garden of Gethsemane, where Jesus sweated blood; can this cup be removed? Thy will be done.
- The dungeon where Jesus was kept before His trial before the high priest, and a statue of Peter denying Jesus three times.
- The Place of the Skull (where crucifixion was held) and onto the Garden Tomb. He is not here; He is risen!
- Walking the wall around Jerusalem from Damascus gate to Joppa gate, with soldiers on the wall as we go down into the Muslim quarter.
- A step into the Christian quarter, where we found a Lutheran church (just for Bill).
- Shopping in the busy Armenian quarter.
- We visited locals who knew our friend in Santa Barbara, on the west side of town.
- A friend of ours who grew up in Egypt (Coptic Church), now a Christian missionary, was able to come and see us as well.

So we traveled many miles during our two-week pilgrimage and learned so much about the history, geography, and biblical significance of the places we visited in the Holy Land. We do hope to return someday.

CHAPTER J

James (Our Son, Kings, Apostles)

When I started reading the Bible, I noticed that the book of James came just after the book of Hebrews, often called the hall of faith. Now that made sense to me since it takes a lot of faith to raise a James! In all seriousness, there were many guys named James in the Bible, so I will touch on each of them, but I must start with our son James. So what does this name mean? Here is what it says in www.babynames.com. The meaning of the name James is "that which supplants, undermines, the heel." So what does *supplant* mean? It means "to take the place of (another), as through force, scheming, strategy, or the like; to replace (one thing) by something else." Yes, the same derivative as the name Jacob—the one who stole his brother's birthright!

Well, for such a great name, that is a rather-strange meaning. After all, there have been so many famous people named James. Here is some history from www.BehindTheName.com. This name has been used in England since the thirteenth century, though it became more common in Scotland, where it was borne by several kings. In the seventeenth century, the Scottish king James VI inherited the English throne, becoming the first ruler of all Britain, and the name grew much more popular. In American name statistics (recorded since 1880), this name has never been out of the top twenty, making it arguably the era's most consistently popular name. It was the top-ranked name for boys in the United States from 1940 to 1952. Famous bearers include the English explorer Captain James Cook

(1728–1779), the Scottish inventor James Watt (1736–1819), and the Irish novelist and poet James Joyce (1882–1941). This name has also been borne by six American presidents. A notable fictional bearer is the British spy James Bond, created by author Ian Fleming. So how did *our* James come into our family?

We were married in February 1995 and tried to have our own child, but it is a difficult challenge for a woman over forty years of age. After one year, we decided to adopt children and became certified foster parents in 1996. We asked for a child no one wanted—no living relatives with any claim or interest in the child—because our goal was to adopt our child and avoid all that visitation mess. So we were introduced to our James in June 1997. He was three and a half years old and such a beautiful young boy. He had suffered abuse from his birth mom, who was schizophrenic, so when he came to us, he had no words, was not potty-trained, and was lacking fine and gross motor skills. But he loved our home and our dogs (golden retrievers), so we decided to take him in as a foster child. Dear James, this chapter is being written to give hope by sharing your success story. You even said, "Be sure to tell them that I was the one who was not supposed to amount to anything but found a way to overcome." We are proud of you, James.

During our first medical visit with his pediatric neurologist, we were told he had cerebral disorganization with Billy Budd syndrome (like traumatic brain syndrome), and the doctor told us it was okay to be his foster parents but we should *not* adopt him since he would probably end up in jail or an institution. What? Such a horrible prognosis for one so young, so we decided to follow our hearts and cover the situation with a lot of prayer! No one had ever heard of this diagnosis, but years later, he would be qualified for special education under the diagnosis of traumatic brain injury (TBI). So who was Billy Budd? (His other syndrome.)

Here is the definition according to Wikipedia. *Billy Budd, Sailor* is a novella by American writer Herman Melville left unfinished at Melville's death in 1891. Acclaimed by critics as a masterpiece when a hastily transcribed version was finally published in 1924, it quickly took its place as a classic second only to *Moby-Dick* among Melville's works. Budd is a handsome sailor who strikes and inadvertently kills his false accuser, master-at-arms John Claggart. The ship's captain, Edward Vere, recognizes the innocence of Budd's intent, but the law of mutiny requires him to sentence Billy to be hanged. So an innocent boy gets nervous and strikes out at someone and gets hanged? We are not going to let this happen to our James!

Since I was working full-time, I had to find a day-care center that would take care of him during the week. Gratefully, the hospital where I worked operated such a facility, and they took on James. His first teacher was Ms. Sandy, and she really liked him. In May of 1998, she had all her kids make a Mother's Day gift from an old men's T-shirt with a handprint from the child and the words "I love my mom," May 1998. To this day, I wear that shirt every Mother's Day with great pride! I will darn it until the day I die.

Unfortunately, James had an abusive side to his personality (Billy Budd syndrome) and would threaten other kids in the day-care setting. This, of course, led to other parents asking for him to be removed. So we went through several caretakers until he started kindergarten in the special education program. During that time, we tried every kind of therapy, including one called play therapy. The therapist would have James use little toy soldiers in a sandbox to re-enact what had happened to him. This, of course, made him even more agitated. She thought it would make for a great clinical paper she could write. So we ended that treatment.

Since there was a child development center at the hospital where I worked, I asked the director if there was any way they could accept James into the center. Since his primary insurance was Medicaid (as was the case for all foster children), they could not accept this insurance. So we talked about options and she asked if he had ever been abused. I said yes, and we found several hospital emergency room records to validate this, so we applied for Victim Assistance Funds from the state of California and were awarded $10,000 to help James. So that was our payment for two years of occupational therapy for James. God is so good! His protection and provision once again.

We were able to adopt James by the end of 1998, and that was quite a celebration. We have friends who adopted five children from orphanages in Romania, and they told us about the tradition where they celebrated the day they got each child as the "gotcha day." So each child had a birthday, a gotcha day, and an adoption day—isn't that cool? In kindergarten, his teacher would say she had eleven children and one James. Yes, his behavior took some extra effort. I remember one teacher gave him a quote that we use quite a lot: "You get what you get and you don't throw a fit!" How sweet is that? By fourth grade, he was transferred to another elementary school in the area and was generally in a classroom with a ratio of one adult for every two students. By the end of sixth grade, he was selected as the class president. How fun is that? The local newspaper even came out and did a story on James since they knew he was adopted from foster care. It was exciting to see his story in print—such an inspiration to other fost-adopt parents.

We decided that two are better than one, so we applied to accept a second foster child in the summer of 2000. (we needed three years to understand how to work with James.) We were told that our house was too small; each child had to have their own bedroom, so we moved from Moorpark to Simi Valley, California, to a larger house. We also joined a church closer to our home that had good programs for young children, including youth sports. In the summer of 2000, Josiah came into our lives (see his chapter). It was also the summer our foreign-student "adopted son," Gabriel, came to stay with us. So our family went up to three boys, two dogs, two adults, and a lot of fun!

We enrolled both our boys in Grace Brethren Youth Sports (our church program), so they both played baseball and soccer from ages five to twelve. The good news is that every child got to play even if they did not have a lot of talent. Watching them in tee ball was one of my favorite memories—such a fun way for little guys to learn to hit a ball! They also enjoyed playing soccer, but all the running became quite a challenge for James since at age five he was diagnosed with asthma.

I can still recall the day I took him to the county clinic on a Saturday for wheezing, and the PA thought he just had a cold and sent us home. Within two days, we were back at that clinic, and the primary care doctor immediately could see that he was in acute respiratory distress and he started him on treatments for asthma. I spent several hours with James and the doctor before he was transferred by ambulance to the local hospital. He would be hospitalized eight times in the next three years, and the emergency room staff got to know him well. He always was able to recover, but when I think back to that first long clinic visit, I realize how close we came to losing him. We were so blessed that he recovered every time. We did buy a nebulizer and took it with us everywhere, as well as a portable generator for our car. Our second son was also diagnosed with asthma, and when we moved to Colorado, all of us were diagnosed with mild asthma. Thank goodness for the experience with James! We became experts in responding to respiratory distress! Again, God is so good, and He always provided for our every need.

We moved to Colorado the year James started middle school, and we were not sure what to expect. He was still qualified for special education, but as bad luck would have it, the middle school he attended was the only one in town and very overcrowded. As such, the special education teachers would get exasperated with their large caseloads and just send James down to the principal's office for misbehavior. Everyone in the administration office got to know him well! During the last week of his seventh—and eighth-grade years, he was sent home one week early as we were told, "We have too much to do to deal with James."

We tried several tricounty resources in our new area and met a PhD called Dr. John Barton. He told us that the treatment James received at this middle school was actually illegal, but we chose to go forward and not try to blame the school. We considered "tough love" and taking everything out of James's room and having him "earn things back," but again, Dr. Barton said this was not a good approach for James. Needless to say, we tried several therapists to work with James. As he got older, he got more belligerent about going to therapy, so we had to let it go.

When it came time to enroll James in high school, we had two choices. We could enroll him in the new high school just built, or open-enroll him into the oldest high school in our district with a long, strong record of an excellent special education program. So we chose the latter. When we enrolled him in Douglas County High School, the new practice in special education was *full inclusion*, so his special education teacher tried to mix his schedule with some regular classes and some special education classes. So here was a young man used to a two-to-one student/teacher ratio going into large high school classes, often with no paraeducator (para). Little did we know that this led to such frustration that he would just leave the campus and get on the local town free shuttle and go down to the local library and hang out with the dropouts—yikes!

It was early in the fall of his freshman year that a fellow student dared him to pull the fire alarm, and he did. This led to the entire school being evacuated and the police and fire trucks responding on-site. When they asked who pulled the alarm, they were told it was James, a special education student. They did not arrest him, but he was ordered to appear in court and go through the diversion program. In the meantime, we had a big meeting with the principal and her staff, including the social worker, to try to figure out what to do with James.

During this meeting, one staff member asked, "What about SSN?" So we had to ask what those initials meant. No one immediately knew, but they did call the teacher in charge of the program (Mary Joy), and she came down to the meeting. We then learned about the Significant Support Needs (SSN) program. According to the Colorado Department of Education (CDE), students with significant support needs are highly diverse learners with extensive needs in the areas of cognition and/or learning, communication, movement, and social/emotional abilities. The individual may also have concurrent health, sensory, physical, and/or behavioral disabilities. Yes, James fit several of these qualifications!

The day we met Mary Joy was a turning point in James's education and in his life. We often told others she was a combination of Mother Teresa and a Marine drill sergeant! There was also a social worker in the school named Desi. When James would have his meltdowns, Mary Joy would often send James to visit with Desi. She became our second savior. During that nineth-grade year, these two women were very patient with James, and we had many conversations during parent-teacher conferences about how to best help James learn. As God would have it, several years later, Desi would ask Bill to volunteer to help her with her at-risk kids, and he became a mentor in the high school, a paid senior volunteer. This program has helped many other students since the end of that first high school year for James in the spring of 2009. So God.

By the time James reached his junior year, he was enrolled in a basic computer class, which he loved. During the back-to-school night, this teacher told us that James had a great aptitude for computers. He told us about a program that had just started at a neighboring, new high school that was a combination high school and community college class for A+ certification to become a computer repair mechanic. He offered to write a letter of recommendation for James to enter this class in his senior year, and he was accepted.

We had to drive James every day to/from the neighboring town (Parker) for this 8:00–9:00 a.m. class, and as God would have it, the teacher used to be a special education teacher! How good is God? He paired James with one of the smartest kids in the class, and by the end of the year, James earned a solid C grade with no para. He also earned dual credits for high school and college and was able to graduate from high school with a 3.0 GPA and eight college credits. How sweet is that? On top of that, he was awarded several scholarships and awards upon graduation that allowed him to attend the local community college to learn more about computers. God is so good.

Again, as God would have it, it turned out that the husband of Mary Joy (Russ) had a career in computers and offered to be a tutor for James in high school and college. He also told us that James had a real aptitude for computers and was able to understand some pretty high-level concepts. Amazing! So now we became very close to this husband-wife pair. Mary Joy told us that when she wrote a letter of recommendation for James to get a scholarship in his senior year, it was the proudest moment in her teaching career. What a blessing for all of us! He even got to attend the honors convocation during the spring of his senior year and was awarded the PAWS award from Mary Joy. Pride, achievement, worthiness. Boy, would I like to find that pediatric neurologist who said James would not amount to anything! We were sure proud parents!

During high school, James did some part-time work as a clerk at a local grocery store. He also wanted to get a driver's license, but we wondered, How could we find a program that would train someone with TBI? As God would have it, we heard about a program in Colorado Springs, just south of us, that was set up for soldiers with TBI and PTSD. It was a hospital-based program, and we were able to enroll James. He passed the classroom instruction with various assimilators and then passed the behind-the-wheel test. Yes, James got his driver's license before he graduated high school, and we helped him buy his first used car. He got his independence! Now, how about that for God's provision in his life?

After high school, James did attend the local community college and take some computer classes, but he hit a wall when it came to the advanced math classes he had to take. As God would have it, we were at the high school graduation party for the son of our friends who had adopted the five children from Romania. This young man (Scott) told us he was going to attend Job Corps to become a certified auto mechanic. We asked, "What is Job Corps?" At that time, we did our research and found out it was a federal program that offered technical training for students in various areas of study. According to www.jobcorps.gov, Job Corps is a voluntary program administered by the United States Department of Labor that offers free-of-charge education and vocational training to young men and women ages sixteen to twenty-four. Again, God intervened. There was a Job Corps Center in the Salt Lake City area where James's birth brother lived! He applied and got accepted into the program to become an A+ certified computer repair mechanic.

Once again, James was not able to pass the math test to get into the program, but he did spend a year getting a certificate in business and learned all things PC and Mackintosh. It was also an opportunity for him to live in a dorm on campus with roommates and learn about living away from home. At first, the adjustment was a challenge since he had to interact with so many inner-city kids who had come from gang backgrounds. The pep talks to "stick it out" came from both us and Mary Joy and her husband, Russ, so that was what he did. He graduated in January 2015, just after turning twenty-one years old. By April, he was hired by our local school district to be a transportation educational assistant to help special education students on the bus. As I write, he just hit his five-year mark and is now vested in his job. Way to go, James!

The other blessing is that he was able to spend time with his brother (Paul) and his adopted family in the greater Salt Lake City area. James learned to use the local transportation system, including the buses and local trains and light rail system. He was also able to take flights to/from the city on his own and navigate airports and local transportation. He even taught me how to put an app for Uber on my cell phone so we could use this service when needed. In fact, James has become our family computer expert and helps with all electronics, including cell phones. I know that Paul's parents loved his visits and were so happy that he always stayed in close touch with his brother.

So the story of our James is one of many miracles and many provisions from God. James has a good heart and is accepted everywhere he goes. The first bus driver he worked with did retire, but they continue to be friends—he is almost like a second father to James. He often told us that all the kids loved James. The current bus driver who works with James is a strong Christian and has been with the district over thirty years. The ongoing positive influence from this man is also a huge blessing for our family. They work so well together. As James says, "If you work with the best, you have to be the best." So he does just that. God certainly looks out for him in so many ways. Our church members also love him. He attends the men's Bible study, and the guys get a kick out of him. God bless their hearts!

We have learned a lot as his parents for twenty-three years. It has stretched our patience at times, but we are so proud of how far he has come; we never regret any of the challenges along the way. I am sure the Holy Spirit has been guiding us. We now pray for a special someone to come along with whom he can share his life. Bill was forty-three years old before he got married, so it may take time for

James as well. But we know God will provide. From the book of James 1:2–4 we are told, "Consider it pure joy, my brothers and sisters, whenever you face trials of many kinds, because you know that the testing of your faith produces perseverance. Let perseverance finish its work so that you may be mature and complete, not lacking anything." Our prayer. Our James.

A quick note about those biblical guys named James. Did you know that two of the twelve apostles were named James? When morning came, He called His disciples to Him and chose twelve of them, whom He also designated apostles: Simon (whom He named Peter), his brother Andrew, James, John, Philip, Bartholomew, Matthew, Thomas, James (son of Alphaeus), Simon (who was called the zealot), Judas (son of James), and Judas Iscariot, who became a traitor. (Wikipedia). James and John were called the sons of thunder. Along with Peter, they became Jesus's inner circle and came to know the Lord most closely.

Jesus also had a brother named James who did not believe that Jesus was the Lord and Savior until after His resurrection. This James then became head of the church in Jerusalem and a strong evangelist and leader. So what's in a name? A lot for James. We are so glad he is a part of our family and is a big teddy bear to all he meets. One special gift from God.

Jean (She Showed Me the Bible)

During a recent Bible study that I was leading, one of the ladies asked what led me away from the Catholic Church into an Evangelical church? I said I was knocked off my horse just like the apostle Paul. No, Jesus did not audibly speak to me, but He had to completely empty my life so I had nowhere to look but up. At that time of a major clinical depression, I did not know the Bible, and the only verse that came to my mind was, "My God, my God, why have you forsaken me?" that Jesus spoke from the cross. This was at the time of my first job loss in 1990 (see job loss). As God would have it, He had put a female friend into my life many years earlier as a colleague in the profession of medical records administration, now called health information management. Her name is Jean, and as it turned out, we had a lot more in common than we knew at that time.

So what does this name mean? According to www.BabyNames.com, the name Jean means "God is gracious" and is of English origin. Boy, did I need a gracious friend in my life! Jean was also raised in a Catholic family with a mom who suffered from depression. The difference was that during much of her childhood, she had to visit her mom in a psychiatric hospital because she was admitted so often. Ironically, I can remember my own mom saying to all of us kids when we were growing up, if we did not behave, we would send her to Moose Lake. What? That was the name of our state psychiatric hospital in Minnesota. Perhaps she had spent some time there? Who knows. But we definitely knew she thought we would drive her crazy. Both Jean and I went through our own episodes of major clinical depression, and we came to find out our brains lacked a certain chemical called serotonin. Ah, a new medical word to us!

While I was working at a hospital in Arizona, Jean came to visit, and I took her to a medical staff meeting with me. After the meeting, she remarked, "Those folks are surely hostile to you." What? Later that year, one of the physicians I worked most closely with told me they thought I was going to hire her and someone might be out of a job. What? How easily people can jump to wrong conclusions! When I lost that job and reached out to Jean, she was the one who told me about the book *Feel the Fear and Do It Anyway*, but my brain was too messed up to even read more than a few pages of any book. When I did finally return to California in April 1990, she introduced me to an even more important book, the Bible. This was the book that gave her greatest comfort.

She brought me to her Bible-based community church, and I attended my first Bible study. That would be the place I would meet my current husband. I swore every week when the pastor preached, he was talking to me. I ended up getting a job as the medical record director at a hospital near where she lived and where she had once worked. I actually ended up hiring her for a position about two years later, but it did not work out and I had to let her go. I learned another life lesson: don't hire friends! Keep work and personal life as separate as possible.

So, Jean, wherever you are now, if you are reading this book, I want to offer you a big thank-you for introducing me to the Bible, which led to me accepting Jesus as my personal Savior. I have been studying that book every year since! So from a heavenly perspective, it was a pretty special friendship indeed! One final shoutout to Bill's aunt Jean. She was married to Uncle Don and lost her battle to cancer in 2005. She was a dear, sweet lady, and I was so blessed to have her in my married life for ten years. I will see you in heaven!

Jewish Governess (Eye-Opening Summer Job)

During my freshman year of college, I was talking to a fellow student about possible summer jobs, and she directed me to an organization that was seeking "mothers' helpers"—they seemed to really like girls from large Midwest families. So I applied. I was offered a job to work for a Jewish family near Trenton, New Jersey, with four children aged two to twelve, three boys and one girl. I accepted the offer, and I was sent my first airline ticket to fly from Duluth, Minnesota, to Philadelphia, Pennsylvania, and then a commuter flight to Trenton to meet my "summer family," the Lichtensteins.

In order to paint the picture of my journey, you need to understand that my all-time favorite movie was *The Sound of Music*, and I think I pictured myself as Maria going to be a governess for a good family. I had taken a beginning guitar class, so I took my guitar with me. I was dressed in a denim outfit with a matching hat, carrying my guitar—all ready for the challenge that awaited me. (I can just hear Julie Andrews singing "I Have Confidence in Me"!) This family became dear to me, so I kept in touch for many years. When Steve and Carole retired, they moved to Stowe, Vermont, which became the American home of the Von Trapp family singers (the real family upon which *The Sound of Music* was based). The granddaughter of Maria Von Trapp became a good friend to Carole. While on the East Coast for a wedding in the summer of 2014, we went to visit Steve and Carole, and they took us to the Von Trapp Family Resort, and I got to meet this granddaughter to Maria. Talk about the circle of life!

But I digress. Let me get back to my summer experience. The eldest son (Lee) was having his bar mitzvah that summer, and I got to attend a celebration that was more lavish than any wedding I had ever attended! It was quite an experience to dive into the coming-of-age experience for a young Jewish boy, let alone the firstborn. On most Sundays we would have dinner at the Jewish country club to which the family belonged. What a treat! The family had a house-keeper as well as a cook, so I was one of several women who were serving the family. My only job was to take care of the children, especially the youngest boy. Since I grew up as the eldest girl in a family of seven, I had a lot of experience in doing this kind of work. I got free room and board and two days off a week and earned $75 per week ($300/month), which was a lot of money for me. I got to do a lot of exploring on my days off, with trips to New York City, Philadelphia, and Boston. Such fun!

The actual city where we lived is Lawrenceville, New Jersey. It is quite close to Princeton University. Here is what www.niche.com has to say about this town: Lawrenceville is a town in New Jersey with a population of 3,546. Lawrenceville is in Mercer County and is one of the best places to live in New Jersey. Living in Lawrenceville offers residents a dense suburban feel, and most residents own their homes. Many young professionals and retirees live in Lawrenceville, and residents tend to lean conservative. The public schools in Lawrenceville are highly rated. A great place to live! Carole grew up in New York City, while Steve was raised in Roanoke, Virginia, so they had different upbringings. I came to understand this when I met members of their families.

It was the summer of 1973, the time of the Watergate impeachment hearings against President Richard Nixon. Steve's mom came to visit. She was a sweet Southern lady. We would watch these hearings together, and she would comment, "Poor Mr. Nixon, they are being so mean to him." I took this to mean that the family where I was living was also conservative Republicans. At that time, I was a Democrat from Minnesota who strongly supported the man who barely lost to Richard Nixon in 1968, Hubert H. Humphrey. In fact, that election was during my ninth-grade year, and we had a mock election. I led the Democrats. The guy I had a crush on (Joe) led the Republicans. Humphrey won in a landslide at Bovey Junior High, so my view of Richard Nixon was quite polarized. Years later, I would become conservative, while this family became liberal.

This puzzled me when we went to visit Steve and Carole in 2014. The possible candidates for the 2016 presidential election were starting to form, including Hilary Clinton. Steve and Carole were also living in the state of Bernie Sanders—they loved him. They also liked Hilary. Steve asked me, If she ran, would I vote for her? I said of course not. He wondered why. I told him that I had an ex-husband who was a lot like Bill Clinton—many affairs. I know Hilary stayed with her husband, but I saw it as a marriage where political aspirations ruled the day. When the accusers of Bill Clinton came forward, Hilary did everything she could to destroy them. How could I ever vote for such a woman? She had no integrity, as far as I could see. I have long wondered why so many Catholics and Jewish people vote Democrat since this party supports abortion, but not Israel. It is funny how our life perspectives change.

Back to summer fun. We spent a month on the Jersey Shore, in a six-bedroom home on the beach. It was awesome! This was my first time at the ocean. My time off included a trip to Atlantic City and its famous boardwalk. I saw pigeons everywhere, so I decided I had to feed them. After all, Mary Poppins did so in her movie (also a Julie Andrews role). I bought some pigeon food (a bag of peanuts in the shell) and began to throw them to the pigeons. They were not interested. A gentleman walked by and laughed as he told me, "You have to shell the peanuts for the birds." What? Those ugly birds with strong beaks could not break the shells? So much for my love of feeding the birds or pigeons. One even pooped on my head during a future trip in San Francisco. Ah, the things we learn along the way!

During our time at the Jersey Shore, Carole's Uncle Bernie came to visit in his Mercedes Benz convertible—wow! He even let me drive the car. It was then that the seed was planted for me to buy a convertible someday. We bought a bunch of "steamers" (clams) that we cooked in large pots on the beach, with corn on the cob. The taste of these clams in hot garlic butter was amazing! So was everything about the shore of the Atlantic Ocean. I had an uncle living in the Boston area, and I got to visit him as well. During that visit, I ate my first lobster in a restaurant on the shore in Boston made from an old ship, called Anthony's Pier 4. What a treat! A winter storm would sink this restaurant years later, but it provided a wonderful place to eat one's first lobster!

As I said earlier, I got two days off a week to explore the area around where I lived, so I opted to take trains to nearby cities. The best was New York City, which was such a great place to explore. I went to matinees on Broadway, walked through Central Park, and ate at a great Italian restaurant called Mama Leones. I learned to walk quickly, as all New Yorkers did, and never had a fear of being alone in a big city. I also went to Philadelphia and got to go to Independence Hall, where the Declaration of Independence was signed. It was a city full of great history and beautiful, tree-lined streets. Years later, I would spend a summer living in a suburb called Norristown. It was only then that I understood the concept "the good and bad sides of a town." I was carefree, and God protected me everywhere I went. One of my college friends was also a Mothers' Helper, and I got to visit her in Rye, New York, home of John Mitchell-Watergate! How interesting is life?

So my summer on the East Coast was quite an experience. It lit a spark in my spirit to go and explore more places in the world. I have stayed friends with the dear Lichtenstein family for many years and consider it a great blessing to be part of their extended family. When they finally got to meet Bill, Carole said, "He is the nicest man I have ever met, except Steve." Now that was a compliment I hold dear to my heart! God connected our hearts.

Joan (My Younger Sister, a Warrior)

Finally, my alphabetic list leads to one of my siblings, my littlest sister, Joan. I was born in 1954, and she was born in 1962, so we are eight years apart. Recently, a male friend of our family said he thought I was a strong-willed woman. What? I said, "You have never met my sister Joan!" I have never met a more straight-shooter in all my life. What you see is what you get! I just love that about her. Her saint plaque on the wall of our home was for Joan of Arc—now that's a warrior! In case you didn't know, here is what Wikipedia has to say about this saint. Joan of Arc is the national heroine of France. She was a peasant girl who, believing that she was acting under divine guidance, led the French Army in a momentous victory at Orléans in 1429 that repulsed an English attempt to conquer France during the Hundred Years' War.

So what does the name Joan mean? According to www.baby-names.com, the name Joan means "God is gracious" and is of Hebrew origin. Joan is a name that's been used primarily by parents who are considering baby names for girls (or maybe wanted a boy named John but got a girl). When Joan was growing up, she loved to do the opposite of what my dad said. This included marrying her high school sweetheart in a non-Catholic church. What? My brother Paul had a shotgun wedding in a Lutheran church, but that was the faith of his bride. Joan, on the other hand, was a bride who had been active in our local Catholic church. I think she did it "just because." Ha! Of our seven siblings, Joan is the one who remains living in the small town where we grew up, and she is very content to do so.

Joan and her husband, Ross, had three girls—Sabrina, Cassie, and Mandy. What nice young ladies! They all became Christians and are raising their children in the church along with their Christian husbands. We love to visit them when we are home. They were raised on a farm not far from our hometown and were good with all types of animals. They also loved hunting with their dad! When deer hunting season arrives, they are as likely as any boy to be in a deer stand with Joan. Hearty Minnesota women! They also go camping every Memorial Day weekend at the same lake since childhood and love boating and fishing. "Grandma Joan" loves spending time with her grandchildren, and she is a great cook. But most of all, she has a big heart.

My mom was a widow at age fifty-six, and Joan was usually the one closest to home to help her with anything and included her during birthdays and most holidays. When my mom started falling down and breaking bones and was in and out of skilled rehab facilities, it was Joan who knew it was time for her to move to assisted living. She and Ross had the horrendous task of cleaning out the house where we grew up. My mom was quite the hoarder of clothes, so all the closets and basement were filled with clothes and other old items. They managed to get it cleaned out and ready for sale. Since we seven siblings were scattered over five states, she became our anchor on the home front.

Since Joan worked in the medical field, helping seniors and those with autism, she had a lot of experience to help our mom. What she never knew was how many facilities would kick out my mom. As the dementia worsened and Mom had to be in memory units, it was usually Joan who had to help make the transitions. Her husband, Ross, was an only child, and when his mom got Alzheimer's, Joan took her into their home as her caretaker. Now that was tough physical work. She always maintained a sense of humor. I remember her saying that when her mother-in-law kept taking off her bedclothes and her wet clothes, she had to use duct tape to keep them on. How is that for Yankee ingenuity! My mom could be just as much of a physical challenge when she had to be moved from one facility to another. Joan just seemed to take it in stride.

When I was in college, I took a beginning guitar class but never played it enough to form the callouses needed to play the instrument, so I gave it to Joan. I am so pleased that she still has that guitar and uses it for praise music in church. Her eldest daughter also inherited those skills (and a beautiful voice), so music always graced their home. She survived several job lay-offs but always got up and picked herself up and started all over again. (I think I know that song.)

When my brother with mental retardation (Michael) got married, Joan was often there to help with their needs. They have lived in three different apartments, and she has helped with every move. I think the only time I saw her flinch was when it involved bed bugs—yuck! When my sister Sue moved back to Minnesota for fourteen years, the two became close friends and worked in tandem to help both Mom and Michael. They say when we get to heaven, we will get a crown with many jewels on it—both Joan and Sue have earned a lot!

One of our brothers has had a struggle with alcoholism, and she is the one who goes and picks him up from his home and challenges him to get treatment and get his life straightened out. She will start with a question like, "Do you know where you are going when you die? I do." She openly shares her faith and gives direct, honest advice that needs to be heard. If this brother does change his current life, I am sure it will be my sister Joan who will be the primary mover and shaker.

When my grandmother was diagnosed with Hodgkin's disease and moved in with my parents, it was Joan who gave her a bath several times a week, including the day she died. Only Joan could handle such a situation with such love and grace. Thank you, Joan, for being such an anchor in our family. Everyone knows you are one of a kind! I may have been the smart one, but you were the tough one, and we love you for it!

PS: About Joan's three daughters. When Joan and Ross went through some tough spots in their marriage, their three girls covered them in prayer and love. They have all married Christian husbands and are raising some great kids, but I have to salute Joan for being such a great mom and raising such great girls. To my nieces, thanks for being such solid Christian women!

A Bible verse for my sister Joan.

> Let us not become weary in doing good, for at the proper time we will reap a harvest if we do not give up. (Gal. 6:9 NIV)

Keep doing all the good that you do!

Job Losses (Failures or Learning Experiences)

As I stated earlier, I was voted most likely to succeed in my high school class. If my classmates only knew how many times I had failed, I think they would have taken back that award. During my most recent lay-off, a fellow worker proudly said, "I have never been let go from a job." What? As if being laid off was my fault? I almost wanted to brag to her how many of these incidents I have had to survive, but I held my tongue. When my nephew Matt was laid off from his first job as an aerospace engineer (2009 recession), it was a real blow to him. His grandpa Joe said, "Just remember, it is not how often you fall down in life that counts, just that you get up." Such wisdom.

Job Loss 1

When I received my master's degree in May 1986 from USC, I was so excited about the future job possibilities that lay ahead. I got a promotion at the county hospital, where I worked to be an administrative officer, but one year later, when severe budget cuts were made, I had to give up that promotion. Many folks in management left and found jobs elsewhere, and I was one of them. I got an offer from the Scottsdale Memorial Health System when Mayo Clinic came to town to become an assistant hospital administrator. My sister and her family lived two hours east of Phoenix so I could be a closer Aunt Kathy, so I took it. Eighteen months later, it was gone.

I must interject and talk about losses in life and how that can affect your mental health. I had gone through a divorce in 1984, including a painful situational depression. Both my grandmother and my dad died in 1986. I had worked for the Ventura County Medical Center for nine years, and even though I voluntarily vacated my job as director of medical records, it was a loss to leave an organization and area where I had a lot of friends and support. I had also fallen in love with a guy who said. "If we spent any time together, we would fall madly in love and have to spend the rest of our lives together." So he kept his distance. I was heartbroken. Another loss.

I was hired as the first female into an all-male administrative team, a role that several inhouse staff had coveted, but no one had broken the glass ceiling. As such, I was resented from the time I set foot in the hospital but was too clueless to notice. I did feel disconnected in my new surroundings but did not give it much of a second thought. My first six months were during the fall and winter, when the weather is lovely. I rented an apartment for six months and then bought a home and thought I was flying high. Then the heat hit, and I was transferred from the main hospital to the north hospital, where the *Scottsdale v. Mayo Doctor* feud was heating up, and my job placed me in the middle of it. Again, I was resented but did not even know it until a friend came to visit from California (Jean) and I took her to a medical staff meeting with me. She said, "Those people are really hostile toward you." What? She could feel the tension that I was not noticing.

I was on the board of the local Franciscan Renewal Center, and this was the source of my local friends. I was even on a retreat team. I also got to spend most weekends with my sister Sue and her family and really enjoyed that time. I also had friends from college (a couple) who had just moved to Scottsdale, and they were like extended family to me. Those were my positive anchors. The only person I knew in my neighborhood was my male neighbor—he would occasionally pop his head over the fence when I was swimming late at night, so we chatted. I did consider a couple of the managers at the hospital(s) my friends, but several would stab me in the back. The director of nursing at the North Hospital was let go before me, and she warned me that the administration could be quite vicious. She was the one who told me to no longer share anything personal with staff—it was going around in the gossip mill of the hospital. Oh, dear.

I decided to take a couple of classes at Arizona State University in economics and marketing. In the fall of 1988, I began to have difficulty in concentrating. This felt familiar to some of my studies at USC while I was going through my divorce. But I plugged along; I was sure it would pass.

When it did not pass, I decided to see a counselor. My depression was getting worse, and one day, I just fell apart and began sobbing. That night, I had a huge panic attack and thought it was a heart attack, so I called my best friends in the area, who called 911. The ambulance came, and my blood pressure was off the charts, but they confirmed it was just a panic attack. Unfortunately, I worked for the very hospital where these paramedics came from, and before the day was out, several doctors I worked with knew of the incident. What confidentiality?

Since my health insurance covered 100 percent of a hospital admission but not much for outpatient visits, my counselor referred me to a psychiatrist, who thought it would be good to take a leave from my job and get some intensive therapy at an inpatient psychiatric facility in the area. So I asked our human resources director for a medical leave, and they sympathetically approved. In January 1989, I would spend my birthday in the hospital. My sister and family came to visit a couple of times, but it was a pretty closed environment.

They say physicians, particularly psychiatrists, practice medicine, and that was just what happened. They started giving me different types of psychotropic drugs to see what would work. I felt like a zombie a lot of the time. I had two roommates during my stay. The first one got regular shock treatments—oh, dear. Was I in a cuckoo's nest? The next one had formerly had my doctor and said he was no good. Yes, the inmates chat a lot, and when you are looking for answers, you start listening to everything.

One of the distinct experiences I remember was attending "psycho drama," where staff would act out a drama that often involved abuse at home, with lots of yelling, a way to trigger feelings that patients might be holding in. Such was the case for me. A yelling dad who would snap his belt at the children brought back childhood memories. Again, I started sobbing. My doctors were not sure what was going on. After nearly four weeks, I was getting tired of all the therapy and drugs and asked my doctor to discharge me back to work. He did not think I was ready, but I did it anyway. In medicine it is called against medical advice (AMA). I should have known better. But one of the expressions we often heard was, "Don't should on yourself." I was not a very compliant patient; I just wanted out.

When I returned to work, my anxiety and depression did not allow me to function very well, and the staff around me knew it. The administrative team decided to cut their losses and let me go with a six months' severance payment since I was not able to do my job. I conferred with the nursing director, who was let go, and she told me to tape-record all that they said. This only made things worse. Good friends from California sent me some money to see an attorney, but I found out that Arizona was a right-to-work state, which favored the employers in all matters of termination. So I did not have any legal grounds to fight the issue. I completely fell apart. Years later, I would reflect on the bigger picture, and I realized that the CEO for the hospital had treated me as a favorite, so the staff resented me. When administrative team meetings were held, he would leave the meeting for a while, call me into his office, and then send me back into the meeting. Killer glares. But I was clueless until a member of that team brought it to my attention. She called me to see if I was doing okay. Such was the case when I was the "favorite" in my family of origin. Sibling disgust. But I was clueless. I needed to get my antennae up.

Even though my California friends said I should sell my house and come back to California, I was not able to make a decision—my body was filled with fear. I stayed in that home for thirteen months and did a little part-time work. I changed psychiatrists and did some more inpatient work, but it did not seem to help. I got a ticket to fly home to Minnesota to be with family but drove to the airport on four different days before I got the nerve to get on a plane. My family was shocked at my condition—anxious, depressed, and losing weight. When they called my psychiatrist, he merely said I needed to stop beating myself up (mentally) before I could ever recover. I did go back to Arizona, but my erratic behavior led to my sister saying I could not see them for three months. I was truly alone. The one thing that kept me going was attending daily Mass at the Franciscan Renewal Center since those friends were always there for me.

My sister had a newborn at home (her fourth child), and she could not manage me as her "fifth child." Gratefully, she was in contact with my best friends in California, who drove to Arizona and "kidnapped" me in a big RV and brought me and my personal items and clothes back to Santa Barbara. Sue and Jeff packed up my home and put everything in storage. Gratefully, I was able to find renters for my property with a lease purchase agreement. My California friends gave me ninety days to stay with them and find a job (April, May, and June of 1990). As God would have it, that friend who had come to see me and attended that medical staff meeting said there was an opening for the director of medical records at the small hospital near where she lived. So I applied, and I actually got the job. I started in May 1990, and gratefully, most of the work was "automatic" for me to do, but it was a jittery time to be supervising a staff of ten. God took care of me in so many ways. Manna.

That friend who found the job also had been through a deep bout of depression, and she had a mom who was chronically depressed and hospitalized most of her childhood. We both grew up in German Catholic families, and we had much in common. She, too, had been a medical records director but had to leave her job in Northern California to "come home" to be cared for at the very hospital where I worked. They called it the med stress unit (like club med) and even had cute T-shirts that they wore. How could anyone take major clinical depression so lightly? She also told me about the new wonder drug called Prozac, so I started taking it. Slowly but surely, I started to feel better, and I spent three years in that job. More importantly, she introduced me to her greatest source of comfort, the Bible. She introduced me to a Bible-based church and got me started in a Bible study; in many ways, that was the beginning of my salvation. I was blessed with a kind assistant called Elaine, who was there for me. I was able to completely remodel the department and get it all organized. Rumors started that this private hospital was about to be closed, so it was time for a new job.

But I digress. During that summer, I spent three months in Santa Barbara with friends, one month with another friend in Ventura, and then I rented a room at a gals' townhome near the hospital as I began to look for a place to buy for myself. I went to a townhouse auction, and that was where I met Don (see chapter D), who did buy a property and invited me to dinner. We started a wonderful dating relationship. Later in the fall, I did find my own condo at an auction at a price half of what it was worth one year earlier. I moved in at the beginning of December and was once again given a new start by God. Don even attended the same church as me. So much manna.

Don and I went to Durango, Colorado, over New Year's Weekend, and that was when I wrecked my left knee—I blew out all the ligaments. By January 1991, I once again spent my birthday in the hospital, but this time for an anterior cruciate ligament (ACL) repair. The guys in the lab told me they used more blood during my surgery than they had ever seen, but it all seemed to go okay. I was on a short medical leave but able to return to work within a few weeks. I did spend Superbowl weekend with Don, but shortly afterward, he would break up our relationship since his wife had fired her first divorce attorney and was coming back at him with all kinds of new demands. Just as it had been too much for my sister, it became too much for Don to juggle both. But God still looked out for me.

I would have four knee surgeries in 1991, which was quite unusual for an ACL repair. The first surgeon had me in a full leg immobilizer for two months, so by the time I started PT, my knee was literally stuck with adhesions. The PT staff tried all they could, but x-rays revealed that the screws that attached my new patellar tendon graft to the back of my knee had started to move. So I had my second surgery in April 1991. The anesthesiologist would come to my postop room and tell me he had never seen my surgeon so upset—the scarring in my knee was a mess!

The PT staff insisted I get a continuous passive motion (CPM) machine that would keep my knee in motion every night when I slept. They worked tirelessly with me to get my knee to move, but I could barely get enough range of motion to ride the exercise bicycle we used to warm up every time I was in PT. As God would have it, my primary care doctor was a female internist who had just moved to the area from Los Angeles, and she knew the *best* knee surgeon in the country—he was the team doctor for the LA Rams and was part of the Kerlan-Jobe Medical Clinic. She got me a personal referral, so I started driving nearly two hours south to see a most remarkable orthopedic surgeon and genuinely nice man. Dr. Clarence Shield. Such a God thing.

As a sidenote, there is a bit of history about the Kerlan-Jobe Clinic from www.kerlanjobe.com. In 1958, the Brooklyn Dodgers moved to Los Angeles. Dr. Robert Kerlan became the Los Angeles Dodgers' first team physician. In 1964, after serving as medical staff sergeant in WWII with the US Army, Dr. Frank Jobe returned home, received his medical doctorate, and joined Dr. Kerlan's practice, then named Southwestern Orthopedic Medical Group. In 1974, Dodgers pitcher Tommy John permanently damaged a ligament in his arm, potentially ending his career. Drawing on his knowledge treating polio patients, Dr. Jobe proposes a radical new procedure. John agrees, and Dr. Jobe performs the world's first ulnar collateral ligament reconstruction surgery. The procedure is a success. Tommy John goes on to pitch in the Major Leagues for fifteen more years, and the procedure is now commonly known as Tommy John Surgery. World-class athletes from around the world flew into LA to go to this clinic, and "miraculous" surgeries were performed that got many athletes back on the field. I found my own miracle at this clinic. And to think that four years later, I would marry a polio survivor who also had a miraculous surgery experience. It was another world-class center in Los Angeles, but we were both in the right place at the right time. God is so good.

Dr. Shields performed surgery on my knee on Labor Day weekend of 1991 and came into my room postop to tell me that he only works on injured knees and mine was the *worst* he had ever seen! What? He said it was like carving out cement—so many adhesions. He put me into PT daily for the next two weeks, and I would have to work through the pain to start getting more extension for my left leg. By December, I had still not reached the goal of zero degrees, so he did one more surgery to "snip" that original reconstructed ligament to give me more motion. He even created a special brace that would enable me to ski again. How good is God that He put this special doctor in my life at just the right time? Just as the angel named

Clarence "saved" George in *It's a Wonderful Life*, I also had an angel named Clarence. God is so good.

Job Loss 2

So back to that hospital that was rumored to be about to be sold. Remember that PT center where I went for all my knee therapy? The owner was a fellow manager at the hospital, and he saw me as one who could help with a new business he was creating, one that would offer a sports medicine model to those with Workers Compensation injuries. So I took the job as the administrator of this business in the summer of 1993. As God would have it, I met the owners of the National Association of Occupational Medicine located in Santa Barbara. I told them about our unique model for treating Work Comp injuries.

They invited me to speak at their national conference being held in New Orleans in 1994, so I took my sales manager for a trip to this interesting city that is literally below sea level. We stayed in the French Quarter and had a fun time. I was able to use my knee sports injury incident to begin my PowerPoint presentation. I still remember my opening line. "I blew out all the ligaments in my left knee while skiing at a resort near Durango, Colorado, called Purgatory. As a good Catholic, I should have known better than to go to a place called Purgatory. Ha!" I went on to say I was treated by a traditional orthopedic surgeon who wanted me home at rest until I found a sports medicine specialist who wanted me back on the field, and that made all the difference. That presentation was so well received that I was invited to speak at their national conference in the following year in San Francisco. My presentation was just after lunch, the time when the verdict for O. J. Simpson had been announced. Talk about a distracted audience! But God led and protected me during all these adventures.

During all this time, I found out that the business owner (Richard) had gone bankrupt in his first business north of Santa Barbara. Although we created a business plan to sell our model to some larger businesses, we were not successful because this second business had to file for bankruptcy. It was filed in Santa Barbara County. Yes, I went to those court hearings and actually saw my ex-husband from a distance in that very place where he worked. I continued to make calls on behalf of Richard to try to find buyers. One such conversation was overheard by our nosey young book-keeper, who told Richard I was trying to sell out his business from under him. What? I was let go the next day. This was my second sudden job loss.

As God would have it, our medical director (Dr. Miller) was a strong Christian, and we were in a long car drive together the day before my termination. We were on a trip to share our business plan. When he found out that I had been terminated, he caught me in the parking lot as I was about to leave with all my belongings. He said, "Don't let the accuser of the brethren fill you with lies that this was your fault. It was not." Who was this accuser? I had never heard such an expression. He then told me about the father of all lies, Satan, and I began to look at the spiritual nature of what was happening to me.

Also, as God would have it, the year I got fired was 1995, just six months after I was married to Bill. So I had a husband with a job, a home, and health insurance. So I was able to file for unemployment and be protected during my next search for a job. I had also stayed in touch with the assistant administrator from the hospital where I worked, and he introduced me to the health-care executives of Southern California, based in Ventura but covering all the LA area. I was asked to be on their board of directors and served this organiza-tion from 1995 to 2006 (when we moved out of California).

As part of this board, I got to give a presentation to local hospi-tal administrators in Ventura County, and I met the CEO from Simi Valley Adventist Hospital. He liked what I had to say, and he hired me in the fall of 1996 to help him establish an occupational medicine clinic at his hospital. I then helped him do marketing for their emer-gency medicine department. He hired a marketing director who used to work for the *LA Times*, and she taught me a lot about marketing. During this time, the hospital decided to create a cancer services pro-gram based on their existing Nancy Reagan Breast Center, and they hired me as the director for this program. So I then learned a lot about the cancer world and made trips to visit large tertiary facilities to see if one would partner with us.

I was asked to serve on the board of the local American Cancer Society board and ended up as cochairman for two Relay for Life events, during which we raised over $300,000 during each of the two twenty-four-hour events. So I learned a lot about fundraising as well as cancer. During this time, we were working with the local school district to set up a stop smoking program at the local free clinic. During this effort, a school nurse asked me to help apply for a Community Development Block grant, so I wrote the grant. She asked, How long did that take? I said a couple of days, and she said you should do this for a living! We got the grant!

I also got involved in a county-wide task force for breast cancer early detection and prevention. I became the chair of this group and worked with professionals across Ventura County to get and set up a mobile mammography unit that would help the underserved populations. I was introduced to the Ventura Community Foundation that helped fund local grants from a member of this task force who was director of the Ventura County Resource Foundation (Paul).

So as God would have it, by the end of 2001, I was very well connected across the country in the area of cancer prevention and grant writing as well as marketing. I was now a chamber ambassador in Simi Valley and part of the leadership academy for the county. I was also a member of the local Kiwanis Club and made many professional friends. Then out of left field, the hospital administrator was offered a job at the corporate headquarters in Northern California and a new administrator from out of the area was hired.

Job Loss 3

The new CEO hired a new CFO, and their first task was budget cuts. She did not have the same vision as the previous administrator about cancer services and thought cutting my position would be a good first step to saving some money. So the human resources director appeared at my door at the beginning of 2002 with boxes and said my job had been eliminated. I was actually escorted out of the building. Really? I remember how shocked the medical staff was as well as my work colleagues. Even cancer survivors that I had served started calling me and saying I should sue for illegal termination. But I did not.

Job Loss 4

As God would have it, that director of the Ventura County Medical Resource Foundation knew I had good grant-writing skills, and he asked me to come to work for him as their grant writer at the beginning of 2002. So God provided and protected me once again. However, by the end of the year, he was suddenly fired from his job, and their board asked me to be the interim director, which I did. They decided to bring back a previous manager, and they made me the grants person. Within two months, this new person was so jealous of how well liked I was that she tore down all my plaques and she fired me. I prayed for God's help.

As God would have it, while serving jury duty, I met one of my fellow ambassadors from the Simi Valley Chamber, and she could see I was really stressed. She encouraged me to apply for a workers compensation stress claim that was approved one day before I was fired. So I was able to collect funds for my time off work. During the next two years, every single person whom I had worked with at the foundation left. Every time, they called me and said I should file a libel suit against this new boss since she spent all her time badmouthing me to everyone. It was not until the very last person who left told me that I did decide to retain an attorney. In the meantime, this badmouthing had prevented me from obtaining another full-time job. Gratefully, I did grant writing or a lot of different organizations. God once again protected and provided for me.

All my previous staff were interviewed and gave testimony to my claims. Unfortunately, I could not get anyone to specifically state they had not hired me because of this slander—they were all directed to keep quiet by their own employers. By the end of 2005, my case was sent to arbitration, and I found myself in a legal office, me in one room and the other party in another room. The attorney would go back and forth between the rooms, and he finally came back to me and said they had made an offer to settle. He also said, in all cases he had ever done, this was the strangest one he had ever seen. Most plaintiffs (my position) were the angry ones, but I was a bucket of tears while the other party was the one filled with anger and vitriol. I got this settlement check in January 2006, enough income to cover the year. As God would have it, that was the year we decided to move out of state, so I was not stressed to find a job. God is so good. He was always with me to provide and protect me no matter what. I could now empathize and help others who lost jobs. God comforts us so we can comfort others.

According to 2 Corinthians 1:3–7, "Praise be to the God and Father of our Lord Jesus Christ, the Father of compassion and the God of all comfort, who comforts us in all our troubles, so that we can comfort those in any trouble with the comfort we ourselves receive from God. For just as we share abundantly in the sufferings of Christ, so also our comfort abounds through Christ. If we are distressed, it is for your comfort and salvation; if we are comforted, it is for your comfort, which produces in you patient endurance of the same sufferings we suffer. And our hope for you is firm, because we know that just as you share in our sufferings, so also you share in our comfort." I now think this has become one of my life verses. God has comforted me, protected me, guided me, so now I can help others.

Job Loss 5

During my time at the school district, I changed positions from the audiology team to the District Library Media Center. Two years into the position, our department of six members was slashed in the budget to only three staff. My job was one of those eliminated, so I was given notice in March 2018 that my job ended in June 2018. This was the week before my mom died, so it was a challenging time. I chose to stay and help my director and was able to find another job at the local high school as the administrative person for the international baccalaureate program. Again, God provided a smooth transition for me during yet one more job loss. My son James likes to say that he thinks one of the reasons I was hired was my loyalty to the boss at the place of layoff. I could have left and taken the severance, but I chose to stay and help. I think Jesus would approve.

It was another job and another opportunity to learn new skills and to make an impact in the lives of high school teenagers. Our school mascot was the Huskie, so I participated in all things Huskie, from sporting events to being a chaperone at homecoming and prom, to being a judge for speech and debate meets, providing leadership in the Fellowship of Christian Athletes (FCA) and the annual international week and even acting in an improv event for our high school theater. When I retired from my job in June of 2020, we published our final IB newsletter, and here is what my boss had to say in his "Coordinators' Corner" article:

> Amidst all of the unusual circumstances bringing this year to a close (COVID), I want to recognize the retirement of Kathy Kramer. Kathy serves as the IB administrative assistant and has been an invaluable help to our Diploma and Middle Years programs.
>
> Kathy embodies the ideal of "everyone a huskie" with her dedication to all things Douglas County. She attends athletic events, dramatic performances (even participating on the staff team on the improv night), she volunteers to judge competitions, works tirelessly to set up events on the weekends and evenings and attends to all of the duties required of her position. Her dedication and school spirit are nothing short of remarkable.
>
> Kathy is also a model of the "Learner Profile" from risk-taker to communicator. Her

willingness and ability to come to understand a complex program in a short time helped to build our program and its connections within our community. Of all the profile traits, "caring" most suits Kathy. She genuinely cares about the people she works with. She went out of her way to promote the accomplishments of students by writing articles and creating posters. These human connections arise because her genuine kindness comes from who she is as a person and how she values those around her.

Kathy wrote an extensive "TOK" journal exploring perspectives and reflecting on her past. Her genuine curiosity and willingness to examine situations from multiple angles define what our program is all about. Kathy plans to continue her involvement in our building by substitute teaching and we will be sure to leave a bowl of candy out for when she stops by the office!

So when I hear that someone is losing their job, I can most certainly relate. It is clearly high on the list of life stressors, yet it can be a gift of new opportunities along the way. Thank goodness for His peace that passes all understanding during all these transitions.

Jobs Kept (Good Things I Learned)

So now that I have told you about all my job "failures," I must say a few things about the other jobs I have held along the way, what I learned, and how God helped me.

Softball Coach

We all remember our first paid job. Outside of some babysitting, of which I did a lot, the first time I had a real job and had to get a social security card (for taxes) was the summer before I started high school, at age fifteen. I worked for our local town as the girls' softball coach with a good friend named Margaret. I can still remember hauling a big canvas bag full of bats and softball items up the street and over the railroad tracks to our local baseball field located by our town dump.

I was a pretty good athlete as a child but had never been a coach so this was learn-as-you-go. The most challenging thing was that the mediocre athletes always seemed to show up for practice, but the best ones did not always come. So when game day came, we had to decide if we would play our best players or the ones who tried the hardest and came to practice. We did both. Of course we wanted to win, so the best ones got to start the game, but by the end of the game, every girl got to take the field. I now have grown nieces and nephews with children who are good athletes. One such niece has a well-built son who was asked to be captain of his football team. What she said? He is good on the field, but off the field he is constantly in trouble with the law and hanging with the wrong friends. She went to the coach and asked to please not allow him to be captain. He was not a good leader or role model. Good for her!

I also learned how to manually score baseball. You know, balls, strikes, walks, hits, runs, with a pencil in a scorebook. Many years later, when I was a partial season ticket holder to the LA Dodgers (ten people shared the seats or eight games for each season), I got to sit in the second deck behind third base and score the games. Isn't that what everyone did? Start with a program and keep track of what was going on? I can remember guys sitting behind us, asking me how I learned that. I would say I thought everyone knew how to score a game! I can do the same for bowling! So if the internet goes down and all electronics are not working, these fun skills may come in handy! What the Lord showed me in coaching paid off when I became a manager of people. Take care of everyone and pay attention to details. Thank You, God! I did go on to becoming an A&W Car Hop for other summers. Oh, to never want to be a waitress for a long-term job—it kills your feet and back! But serving is an honorable thing to do.

College Summer Jobs: Selling Books Door-to-Door

When I was in college, I worked in a different state every summer. I already told you about my first summer as a Jewish governess in New Jersey. You won't believe what I did the next two summers. I sold books door-to-door! What? My parents thought I was crazy. During my sophomore year of college, I saw an ad to work for Southwestern Book Company, including a week of sales training in Nashville, Tennessee, a chance to earn much more money than my $1.25/hour job as a carhop. So I signed up!

I made my way to Nashville to learn how to do sales. This company had quite a well-oiled training program! It was fun and energizing to be around so many other college students who were learning "you can do it, never give up!" I was assigned to join a group of girls going to Dallas, Texas, to sell cookbooks for $10 each, where we made $5 for every book sold. When we arrived in Texas, we were taught to go to a local church of our choosing and ask if there were any church members with a room to rent, and sure enough, my partner and I found a room to rent. She was a very religious person who read her Bible every night. I never asked much about her habit, but I do know a great deal of the males in this work were selling Bibles door-to-door, and they made the big bucks!

I made it through ten weeks of working eighty hours a week and made a net income of nearly $2,000. That was a lot of money for me. I had a goal to earn enough money to buy my first used car, which I did, a Chevy Malibu. I learned it is good to have goals and keep your eye on the prize. We got every Sunday off and met other teammates at some fun place like Six Flags over Texas, so after church on Sundays, we always had a blast. All work and no play makes Jill a dull girl. Yes, we got a day of rest and fun. Amen! I did very well (for a female), so the guys asked me to come back the next summer and lead a team. What? I had to find a new goal.

The guys called me up during my junior year in college and asked if I wanted to hang with them again, this time in January 1975, to drive to Steamboat Springs, Colorado, and go skiing. They took care of me—car/gas, room, and board—and were all Christian gentlemen. Yes, these were the Bible salesmen! We had a week of pure fun learning to ski, after all the holiday travelers had left the slopes. These guys were all from the South with such sweet accents. They had the ski instructors in stitches most days—what good, clean fun! I also got my first taste of real Colorado powdered snow—nothing like Minnesota! I think a seed was planted to come back to the Rocky Mountains. The next summer, I would sell dictionaries in the Philadelphia area.

I recruited a team of all women, and when I arrived at sales training, the guys thought I was crazy. Most women could not handle work this intense for ten weeks straight. They were right. By the end of the summer, most of my team had quit and gone home. But I had a new goal to spend the next summer in Europe, so I pushed on. Again, I found us a place to live at the local church where the local mortician offered a three-bedroom apartment above his mortuary for a real deal. So three of us lived there—it was amazing. We were actually in an area called Norristown, and there were a lot of African Americans in our neighborhood. We were told to be cautious, but you know what? The fact we lived over a mortuary kept them all away. They did not want to be near dead bodies. I told one of the gals just before she left that I now knew what Jesus must have felt when all His disciples deserted Him. It was lonely.

It was also the summer I learned my dad was having an affair, and I was called home for an important family meeting to decide how we siblings would respond. (Yes, I had extra funds for a flight home and could take a week off—my sales manager was very kind.) As I flew home, I was lost for what to say to my dad. Obviously, it was wrong for him to cheat on my mom, yet I did understand how hard it must have been to be married to someone who never showed him any affection (my mom), nor did she do anything with him except the "work" to raise a big family. I guess she never learned "all work and no play makes Jill a dull girl." My brother with children told my dad, if he left our mom, he would never see his grandkids again. How sad. Dad loved being a grandpa, so he gave up the affair and stayed with my mom. Those sales guys were there for me before, during, and after that huge event in my life. I think God had put them in my life so I could see the value of knowing His Word (the Bible) and how people live their lives. It would be fifteen years later before I owned a Bible. These guys were precious. More manna.

Center for Disease Control

So I already talked about the summer after college where I went to Europe for twelve weeks for only $1,200 all-expenses paid. But when I came home, I had to find my first "real job" after college, so I started looking at jobs being posted in the *Journal for Medical Record Administrators*. I only looked at states that were warmer than Minnesota. This would lead to my application for three different jobs. The first in Fort Myers, Florida, but I quickly learned it was a community for retirement folks and not young professionals. I also went to Gainesville, Florida, and interviewed at their large teaching hospital, but I realized it was a very big job, and my love for Florida was waning. I learned how hot, muggy, and buggy the place was! So my third job interview was in Atlanta to work for the Center for Disease Control (CDC) to work on the SENIC project—the Study of the Efficacy of Nosocomial Infection Control, which means hospital-acquired infections. I had friends from my European trip who lived in the Atlanta area, so I took the job.

It was a perfect first job out of college! I was given a good salary, but I could save all this money because all my living expenses were paid. Hotels. Meals. Flights. A government car to use wherever we went. During the fall of 1976, I traveled to the East Coast with a couple of guys, and we did interviews of hospital administrators from New York to Washington, DC. Great fun! Every city was a chance for exploration! I also had time to fly to Boston and see my uncle who lived there. I loved all of it. By the beginning of 1977, I was assigned to a team of women to do data collection at hospitals, which meant one week per town reading tons of medical records. This was not as much fun. Our team was sent to Kansas City, Missouri, and we worked our way east to Hannibal, Missouri. We watched a few tornados from our small-town motels.

As God would have it, my college roommate from Tennessee (Marybelle) was living in Memphis, where her husband was going to optometry school, so I flew there to visit her over the Presidents' Holiday weekend. While on the flight back to Kansas City, I met a guy on the plane, and I told him I wanted to explore Kansas City, but all the gals on my team wanted to order room service and sit in their rooms and read. Really? He said he had a friend I might enjoy meeting named Bill. He warned me that he was not the type to settle down just yet, which was fine with me—I just wanted to explore Kansas City. One week later, I got a call from the bar in our Howard Johnson Hotel from Major Bill—he asked me to have a drink with me. So I did.

It seems a bunch of Army officers were in the area studying at the Army War College in Leavenworth, Kansas. Here is how it is described by Wikipedia. Fort Leavenworth is a United States Army installation located in Leavenworth County, Kansas, in the city of Leavenworth since it was annexed on April 12, 1977, in the northeast part of the state. Built in 1827, it is the second oldest active United States Army post west of Washington, DC, and the oldest permanent settlement in Kansas. Fort Leavenworth has been historically known as the Intellectual Center of the Army. Wow. He was getting his master's degree and learning a whole lot about moving up as an Army officer. They say that is hard for a single man, but he did it. And he was probably one of the most interesting men I have ever met in my life.

As we headed east through several small towns in Missouri, he would come and see me and take me to dinner. He had served in Vietnam as an officer and paratrooper and was one of the only people who had anything good to say about that war. He was married just before he enlisted, but she left him for another guy and he had no wife when he returned from Vietnam. I rather think he became "married to the Army," and he certainly had much more worldly experience than me. Yet he was an officer and a gentleman when it came to the way he treated me. When we found out our team was being sent to California, I called to tell him my exciting news, but his phone had been disconnected. I did have an APO forward mail address, so I wrote him a scathing letter to say I thought we had something going, but he just disappeared on me. So strange.

When we arrived in Los Angeles, it was Memorial Day weekend, and I got my government-issued car and began driving the LA freeways—no problem. I was getting tired of living out of a suitcase, so I searched the *LA Times* for job openings and found two that had positions for a director of medical records. One was a huge hospital in Beverly Hills–Cedar Sinai Medical Center. I think the previous director was leaving with a nervous breakdown—ha! Not for me. So I rented a car and drove north to the second job interview in Santa Barbara. Now that was completely different from LA and one of the most beautiful places I had ever seen. So I accepted the job at the county hospital and went back to Minnesota and packed all my belongings into my Chevy Malibu and began the drive west. I took with me my sister Sue, who had just graduated high school (1977), and we had a fun road trip. Once I reached LA, I put her on a plane back home, and I settled into a one-bedroom apartment and began my new job, in paradise.

Shortly after I started, I met my ex-husband, who was working for the local district attorney's office. He served me a subpoena, and we started dating. Within a couple months, Major Bill called me out of the blue and said he had received my letter and wanted to see me. I told him I was dating someone else, but perhaps we could meet at Disneyland and spend a day together. He then said he wanted to see me and not California, so I had to let go. Later on, I would find out that he was now stationed at Fort Bragg, North Carolina, as a colonel and was a commander in the Eighty-Second Airborne. They were often sent on "black ops" and could not tell anyone where they had gone. In the spring of 1977, he was somewhere in Europe, learning how to fight terrorism. If you remember the Iran hostage crisis that occurred in November 1979, you may recall that President Jimmy Carter had sent in Delta Force to rescue the hostages. He led that group! The mission was a big mess, but he survived and would later go to LA to help then police chief Daryl Gates teach his officers how to fight gangs like they fought terrorists. They would become good friends. Gulp. He was a very important man. What did he ever see in me? But this relationship would be continued after my divorce, when I saw him on ABC World News Tonight. No lie. The only military guy I had ever dated would go on to become a general, and all those years, he still remembered me. That Segway during my CDC job was quite something.

County Hospitals—Santa Barbara and Ventura

I ended up working as the director of medical records at Santa Barbara General Hospital from 1977 to 1978 and took the same job at Ventura County Medical Center from 1978 to 1987. I was thrown into the world of managing women—first, a group of twelve, and then thirty-two ladies who worked 24-7. Now that was a learning curve! I knew my stuff when it came to medical records management, but how do you prepare to manage women of all job types, from filing clerks to transcriptionists to coders? So I learned on the job and came to be respected as quite a good manager and one who completely organized and transformed the departments I led.

Within one month of my taking the job in Santa Barbara, the hot Santa Ana winds came to town and burned down over 250 homes in the rich area called Montecito, so the city was declared a disaster area. By the winter of 1977–1978, the rains came and never seemed to stop, so mudslides cut off the roads both north and south of Santa Barbara. Another national disaster. By spring, I experienced my first earthquake. Another disaster. And then at the end of June in 1978, a ballot initiative called the Jarvis-Gann Act (Proposition 13) passed, and within a week, the hospital where I worked closed its doors. Yes, another disaster for me. Really? Four times in one year?

We still had clinics to run, but I had to lay off staff, and the whole job became quite sadly boring. If God was telling me to leave California, I certainly was not listening! How could I leave paradise? Especially since I was dating a handsome guy with a great job who then asked me to marry him. So I said yes, and I took a short administrative leave to help a local nonprofit who did outreach to the poor orphans in Tijuana, Mexico—my first mission effort! Within a few months, my boss in Santa Barbara recommended me for the medical record job in Ventura, and so I interviewed and was accepted. It was just thirty miles south, with the same beautiful ocean breeze and mild climate. Houses cost less than half as much, so it was a good move for me and for us.

As for the medical record manager job in Ventura, I followed a gal who had been there nearly thirty years, so they were in need of new leadership. Our file room, located in the basement, was called the chart room, and the files were literally falling on the floor. I had to immediately set up a system where every member of my staff had to work in teams of two, every two weeks, to start purging old records. The other managers in the hospital were amazed. Since our primary purpose was the quick retrieval of data for medical care, we could finally meet that challenge. The staff also got to learn real teamwork, and they came to enjoy that day off from their regular routine to do something completely different and come to work in jeans! The managers had a monthly meeting to learn what was going on in the hospital, and I would have a staff meeting the following day to fill everyone in. The director of our hospital auxiliary would tell my staff, "You guys know more about what is going on than anyone else in the building." They liked that. You might say I was an open book about sharing information, and I really cared about my staff.

One year into my job, I needed a supervisor for that large chart room, and I interviewed a gal named Paula, who had raised seven children and several grandchildren but had never worked out of the home. Since I came from a family of seven children, I knew how much work that was, so I hired her on the spot. She became a wonderful employee and dear friend. After nine years on that job when I made an upward career move, I kept in touch with her, and we have remained friends to this day—over forty years! When I married Bill, I introduced him to Paula and her family, and we would go to her home every Christmas Eve for homemade tamales—her family treasured that tradition we shared. When we adopted two boys, they became like her own grandchildren, and she was so kind to them. She would tell Bill stories about how much I had helped all the staff to learn things like medical terminology and how to move up in the world. The things I took for granted had long been remembered by Paula, and it was sweet music to my ears to hear "Well done, good and faithful servant." I guess God had already come to live in my heart, and it seemed to show to all those around me.

I also got involved in many things at the hospital. I was named the chairman of the employee participation committee, and we raised funds to augment our budget for extra things, including a care room for those who had to hear bad news and needed a private room in which to meet. To this day, when I go back to that hospital, I still see my name on a plaque by this room, and my heart feels grateful I got to be part of something important. In 1984, we celebrated the one-hundredth anniversary of the hospital, and I was asked to lead a group to put together a time capsule, for which we collected current event items and buried them. It was the year we launched the building of a new hospital adjacent to our old building, and it was a great thing to be part of. Our hospital auxiliary leader would put on annual melodramas with musical numbers between acts, and I always got to act, sing, and dance with the rest of the cast that included our residents in family practice medicine. What fun! I was on a bowling team; we were awful but laughed a lot. We also had golf tournament fundraisers and wine-tasting events, all of which I got to help organize and participate in. In so many ways, it was the best job I ever had! So why did I leave?

It was the summer of 1987, and we got a new hospital CFO and he found out our finances were in a big mess. Massive layoffs occurred (over two hundred staff across the hospital), and many managers, including myself, took the chance to move on to other jobs. This even included our hospital administrator and many of my friends. So with my master's degree in hand, I took that job in Scottsdale,

Arizona, which ended up being the worst job I ever had! I certainly learned that following the money is not as important as following your heart. If I had stayed twenty years, I would have earned a full retirement and been able to do other things after that. But I did not look at life in those terms. I was only thirty-three years old when I left Ventura, and retirement seemed a long way off, so those thoughts never occurred to me. I was too ambitious. God needed to humble me. You already know what happened in Scottsdale (first job loss), so let's move on to my next medical record manager position when I came back to California in the spring of 1990. I had to take a step back in terms of prestige, but as God would have it, I was offered the same annual salary I had been given in Scottsdale. I was a mess, but God watched out for me.

Private Hospital Manager Job

I have already talked about landing the job as the director of medical records in May of 1990, partially due to my friendship with Jean, the one who also introduced me to the Bible. It was a smaller hospital, and I had fewer staff, but it was just the right size to recover from my Arizona time of depression. I stayed in this job for three years and did well to completely remodel the department and make everything more efficient. When it looked like the hospital was going to be sold or closed and I was taking another job, one of the doctors on the staff told me that he had never seen one person make such a positive difference in such a big way. Really? I left that job to go work for my fellow manager who ran the outpatient physical therapy department and was getting ready to start a new venture in the world of occupational medicine. You already know how that turned out two years later—my second job loss.

So as I look back at those three years as a manager, what did I learn? First, I had jumped into a situation where I had a witch on my staff, literally, a Wiccan. She worked on our evening shift as a coder, and the other evening staff would tell me stories about what a wicked person she was and how she was constantly "staff splitting." What? I had never known that such folks really existed in this area of spiritual evil deeds. I was able to collect enough documentation of her poor performance that had caused the hospital money (incorrect coding), so I was able to let her go. As I went to my new job, I had another male witch who was putting satanic things into our computers. It was a good thing I was in a small church group at that time, and they told me to get rid of all of it and flee—this was serious business! So God protected me against these evil forces that were literally working against me in another very affluent area of Southern California. Gratefully, the medical director at my new job was a believer, and he prayed over me that the accuser of the brethren would not get to me. What? Yes, Satan himself. I never knew such forces even existed in my world, but God certainly protected me in ways I never knew. More manna.

Simi Valley Adventist Hospital—Many Roles

As you know, after I was let go from my occupational medicine job (loss number 2), I happened to be serving on the board of the health care executives of Southern California. The assistant administrator from my previous hospital had lost his job when the facility closed, but we kept in touch and he introduced me to this group. So for nearly a year, as I collected unemployment and searched for a job, I had been put in a perfect place to meet leaders in my field, where I got to make presentations and kept well networked. God kept me in His eye the whole time.

It was the fall of 1996 when I met the hospital administrator from Simi Valley Adventist Hospital. He knew of my experience in setting up an occupational medicine program and asked me to do the same at his facility, so I accepted his job offer. I spent a year helping launch the hospital-based program and got to meet employers from all over the area. Before I knew it, I was serving on the local Chamber of Commerce as an ambassador and even did ribbon cuttings when all new businesses opened. Before long, this CEO asked me to set up a marketing department for him, and he brought in a great gal who had worked for the *LA Times* to lead the department I had set up. Within a year, this same CEO wanted to expand their cancer services program, so I was offered the job to lead this effort so I moved up. I then got to sit on the board of the local American Cancer Society and led two Relay for Life events. I was the most plugged in person you ever met! Sadly, the CEO moved up to the corporate office, and the new CEO eliminated that program, and I was laid off in a budget cut (loss number 3). But God continued to provide.

During the last six months in my cancer services director role, I met a school nurse who wanted the hospital to work with her and the local free clinic to set up a program to help teenagers quit smoking. In lieu of detention, they were sent to me and we spent the better part of the day talking about the evils of smoking from a health perspective (black lungs) as well as a social impact on their lives. She found out that their Community Development Block grant funds were becoming available and asked if I could write the grant. I had never done this, but as a nonprofit organization, we certainly qualified, and I put together a grant package on behalf of our three entities—the hospital, the local high school, and the free community clinic. We got funded! That was a fun experience for me. At the same time, I was asked to sit on a county-wide task force to develop better mammography screening for poor women, so I also made new friends and colleagues across the county. So when my hospital job suddenly ended, I was able to find a job quite quickly through these connections. One of the members of that task force asked me to come and write grants for his foundation. That started my jump into the grant world, where I would even be asked to teach a class on grant-writing at the local community foundation. This would really help sixteen months later, when a new CEO was hired and she ended my position. I learned so much about so many things and made so many connections during my hospital job, that God opened doors for me. So much manna.

Ten Years of Grant Writing

During high school and college, my favorite subject was math, not English. Although I did well at both, I never thought I would end up writing for a living. But from 2002 to 2012, that was exactly what I did—I became a grant writer and managed some of the programs I got funded. I got to act as a consultant to many nonprofits. I ended up working with over fifty different organizations. Wow. During that awful Arizona job, I had taken a class in executive writing, and it helped me. I also made friends with a gal who ran a grant-writing business, and she became a good mentor to me. It was during this time, I think, that I grew to love writing and being able to tell a story that would capture those reading my proposals. God had also given me a diverse group of professional contacts. Talk about manna! Here is a list with so many stories to tell:

	Company Name	Type Work	Years
1	American Red Cross, Ventura County	Disaster preparation and response	2008–2010
2	Barbara Johnson Foundation	Support—family crisis, gays, suicide	2007–2009
3	Bone Cancer International Inc.	Information on bone cancer for MDs and patients	2005
4	Café on A—KEYS Academy	Hispanic teens at risk programs, including art	2005
5	Channel Islands Community Church	Community development on church land	2004–2005
6	Children's Enrichment Program	Conflict resolution skills in kids	2004–2006
7	Children's Hunger Fund	Food distribution for poor kids/families	2005–2006
8	Connect 2 Ministries	Connect and train churches—overseas missions	2012–2013
9	Consumer Credit Counseling Services	Credit, debt, budget counseling/education	2004–2005

10	Denver Ignite	Help to refugees in greater Denver	2013
11	Eagle Ridge Camps and Conference Center	Christian Camp and Conference Center	2004–2005
12	El Concilio del Condado de Ventura	Outreach to Ventura Co Latinos	2005–2006
13	Employment Aptitude and Placement Association	Jobs for unemployed / low income	2005
14	Evangelical Friends Church SW	Christian missions, camp, inner city	2005
15	Family Health Support Network	Foster Family Agency, Palm Springs area	2008–2010
16	Family Life Foundation	Diabetes program; family violence	2004–2005
17	Food Share of Ventura County	Food distribution for poor	2004–2006
18	Girls Club of LA	Reggae, rock and jazz festival	2005
19	Glass Hearts	Restore lives, Fatherhood Project	2012
20	Golden Rainbow Senior Center	Senior Center in Palm Springs area	2008–2009
21	Grace Brethren Church and Schools	Christian education and athletics	2006
22	Greater Hope—Church of God in Christ	Low-income housing	2005
23	Horseback Miracles	Equine therapy for hurting kids	2013
24	Inner-City Child Development Foundation	Day care for low-income children	2005
25	Kids to Kids	Restoration house, for teenage girls	2004–2005
26	Kiwanis Club Santa Susana	Pediatric Trauma Prevention	2003–2006

27	Kiwanis International Foundation	Regional Pediatric Trauma Prevention	2005
28	Mossy Foot Foundation	Ethiopia—foot disease care and help	2005–2006
29	New West Symphony	Music education and performance	2006–2008
30	Ojai Christian Academy	Christian school expansion	2005
31	Ojai Church of the Living Christ	Community development on church land	2005
32	Omega Martial Arts and Karate Team USA	Using martial arts—positive influence for Christ	2012
33	Oxnard Downtown Center for Arts	Arts for underserved Hispanic kids	2005–2006
34	Pallets Caribbean Inc.	Barbados new business development	2004
35	People's Self-Help Housing Corporation	Community development on church land	2005–2006
36	Promotores Foundation	Health outreach to Hispanics	2003–2004
37	Restoring Hope Foundation	Chocolate Festival, for orphan kids	2005
38	Samaritan Center	Homeless assistance, day programs	2005
39	Simi Valley Community Care Center	Education and community services—Hispanics	2005–2006
40	Simi Valley Hospital	Cancer prevention, education, screening	1996–2001
41	Tails 'n Twine	Horse Ranch nonprofit application	2008
42	The Lee Fitzgerald Show	Tell a story—cable TV program	2004–2005
43	Total Man International Network Inc.	Low-income housing and education	2004–2005
44	Town of Larkspur, Colorado	Park enhancement project help	2008–2011

45	True Spirit Community Church	Community development on church land	2005
46	United Parents	Severely emotionally disturbed kids/families	2005–2006
47	Valley Video Foundation	Tell a story—video and cable TV	2005–2006
48	Ven Co Partnership for Safe Families	Family violence prevention scholarships	2003–2006
49	Ventura College Foundation	Fundraising and board work	2005
50	Ventura County Community Foundation	Teach classes, grants and research	2005–2006
51	Ventura County Medical Resource Foundation	Health Outreach to Hispanics	2002–2003
52	Voices for Justice Network	Sexual Exploitation Survivor Network	2005–2007
53	We Are All One Foundation	Fundraisers to help orphan kids	2005

Here are some sample stories from this list.

Barbara Johnson Foundation. The founder of this organization had died, so her son was running the foundation. A Christian friend from Northern California introduced us, and I made several trips to their headquarters in Palm Springs to learn more about this amazing woman who was one of the founders of Women of Faith (WOF). Once she discovered her son David was gay and she decided to continue to love him unconditionally, the WOF group decided to drop her from their speaker list. She literally gave away her books at these large events and accepted freewill donations for her work. It all went away, and she spent her last ten years of life fighting brain cancer, always with the joy of the Lord. I got to work with David and learn more about the lesbian, gay, bisexual, transgender (LGBT) part of society. It was eye-opening. As the Bible says, hate the sin but love the sinner. These guys were great fun to work with! So when I look at the book on my shelf, *Stick a Geranium in Your Hat and be Happy!* I always smile from all the splashes of joy she left behind. It was a joy to help those guys.

Food Share Ventura County. Through my grant-writing class, I met the founder of this huge food bank, Jewel. She matched her name! The number one industry in Ventura County is agriculture, yet many of the Hispanic families are poor and undernourished— they don't get to eat the very food they pick. She told me that she and her husband started collecting food for these forgotten poor in their garage. Her entire work was based on a verse from the book of Leviticus 23:22, "When you reap the harvest of your land, do not reap to the very edges of your field or gather the gleanings of your harvest. Leave them for the poor and for the foreigners residing among you. I am the LORD your God." Wow. I learned about the concept of gleaning. When I studied the book of Ruth, it reminded me of Jewel, since Ruth was gleaning the fields of Boaz, who ended up being her kinsman redeemer. I love both Jewel and Ruth. God is good.

Voices for Justice Network. I met this organization founder while attending a grant information session for some funds in Ventura for women. I saw this quiet woman taking notes and introduced myself. She said her name was Juliette. She had written a book called *Memoirs of a Sex Industry Survivor* under her pen name of Anne Bissell. She called her work a fusion-fiction novel about her own life, one where her own dad pimped her out as a teenager to make money from her body. As she states in her cover flap, "For Juliet, the 'life' or the world of prostitution started off as a game. Then the 'game' took over. First she became addicted to the fast, constant, easy money, then to turning tricks into 'sugar daddies.' As Juliet begins to heal from her life as a prostituted teen, she meets other sex industry survivors. Their similarities change her perspective on the sex industry for good. For most sex industry survivors, prostitution is a re-enactment of childhood sexual exploitation."

Juliet founded Sex Industry Survivors Anonymous, with a mission to deglamorize the global, billion-dollar sex industry, which she believes in not a victimless crime. She studied women in the sex industry over two decades and tells some amazing stories in her book.

Wow. Now this was a part of the world I had never known about. She got me to throw away my DVD copy of *Pretty Woman*, which gave such a misleading image of the world of prostitution. Very seldom, there is a prince charming who comes to the rescue. Gratefully, Juliet had a son, and her second husband provided a safe, healthy environment for her own recovery. Then I saw the movie *Taken*, about a retired special-op dad whose daughter was taken (kidnapped) by those in the sex industry and was about to be sold to a rich sheik. This stuff really happens. She told me that this industry makes more money than the drug trade in the USA, with Houston as one of the core cities for this crime. When the Democrat convention came to Denver in 2008, she contacted me and asked me to pray since huge numbers of young girls were being shipped into the city to satisfy the politicians coming to town. How disgusting. So not only did I help do some writing for her, but I also became her friend and a prayer warrior for her cause. Only God could set up such a connection. He was opening my eyes to the real world of darkness that surrounds us. I think I need to write a note to Juliet and make sure she is okay.

When we moved to Colorado in the summer of 2006, I thought I had left my clients back in California, but God was so good—many asked me to come back and continue to work for them, and new clients also appeared. So I got to make many trips for business pleasure to/from Colorado to California for this continued work. I was not always paid for my work, but I do believe I was always able to bless those that I worked with. When the market crashed at the end of 2008, most of this work disappeared, as many sources of funds dried up. Private foundations get their funds from successful entrepreneurs who lost a lot in the stock market. I did some grant-writing work in Colorado and learned who the big foundations were. I also helped several folks start their own 501-c-3 nonprofits. Even now, I offer those skills to the Christians around me who have a need. God was so good to me—how could I not remember "we are blessed to bless others"? So much manna.

Douglas County School District

When my eldest son was in his senior year (2011–2012), I decided I needed to go back to work and find a job that offered benefits since health-care insurance costs were skyrocketing. As God would have it, I was part of a Moms in Prayer group that met once a week to pray for our kids at the school that my son attended. One of my prayer partners, Deb, had a husband with end-stage cancer, and they were getting ready to put their home on the market and move back to Seattle. He was returning to a previous employer who took him back and kept his health insurance active. We Moms in Prayer sisters went to Deb's home to help clean/paint and make it show-ready, and I met Deb's boss, Donna. She was the team leader for all the audiology services offered in the school district. She said Deb was taking a year's leave of absence, and maybe I should come and work for her during that year. So I applied and got the job. It was quite the learning curve for me, but it was also a miracle that the primary women with whom I worked were all Christians! Yes, in a secular school district setting. Not only that, but the church where my current Moms in Prayer group met was where Donna attended. As part of my hiring agreement, I had to ask for leap year day off since I was leading a prayer siege against suicide for our high schools. Donna was so excited. God is so good.

As God would have it, Deb's husband died within four months of her leave, and she tried to come back but found her heart was not in it. In the meantime, another Christian college (Barb) had her cancer return, and she had to take time off for breast surgery. So I stayed to help her. Another Christian colleague (Diane) saw the return of her cancer. By the spring of 2014, Donna retired, and within less than a year, she died of aggressive brain cancer. All these ladies would lose their battle to cancer, and I attended all their funerals. Because of my time working with cancer survivors as well as families who lost loved ones to cancer, I could be present to each of these women during their final months. Yes, I worked on that vision-hearing screening team for four years, but I truly believe my greatest contribution was just being there for these women. I got to be His ambassador in so many ways to so many people. Manna. God's plan.

As God would have it, Donna lived just a block away from our home, so when she got diagnosed, I became the "messenger" between the school district colleagues she knew and her family. During my first year on the job, Donna invited our family to join her family for Thanksgiving, which we did. We reciprocated the following year. At both gatherings, I took one photo of her and her husband and two kids and then of her and her daughter. She loved those pictures so much she asked for the negative. During that last year of her life, her family had those two photos put onto large canvas prints that were on display at the funeral and now hang proudly in their home. I also made sure she was showered with cards for her last birthday in October 2014, and her sweet husband said, "I am sure I know the mouse who spread the word. Both were such a blessing to me. I came to understand the book of Esther better—"for such a time as this."

After Donna retired, the audiology team was not the same. I also desired a better-paying job so I could get a higher average salary for at least three years before I retired. So I got a job as the assistant to our district library media center director (Linda). I knew very little about libraries but had learned a lot about the school district and all the schools we needed to serve. In fact, many of our hearing screenings were held in school libraries, so I knew many of my new colleagues. Linda was raised in a large Catholic Midwestern family, so I think it helped me to understand her personality. It also gave me a "mirror" in which to see that I was once that driven, workaholic person who I now helped, but my role and personality had softened. When budget cuts led to the elimination of my job, Linda was so gracious to give me a great recommendation for my next job.

So last but not the least, I went to work at the high school that we moms had been praying for, Douglas County High School. I guess God brought me full circle. I became the administrative person for the International Baccalaureate Program (see previous chapter). I did this work for two years, until I reached age sixty-six, and could retire and draw Social Security and Medicare. I learned a lot about high school culture for both the staff as well as the students. I sadly realized the school needed far more prayer than when we had prayed for it when James attended the school!

The IB students were very respectful of me, and I enjoyed those relationships very much. On average, the other students seemed to have less and less respect for authority. I saw a really good teacher suddenly let go because he "flicked an earbud" out of the ear of a student who would not remove it when asked. The parents went to human resources, and they took the side of the family. I originally planned to retire in March of 2020 but decided to stay until June for various reasons. This was the exact time the COVID-19 shutdown started. God protected me once again. I got my full pay until the end of June for working only part-time from home. I also did not have to deal with the messy school startup for 2020–2021, which was some in-person and some remote learning. The timing could not have been more perfect. So much learned. So God. So much manna.

John (A Brother, a Saint, Beloved Name)

My mother had seven children in twelve years starting in December 1952 until June 1964. My older brother (Paul) was born in December 1952, and I came along in January 1954, only thirteen months later, the only one of the seven who was premature. Ten years later, my mom had her youngest child, John. Such a difference between being the eldest girl versus the youngest son.

So what does the name John mean? According to www.baby-names.com, the name John means "God is gracious" and is of Hebrew origin. God certainly has been gracious to my little brother, and he rose to be a vice president of a concrete company as a civil engineer. As such, he earned a very good salary and even larger annual bonus. In the world's view, he was the most successful of all us kids. The problem is that when the 2008 recession hit, he lost that bonus. He lost his home. His marriage ended. He was a victim of the recession, just like my sister Sue's husband, who lost his job. The year 2009 forward would be a tough time for John.

Since my dad died while John was still in college, sadly, the day my dad died, he was walking out the front door to go play a round of golf (we lived on a nine-hole course), and he dropped dead of a heart attack. John was the one to find him. His wife, Cris, told me that he was so shaken by this event that he had to take six months off from his college studies. He and Cris got married, and they both worked full-time during this time. It took him over six years to get his structural engineering degree, but he did it. Good for him!

I have had a hot-cold relationship with my youngest brother. When I was going through a situational depression during my divorce, we had a family counseling meeting in Minnesota. I can still remember the kind support he offered—he said that is what families are for. He always had a good heart, and I think his greatest goal was to have a family of his own. During college, his girlfriend got pregnant, so they got married. That is a challenging way to start a family life, but they seemed to do okay as they settled into a home and job in the Twin Cities.

They went on to have three girls and finally a son. Since he was prospering at his job, he spoiled his children. When I flew home for family visits, I often stayed at John's home before making the trip up north. He was very generous in giving me a place to stay. When alcohol became a bigger factor in his life (like our dad), I wrote to John and said I hoped he got help, so I would not have to come home for the funeral of one of my nieces or nephews. He was not happy with me, so there was a time of separation between us.

When his kids grew up and started having children of their own, he became Grandpa John. This war's a role he really loved. To this day, I think he would do anything for his kids and grandkids. But having it all can have a great negative impact on one's life. I learned that firsthand when I reached the pinnacle of my own career just to lose the job and fall into major depression. I have heard it said that those who reach the highest highs hit the lowest lows.

I am reminded of the wisest man who ever lived, King Solomon. When his dad (King David) died and the Lord asked him what he wanted, he asked for wisdom and discernment to lead his people. God was so pleased that he also gave him great riches. Leaders from all over the world would come to visit King Solomon to meet this amazing king in person. Yet he would go on to have over seven hundred wives and three hundred concubines, who brought idols into the king's palace, and he stopped worshiping just one God. By the time of his death, he wrote, "All is vanity under the sun." He never had contentment no matter how much he acquired. King Solomon concluded that you need to fear God and keep His commands as the only hope for a good life. I don't think my brother John ever learned the secret of contentment in his life. I hope he will someday.

The apostle Paul would also write about the secret to contentment in life. He wrote in his letter to the church of Philippians 4:11–13, "I am not saying this because I am in need, for I have learned to be content whatever the circumstances. I know what it is to be in need, and I know what it is to have plenty. I have learned the secret of being content in any and every situation, whether well fed or hungry, whether living in plenty or in want. I can do all this through him who gives me strength." I can do all things through God. This is the key.

Ironically, the youngest apostle was John. He was just a teenager when he followed Jesus all the way to the cross. His mother (another Mary) had two sons who followed Jesus (James and John), and she wanted the Lord to let them sit at His right hand when He reigned in glory. Jesus responded that it was not His place to do this—only God could make this choice—and the price of following Him would be great. I have a theory that when all the other disciples fled during the crucifixion of their Lord, John stayed with Jesus to the cross since his mom was there and probably said, "You are coming with me." He was called the disciple Jesus loved. From the cross, Jesus asked him to take care of his own mother (Mary), which he did. He was the only apostle not to die as a martyr. He was exiled to the island of Patmos for his faith where he was given the revelation by the Lord of the end of the story of the world. John also wrote one book of the Bible, and his book is about Jesus as all man and all God—a god of love. So John is a pretty special saint from which to be named.

John raised his children in the Catholic Church, but this meant in making sure that they were all baptized and received first Holy

Communion and Confirmation. Like most young adults, his kids all fell away from the church. When my sister Sue had to send my mom back to Minnesota to a good memory care unit, it was John and his daughter Allison that found a good place for her to live—so sweet. He would pick her up on Sundays and take her to Mass. I was so pleased. He became the youngest one to look after our mom. (Just like the apostle John.)

But as her condition deteriorated, so did his commitment to this Sunday ritual. When she died, he came and left her final room in hospice before the rest of us siblings came, but he had to leave before the rest of us arrived. I am sure it was not easy to see the shell of a woman we called our mom (soft heart). We got to gather in her room. To share songs and love. To go out to lunch and get the word she has passed together. He missed this experience. We had to call and give him the news. He missed sweetness.

Dear John, I pray for you. At Mom's funeral two months later, he was intoxicated and peeled out in his car as he came to and from the cemetery. Our son James said, "What is wrong with Uncle John?" We could only reply, "Who knows? We just need to pray for him." I love you, dear brother John, but I do pray that you will be able to get your life back on track and become that little brother who cared so much for me when I was in a hurting place.

John lost his job in April 2019. The original company owner (his friend) had retired, and the new owner did many cuts. He was let go. He has had a hard year since then, but I think he has now hit his low and is on his way to recovery. We had a sixtieth birthday party for our brother Michael at a family cabin in June 2020; he was sober but shaking and weak. My heart broke for him. This last year had been harder for him than I could ever imagine. He should have called me; after all, I am the family expert at lost jobs!

Ironically, his ex-wife (Cris) is back at his side, helping him since her ten-year boyfriend died. God works in such mysterious ways. She recently called and said John did a reading at the wedding of her niece and he did a very nice job. What a picture of hope! She says his strength is getting better day by day. I continue to pray for all his family. God is not finished with him yet. Thank you, Cris, for your amazing support in times of need in our family—that includes many moves for our mom. Despite your own challenges, you have risen to the occasion for our family at several times, and we appreciate you.

My Bible verse prayer for you: "Let all bitterness and wrath and anger and clamor and slander be put away from you, along with all malice. Be kind to one another, tenderhearted, forgiving one another, as God in Christ forgave you" (Eph. 4:31–32). Go forward. Never look back. Forgive. Be the best father and grandfather ever!

Joni Eareckson Tada (Disability Ministry)

Now that I have covered John, I will move on to an amazing lady who was supposed to be born a boy, to be named after her father, John. Her name is Joni (pronounced John-ee), and I had the pleasure of meeting her in May 1992 at a Mother's Day luncheon at our church. She was the guest speaker and quite famous, but I had never heard of her, read her book, seen her life-story movie, or knew her amazing story, so it was quite an adventure to make such a new friend. After hearing her story, I stopped and asked if I could donate all the durable medical equipment I had used during my knee therapy. This led to a bigger connection than just equipment donation.

So who is Joni Eareckson Tada? She is an evangelical Christian author, radio host, and founder of Joni and Friends, an organization "accelerating Christian ministry in the disability community" (www.joniandfriends.org). Joni and Friends Radio provides hope and encouragement through Joni Eareckson Tada's *Joni and Friends* and *Diamonds in the Dust* radio programs. An athletic teenager, Joni broke her neck in a diving accident when she was seventeen. Her spinal cord was severed, and she became paralyzed from the shoulders down. Despite this enormous challenge, she learned to write/paint with her mouth. She has created many paintings and written many books and leads an international disability ministry located in Agoura Hills, California. This was just south of the church where we met.

At the time we met, Joni was getting ready to launch a church-based disability awareness ministry and asked if I would lead such an effort in our church. Of course. I met with her staff and learned more about why the disabled rarely get to attend church. If you are a parent to a disabled child, getting ready to go anywhere is a chore. Getting dressed, ready, with all equipment on board, and getting to/from in a handicapped-accessed vehicle can be quite the challenge. Sadly, if you do make it to a local church, most church bodies do not know how to incorporate such individuals into their fellowship. It's not like school, where you have trained staff to act as educational assistants to help with the person's needs. Yes, it is the law to provide handicapped access to buildings, but it pretty much ends there. Once you get into the facility, you need a welcoming person who can get you started. Just like schools, these folks want to be "fully included" into whatever programs you may offer, not separated into a special education Sunday school. For those who can't see or hear or speak well, this can be a real challenge.

So Joni and Friends helps churches get started, especially large churches that have the staff and facilities that may accommodate needs the best. Our church had such a facility and staff, so it was a good match. I started with the idea to allow the disabled to come to our dress rehearsal for the Christmas music program at our church—quite the production, for free! Since I was already volunteering time at our two local homes for those with cerebral palsy, I started with an invitation to these folks. They were thrilled. I also asked around at our church for anyone with a disability, including hearing, and made accommodations to get an interpreter for the hearing impaired at the program. It was a big success!

In the fall of 1993, I arranged to have a "disability awareness Sunday" at our church, including an honorary luncheon for Joni. I had just met Bill Kramer, who had polio as a child, and I invited him to come to the event, so he agreed. As God would have it, he and Joni had something in common. They were both treated at Rancho Los Amigos in Los Angeles. Bill in 1956 for his polio, and Joni in 1967 for her broken neck. They even had the same surgeon! Is God amazing or what? It was such a thrill to have them meet each other.

I started a support group for parents with disabled children, and Bill would help facilitate this group. Bill would tell his story and quote Psalm 139, "You are perfectly and wonderfully made," to these moms, who were so touched. We blended it with an outreach for single moms and had some special events on Sunday nights for the kids to "play" and the parents to rest. We got a lot of the Promise Keepers guys to help—it was a blast! By the time we adopted our boys from foster care, we became interested in the family retreat program. We wanted to act as volunteer staff, but since our boys both had special needs, we were invited as a family to participate. The camp we attended was in the Santa Cruz area, and we never felt so pampered. Each boy was assigned a one-on-one helper for the week, so we got to be indulged as parents in respite, including a special dinner. Now that we are retired, we want to go back as adult volunteers for these camps.

We also learned about their program called Wheels for the World. Used wheelchairs are donated to Joni and Friends. They are sent to prisons to be refurbished. FedEx funded the shipment all over the world. Volunteers raised their own support to be staff on these trips. During my grant-writing years, I was introduced to a group of guys in Orange County who were building a youth camp in Big Bear Lake, California. I began writing grants for them and introduced them to Joni and Friends, with a suggestion to build a "handicapped-accessible camp" since none existed in California. (Most are at least seventy years old before ADA existed.) I brought one board member to the International Disability Center and introduced him. He was so excited that he joined a Wheels team and came to love the program. The good news is that the camp redirected its vision to build a handicapped-accessible facility and got the endorsement of Joni and Friends. How exciting is that? The Eagle Ridge Camp and Conference Center is now a dream in process, and I hope when it is completely finished, it will be the perfect place for those with disabilities (including the elderly) to go. Such a God thing.

We have several of Joni's paintings in our home and quite a few of her books. When making wedding plans, we hoped she could come and sing at our wedding, but the date did not match her schedule. She did, however, give us a signed copy of her devotional *Diamonds in the Dust*, and we took it on our honeymoon. It is lovingly signed with gratitude by Joni for my heart. Sweet. I try to go to her center when I am in California. One year I received a blanket from the Cystic Fibrosis Foundation for a donation I had made. Since that is a hard word to pronounce, they say "sixty-five roses," and that is what is on the blanket. I gave mine to Joni. She had never heard that story, so I was thrilled.

When this book gets published, I plan to donate most of my net proceeds to Christian charities, and Joni and Friends is at the top of my list. If you don't know about this amazing woman and her ministry, be sure to go to her website and check it out. You will be glad you did!

Joseph (Son of Jacob, a Good Man)

Of all the people I have studied from the Bible, my favorite is Joseph, the son of Jacob, found in the book of Genesis. Did you know that his story comprises the last third of this book? Did you also know that years after he died, his bones were carried by Moses as they spent forty years going to the promised land? He was also considered a Jesus-like person in the Bible, one who came before the Lord but was like Him in character. As I stated earlier, he was also the favorite son to his father, so he became despised by his siblings (jealousy). How could I not relate to this man? Despite his early naive nature, he grew to be an amazing leader.

So what does the name Joseph mean? According to www.familyeducation.com, Joseph is derived from the Latin form of Greek Joseph, from the Hebrew name Yosef, meaning "He will add," from the root Yasaf. In the Old Testament Bible, Joseph was the eleventh son of Jacob, the traditional ancestor of the people of Israel. When Jacob blessed his sons, he gave a double portion to Joseph's two sons, Ephraim and Manasseh. Even near his death, I believe Jacob showed favoritism to his son Joseph, since he loved him the most and could see that his heart was the purest of all his sons.

According to Genesis 50:20 (NIV), Joseph said to his brothers after his father's death, "You intended to harm me, but God intended it for good to accomplish what is now being done, the saving of many lives." He held no grudges toward his siblings. He had a huge forgiving heart and understood all that had happened to him was for a bigger purpose.

Another Joseph in the Bible was the husband to Mary, who was the mother to Jesus. He was such a good man. When he found out his wife was with child, he decided he would divorce her quietly, to be kind. But an angel of the Lord appeared to him and explained that the child was born of the Holy Spirit and was the son of God and should be named Jesus, so Joseph kept his engagement to Mary and they became husband and wife. He had to travel to his home area of Bethlehem since a census was being taken, and that was when the child came into the world in a stable. We all know the Christmas story. When Herod decided to kill all the young Jewish babies two years and under, once again, an angel of the Lord told him to flee to Egypt to save his son's life, so he did. He eventually returned to Nazareth and raised his family there. One pastor told us they went on to have seven children, five boys and two girls. We hear very little about this carpenter elsewhere in the Bible, but I believe it was a great human role model for Jesus.

Guys with the name Joseph are often called Joe. Did you know that the people of the Philippines were so grateful that America came to their rescue in World War II that they called all American soldiers GI Joe? Yes, the same name as that childhood toy character. They sometimes just say "Hi, Joe" as a term of endearment. When I was in junior high, I had a crush on a fellow student named Joe. In that school, classes were divided into 71, 72, 73, 74, by grade point average, with the smartest kids in the group 1. This was the same in eighth and ninth grade. We were always in the first group, so we had all our classes together. He was a conservative Republican, but I was the daughter of a member of the Democratic Farmer Labor (DFL) party. We used to say the wealthy families were Republicans and all the ordinary families were Democrats. In 1968, when Nixon ran against Hubert Humphrey (Minnesota favorite son), Humphrey won by a landslide in our mock election. By the time Reagan was elected, my dad became a Reagan Republican. So did I. So I guess Joe is also a person of wisdom.

Our school superintendent was also named Joe. My sister Sue married his son Jeff, so this Joe became an extended member of our family. He lived to be nearly one hundred years old and got to die in the house where he raised his three sons. Everyone in our county knew Joe. He was a good man. He also had a keen sense of humor. When his wife died and my dad died, he would sometimes take my mom out for a meal. On one such occasion, when I was home visiting family in Minnesota, the three of us went to dinner together and Joe picked up the bill. He gave the waitress a card, and she came back to our table and said, "Sir, we don't accept Medicare cards for payment." He responded, "My card is not any good?" and he gave her a Visa. As she walked away, he said, "I hope it works. I found it in the parking lot." Ha! After my divorce, he bet me that I would soon find a nice man to marry. I took his bet, and it was eleven years later before I remarried. Our bet was a bottle of Dom Perignon champagne. He kept his word. It was the best I ever had! So Joe appears to be one of high integrity.

My dad's youngest brother was named Stanley Joe. I suspect that he was given this middle name since it was such a highly regarded saint in the Catholic Church. He has always been my favorite uncle. My brother Paul also had a son and named him Joe. Despite challenging teenage years, he joined the Navy and became a pilot and now has a good job and family as he flies for Southwest Airlines. I have a brother named Michael Joseph, and he has always been a special part of our family. So I think my parents knew what they were doing when they gave him that name. He and his wife both have mental retardation, but they have been happily married for over thirty-five years and live an independent life (see more later). So thank you to all the Josephs that have been in my life. This is a name held dear by our family.

Josiah (Our Son and a Young King)

When Bill and I became foster parents, we were amazed that the birth mothers of both our sons gave their sons such biblical names. James was an apostle and a brother to Jesus. Josiah became king at age eight—the youngest ever—and turned out to be a man after God's own heart. So what does the name Josiah mean? According to www.sheknows.com, the name Josiah is a biblical names baby name. In biblical names, the meaning of the name Josiah is "the Lord burns; the fire of the Lord." The name Josiah is a Hebrew baby name. The meaning of the name Josiah is "Jehovah has healed." Biblical Josiah became king of Judah at eight after his father was assassinated. He ruled thirty-one years. For our dear son Josiah, I write part of your story here as one with a good ending, pain overcome, to help others also heal.

God has healed. I like that meaning. Our Josiah's birth mom was a drug addict, so he was born as a drug baby, one whose brain had been affected in vitro. He came into our home at age four after being in one other foster home. He immediately fell in love with our dogs! During elementary school, he was in "regular" education (not special education), but he had a tendency to run away when faced with any challenges. If he got upset, he would run down the street but eventually return and hide in our bushes until we approached him. He needed time to blow off steam. At one point when he was in Larkspur Elementary School, when he got upset, he would go and hide in a janitor's closet. Then one day, he ran off to the large Renaissance Festival property just across the street. Needless to say, he had everyone out looking for him until he was found. I bet he liked that attention. But it made everyone else worried sick. Manna needed.

I can only imagine what it must have been like to be a toddler with a mom who was turning tricks or stealing things in order to feed her drug habit. We were told by the social workers that his mom had become a lesbian and had a female partner at the time of her most recent arrest. She was so afraid this partner would steal her son and take him away from her that she called Child Protective Services to ask that he be put in foster care for protection. Years later, when she had a short time out of jail, we can only hope that she was at peace knowing he had been adopted into a good home. We were told this about the mom to James, that she was glad her son would not spend his life going from one foster home to another as she had done. God is good. He looks over widows and orphans. Just like our sons.

Josiah had also learned another bad habit as a toddler, to be devious and deceitful. Again, I am sure this was what he observed all the time. After our visit to Washington, DC, in the summer of 2002, we were unpacking and came across a small item that Josiah had stolen from the Smithsonian Institute. We asked him why he had done such a thing, and he had no answer. I can remember how Bill took him to see our local police chief (a friend of ours) and to go inside a jail cell and see where he could end up someday. Tough love. I wonder if that ever sunk in. During his time at Larkspur Elementary, his class was getting ready for the fall festival on the grounds of the Renaissance Festival, and he and a friend stole some cheap jewelry from one of the buildings on-site. When they were caught, they had to make amends at the school by doing extra chores on campus. Again, what was he thinking? Was his brain even working right? Probably not.

When Josiah got to high school, he became more withdrawn and disengaged from other students and his studies. Again, we heard this was common for foster kids. We took him to several counselors, and he was usually very quiet and would not participate in sharing what was going on inside of him. He ended up on an individual education plan (IEP) where he was supposed to get extra help during the school day, but this did not seem to help. I reached out to one of the district psychologists to ask about his behavior and what might be going on. He told me that babies with drugs in vitro often have damage to their brain frontal cortex. This is the area of organization and executive function, and he was probably lacking the neurons to put things together. He suggested we get a brain scan to verify this, but the insurance plan would not cover it. Yet I thought this was helpful information. It gave us another piece to the puzzle.

When Josiah went through equine therapy, the guy who ran the ranch said he had never seen a young man with so little get up and go. He seemed to lack all initiative. When Josiah was hired by a local grocery store, he would do fine when the store was busy, but when it got quiet, rather than asking what he could do, he would wander over to Starbucks and get a coffee and take a long break. Within thirty days, he was let go. When he called us to say he had lost his job and we needed to come and get him, he also called his girlfriend at that time to come and console him. She was there when we arrived and was shocked that Bill gently told Josiah this was only his first job; there would be others. She said if it had been her dad, he would have read her the riot act. She came to love our family for the love and support we showed to her and everyone who came into our home. Since I had been let go from several jobs, I knew how he was feeling. Yet his termination was for a completely different reason. It still hurts.

During one summer we attended a Joni and Friends family retreat, he was given a buddy for the week. This man was with Josiah most of the time, but Josiah still managed to climb a high tree and started throwing rocks at the kids below. What? The buddy admitted he had never seen such behavior, and we were also perplexed. What would drive a young man surrounded in kindness and love to want to hurt anyone else? They say when you are hurt as a young child, you may strike out at others, as a way to get even. Perhaps his inner being was off-balance. He certainly did not seem to have a good moral compass. We talked to him and had him go to even more counselors and continually covered it in prayer—our defense against getting angry.

When he was a young teen, he helped with Sunday school and then helped at vacation Bible school (VBS). As I explained under our church experience, he was accused of touching a young lady inappropriately, and we were asked to leave the church and get an attorney. So we did. This attorney was an expert in sex crime cases as a defense attorney. He had seen many males nearly lose everything because of one such accusation, whether there were any witnesses or evidence to support the allegation. Given Josiah's background as a foster child, he told us it would be hard to win any case in a trial. We should just allow Josiah to accept a plea and do a diversion program, see a court-appointed counselor, and pay restitution. We did all this and, many years later, were able to get his juvenile record expunged of the matter. He passed two lie detector tests, and we believed he had not done anything wrong. This was confirmed when we found the ex-husband of the mother in the case. He asked, "Who is she accusing of what now?" Every time he gave his kids a bath, she would call Child Protective Services and report him. This man eventually got a divorce, with the stipulation she would stop filing restraining orders against him. His pain contributed to our healing. We prayed for those two children and their entire family.

During Josiah's junior year in high school, we finally convinced the counseling IEP group that the high school he was in was not a good fit, and we asked for them to support his application to the local alternative high school. This was a year-round school with nine months on, followed by three months off. They had a new semester starting in July of that year, and Josiah took the entry test and passed, so the principal allowed him to be admitted to the school, despite a long waiting list of other students. He later told us he did not think Josiah would make it, and they had a program where your grades were evaluated every three weeks, and if you did not maintain a C average or better, you were out. Josiah exceeded this standard and also started to improve in his behavior. By the end of the year, he was attending prom with his girlfriend and had a new full-time job at Walmart. It seemed like the curve was finally turning upward for him.

This alternative high school (Daniel C. Oakes) had a very special graduation event where every student had to give a short speech about how the experience had helped them in life, as well as thanking their parents for their support along the way. We framed that certificate, and we proudly hung it on our wall. The speech that Josiah gave during the graduation was incredible. He was poised and confident and gave a special shout-out to a teacher who was retiring with his thanks for her help. In his speech, he read a poem about being that odd kid that nobody understood. I went back and listened to that graduation event video and found the TED 2013 Shane Koyczan YouTube video. Here are some key points Josiah picked out:

- We weren't the only kids who felt this way.
- Walking a tightrope in our lives.
- If you don't like what you see in the mirror, get a different mirror.
- Never quit. Remember all the names they called you? They were wrong.
- Continue to cheer on the underdog, just like you.
- Put a cast around your broken heart.
- Sticks and stones may break my bones, but names will never hurt me. Not.
- Sometimes we are one part left alone, one part therapy, some suicide ideas.
- Don't give in to depression and loneliness.
- When you feel like an abandoned car, just go get some gas.
- Our lives may seem like embers, filled with pain, but find the beauty.

We were so proud of Josiah. And so was his girlfriend at that time—she helped him through so many low spots at his last high school. Those times where he wrote dark things from dark music he was listening to. Those days when we got the suicide watch call from the school to come and pick him up and sit with him in the ER. Gratefully, he was never admitted. He was a cutter screaming out for help, but not one with a plan to end his life. Thank You, Lord. It was so hard to reach him through his pain. But he ended well. He graduated with a GPA over 3.0. He loved his senior year in high school. I know they even have a Facebook page where DC Oakes grads keep in touch. I hope he follows friends on that page and is encouraged by success stories. One teacher, Mr. Marti, said, "You can expect great things from this young man." Manna.

Josiah reconnected with one of those lone female friends on Facebook in 2018 and asked that his birthday gift be a round-trip ticket to visit her in Wisconsin. He came back, graduated from the

Job Corps, and said he wanted to move to Wisconsin. Would that be okay? Sure, I said. Then he said something profound. He told me that he needed to get out of Colorado because drugs are too easy to get. So smart. So wise. When did he grow up so much? He has now lived in Wisconsin for over two years, and he and Jen and their other roommate, Joshua, manage to live together in relative harmony. All have a source of income, and all share in everyday life.

As I remember back to 2012 when his favorite subject was Japanese (he liked the teacher and all those Japanese card games), he asked if we could invite a Japanese foreign student into our home to live for one school year. Sure, we said. He looked at the list and picked Yo, who came into our home in the summer of 2012. He had the best English of all the group and was a fun-loving young man. He actually became a better friend to our son James, but I came to find out part of the reason. When Yo made friends at the high school and told them he lived with Josiah's family, they said it was a shame he got stuck with a loser. Really? Kids can be so cruel. So Josiah was also bullied.

That December, we made a trip to California so Yo could see the fun things to be found there, like Disneyland and Universal Studios, as well as meet members of Bill's family. We were staying with Bill's sister Karen, and Josiah and Yo had a big blowup, so we had to separate them for the rest of the trip. We had to find another home for Yo to live at the beginning of 2013, but by his graduation, we all connected again, and he has even come to visit us since then. We also hope to go visit him and his family in Japan someday. He even calls me Mom. But for Josiah, it was just one more painful, disappointing experience.

Such was the case when he broke up with his girlfriend. He lost another job. He was living with two other gals, and they all left their jobs and lost their apartment. It happened again with two other female friends. But in the end, Josiah kept going and moved to Wisconsin. A new start. I think that his frontal lobe is starting to develop for our young son, who is now in his mid-twenties. We still pray for him and believe he will have a good future. The life verse I have chosen for him comes from Jeremiah 29:11, "'I know the plans

I have for you,' declares the Lord, 'plans to prosper you and not to harm you, plans to give you hope and a future.'" Once again God gave our family manna. And hope. Keep growing, Josiah.

CHAPTER K

Katherine (Important Family Name)

Finally, I come to the name that was given to me at birth, Katherine. My mom's name was Elaine Katherine. Her mom was Lauretta Katherine. Her mom was also a Katherine. When I married Bill, I found out his mom's name was Katherine, but she went by Katie. His sister's name was Katherine Karen, but she went by Karen. So many folks with the same name! It must be pretty special. I found out by looking at my family plaque that I was named after Saint Catherine of Sienna. So what does this name mean?

Katherine (also spelled Catherine, same derivative as Kathleen) has a unique meaning. According to www.chrisitanmeaningofnames. com, there are not actually any characters in the Bible named Katherine. However, the name has a rich Christian historical heritage and likely originated with the Greek word *kantharos*, which was translated as "pure" or "clean" in the New Testament. As for Saint Catherine of Sienna, she was a lay member of the Dominican Order, was a mystic, activist, and author who had a great influence on Italian literature and the Catholic Church. Canonized in 1461, she is also a doctor of the church (Wikipedia).

According to www.churchpop.com, here are some interesting things to know about this saint:

1. She had a twin: Though it's not clear whether they were identical or not, Saint Catherine had a twin sister, Giovanna.

They were born prematurely when her mother was forty years old.

2. Unfortunately, Giovanna died in infancy. Her mother had another child two years later and named that child Giovanna as well. (Hey, I was premature too!)

3. She had twenty-four siblings. That's right, she was one of twenty-five children. And yes, they were all from the same parents. Granted, only about half of them made it to adulthood (due to a high infant mortality rate), but still, that's quite the family.

4. She had the nickname Euphrosyne. She was so joyful as a child that her family called her Euphrosyne, Greek for *joy*.

5. She had a mystical vision of Jesus as a young child. An early biography written by her confessor claimed that when she was five or six year old, she was walking home and suddenly had a vision of Jesus enthroned in heaven surrounded by the apostles Peter, Paul, and John.

6. She had a mystical vision of Saint Dominic. The two most culturally accepted paths for a woman in her time and place were marrying or becoming a cloistered nun. Saint Catherine resisted both options. Apparently, Saint Dominic himself appeared to her in a vision, which convinced her to be a Dominican tertiary, something that at that time was normally reserved for widows. She also got special permission to wear a habit.

7. She had another vision of Jesus when she was twenty-one. Initially, she lived her vocation as a Dominican tertiary in silent isolation in her family's home. Then, when she was twenty-one years old, she experienced a vision of Jesus in which he wed her as His bride and even gave her a ring. She was then told by Christ to leave her solitude and serve the poor, which she did.

8. She experienced stigmata. First reported to have been experienced by Saint Francis of Assisi a little more than a hundred years earlier, Saint Catherine received a version of the stigmata in 1375 that, according to the biography written

by her confessor, was only visible to herself per her request of God.

9. She was very politically active, writing letters to rulers and clergy. In her late twenties, she started dictating letters with scribes to various rulers and clergy, begging for peace between states and for the papacy to return to Rome from Avignon, France. She was so respected she was sent on diplomatic peace missions by various governments. (I love writing letters to those in charge! How fun to be a diplomat!)

10. She survived an assassination attempt. In early 1378, she was sent by Pope Gregory XI to Florence, Italy, to seek peace between Florence and Rome. Soon after, however, while she was with Pope Gregory XI, violence broke out. On June 18, in the midst of violence, someone tried to assassinate her, though she survived.

11. She was attacked by demons on her deathbed. Here's what one eyewitness reported: She began altogether to change and to make various signs with her head and her arms, as if to show that she was suffering from grave assaults of demons, and remained in this calamitous state for an hour and a half, half of which time having been passed in silence. (Dear me!)

12. She's a copatron of Rome, of Italy, and of Europe. Wow! Even if you don't believe in all that Catholic saints stuff, this is rather interesting. I wonder how much I am like this most interesting saint. We laughed when Prince William married Catherine (called Kate). We would sign our correspondence to British friends as "The other William and Katherine." Ha! We might even have some royal blood.

Speaking of royal blood, we all know that King Henry VIII had many wives, but did you know his first marriage, which lasted over twenty-five years, was to a woman named Catherine? According to www.biography.com, Catherine of Aragon was King Henry VIII's first wife. Her refusal to agree to an annulment of their marriage led to the creation of the Church of England. Catherine of Aragon was the daughter of Spanish monarchs King Ferdinand II and Queen Isabella. She married Henry VIII but did not give birth to a male heir. Catherine refused to annul her marriage so that Henry could marry again, which led to the separation of the Church of England from the Catholic Church. Catherine died in England in 1536. Her only surviving child, Mary Tudor, became queen in 1553. It is said that Henry loved Catherine very much, but her inability to produce a male heir was a deal breaker for him. Too bad. Isn't history interesting? Ironically, Henry would go on to have three wives named Catherine.

Since his first wife had been married to his older brother who died, he had to get special permission from the church to marry Catherine. Now he tried to reverse that church decision, and he was able to find a church leader to do this. He then married Anne Boleyn. They had an affair while his first marriage was ending. Anne gave birth to a girl named Elizabeth. (Yes, the first Queen Elizabeth.) Henry was so disappointed. Anne got pregnant again and had a miscarriage—it was a boy. She had come from France as a Protestant and was starting to circulate Bibles in English around the land. Henry accused her of treason, and off with her head! Ironically, my middle name is Ann. When I got to visit an old church in York, England, that allowed brass rubbings, I did one of Anne Boleyn. It still hangs on my wall. So Catherine and Anne both turn out to have very royal connections. Catherine was a strict Catholic. Anne was a Protestant. Such similarities to my own family. History is so much fun. God is so good.

As I mentioned, there were another Katherines in Bill's family. My mother-in-law was named Katie. Her maiden name was Schmidt. My mom's maiden name was Schmid. When we went to get our marriage license, which created quite a stir until we explained things—ha! Bill's sister is named Katherine Karen—she goes by Karen. Her husband and Katie's husband died within a year of each other (1990 and 1991), so I never knew them as married ladies nor did I meet those men. Bill told me that this brought Karen and Katie together. By the time I met them, they did many things together including our first outing together going to the Rose Bowl—for UCLA football and a tailgate party. Such fun. I also got to attend my one and only Rose Parade and Rose Bowl game in 1994 when UCLA was defeated by the Wisconsin Badgers. Good fun! Those were fond memories. When Bill and I got married, we had Karen's only daughter, Mariah, as one of our bridesmaids. Lots of bright red satin dresses that day! Everyone looked beautiful.

I know they were all happy that Bill had finally found someone to marry—even though I was a USC graduate and cheered for the Trojans when they played the Bruins. Go, Pete Carroll!

When we got married, some friends gave us each a name plaque. Here is Kathy:

An Excellent Style; Professional in dealing with people.
Persuasive, she loves to debate; Enjoys the simple things in life.
Takes responsibility for her actions; Diplomatic and easy to talk to.
Holds herself in high regard; Demands the best of herself.
Seeks the true meaning of life. Amen!

Since this book is all about my life, enough said about this Katherine. On to chapter L!

CHAPTER L

Larkspur (Colorado Home and Flower)

When we visited Colorado during spring break 2006, we stayed with some friends who had moved from Simi Valley to Castle Rock to plant a church. Our friend introduced us to his realtor, so we explored property in the area. We did not want to live in the California style of wall-to-wall housing and asked her to show us some more rural properties. She suggested we look in the area just south of Castle Rock called Larkspur, so we did. We loved the area! We found one home that was a ranch with a walk-out basement on one acre of land, so we went back to California to see if we could sell our home. That required us to take a bridge loan while we listed our home, in effect having two mortgages! I believe an angel of the Lord woke me up one night and said this was not what we should do, so we canceled our contract on that home. Our California home would fall out of escrow several times, so we are glad we waited. We got a better property later.

So why was this little town and rural area of two hundred square miles named Larkspur? According to Wikipedia, the community was named for the abundance of the larkspur flower near the original town site. Larkspur is also the site of the historic headquarters building of Universal Co-Masonry. According to the town's website, Larkspur's vision statement is, "Larkspur, a small friendly town in Colorado." It is also home to the Colorado Renaissance Faire and the Colorado PGA, located at the golf course less than two miles from our home, named Bear Dance. There is also a historic Frank Creamery that is now a walking trail. So we landed in a pretty special little town with lots of rural acreage of ranches for cattle and horses.

Since Colorado school started in August while California schools did not open until September, I borrowed the RV owned by Bill's brother Jack and lived in the local campground for a month until we knew if our house sold. The house closed escrow on Labor Day weekend, so we decided to rent a home in an area of Castle Rock called the Meadows to get settled into the new area. We took a six-month lease and started our search for the perfect property. To this end, we asked our realtor to show us everything under $500,000, so we looked at a lot of homes! Our original list of wants for a home were so specific that it was limiting the property we saw, and we wanted to see all that was available.

Our original goal was to find a ranch home (single level) with a three-car garage and a walk-out basement. To our disappointment, many of these properties were raised ranches—meaning they raised the foundation of the home to allow for a walk-out basement. Unfortunately, that often meant outdoor stairs to get into the front of the home! So we stumbled upon a two-story home with a main floor master that only had a two-car garage, but it had something better—a ton of windows and light and wonderful elevations. And it was located on a cul-de-sac. Sold! The home was listed as "sophistication in the woods," and we loved it. We found out that a builder had built the home and lived there and now occupied a similar home just a couple of blocks away. As God would have it, this man (Glen) was from northern Minnesota, not far from where Kathy grew up. We got to be good friends to him and his wife, Martha. We discovered several other Minnesota families in the area, including the ones who owned the local pizzeria and had "fresh Minnesota walleye" every Friday night. Kathy was right at home!

There was a small park in town, and Kathy joined the Park and Recreation Committee to explore how to expand this park. When her grant clients from California started to call, she got busy commuting to the West Coast to do more grant writing. In the meantime, Bill became an active community volunteer and also joined the local Larkspur Chamber of Commerce. He donated hundreds of hours to the town! He worked with the local grant writer who obtained funds from Greater Outdoors Colorado to expand our community park. It now includes a full baseball field, several covered picnic areas, toilets, an amazing climbing play structure for kids, and a large grassy area that is used for free summer concerts in the park and a free tree-lighting event in December. Over sixty trees are lit up during all of December and January, and it is such a beautiful winter sight—many folks just drive through our little town to see and feel the community spirit! Those years of volunteer work turned into a part-time job for Bill, and he is now known all over our area—the friendly guy who helps organize all the events! So the Kramers are involved in a big way! It seems God planted us in this little town to make it a better place. Such a blessing.

During Josiah's time at Larkspur Elementary, we also got involved in the parent-teacher organization that hosted two big events each year. One was the fall festival held on the grounds of the Renaissance Faire. Families come from all over to this amazing week-end festival! The Boot Scooting Boogie is held in the spring at a local horse ranch, and this event features a full dinner and live and silent auctions. The two events raise over $100,000 a year! Talk about amazing community spirit! We came to find out that many retired professionals live in our area, so the talent to pull off such events is deep and wide. So we get to live in a rural area with kind and involved neighbors but are driving distance to both Denver and Colorado Springs. We get to enjoy good old-fashioned neighbor get-togethers all the time. What a God thing!

Light versus Darkness (Good and Evil in Our World)

So what is this thing doing right after describing such a positive place in which to live? It's alphabetical, you know! But more importantly, it is a revelation that came to me along the way from God about the fact that there truly are forces for light and darkness in our world. Since I grew up in the Catholic Church, the basic teaching was that most people are good and will end up going to heaven when they die.

Forces for darkness and evil were rarely ever discussed. In many ways, I had to have my eyes opened the hard way.

The Bible has a lot to say about light versus darkness, including the following verse concepts:

Isaiah 9:2
The people who walk in darkness
Will see a great light;
Those who live in a dark land,
The light will shine on them.

Luke 1:79
To shine upon those who sit in darkness and the shadow of death,
To guide our feet into the way of peace."

Matthew 4:16
"The people who were sitting in darkness saw a great Light,
And those who were sitting in the land and shadow of death,
Upon them a Light dawned."

John 1:5
The Light shines in the darkness, and the darkness did not comprehend it.

2 Corinthians 4:6
For God, who said, "Light shall shine out of darkness," is the One who has shone in our hearts to give the Light of the knowledge of the glory of God in the face of Christ.

1 Peter 2:9
But you are a chosen race, a royal priesthood, a holy nation, a people for God's own possession,

so that you may proclaim the excellencies of Him who has called you out of darkness into His marvelous light;

Ephesians 5:8
For you were formerly darkness, but now you are Light in the Lord; walk as children of Light

John 8:12
Then Jesus again spoke to them, saying, "I am the Light of the world; he who follows Me will not walk in the darkness, but will have the Light of life."

Acts 26:18
Open their eyes so that they may turn from darkness to light and from the dominion of Satan to God, that they may receive forgiveness of sins and an inheritance among those who have been sanctified by faith in Me.'

Matthew 10:27
What I tell you in the darkness, speak in the light; and what you hear whispered in your ear, proclaim upon the housetops.

(Source: https://bible.knowing-jesus.com/topics/From-Darkness-To-Light)

The main thing I learned is that Jesus is the Lord of light, while Satan is the prince of darkness. Lucifer (Satan) was a high-ranking angel in heaven, but he wanted to be equal with God (pride), so he and one-third of the angels were thrown out of heaven and sent to earth (Rev. 12:4). Remember the garden of Eden? In Genesis 3:1 it says, "Now the serpent was craftier than any beast of the field which the LORD God had made." This is Satan. He went on to say to Eve,

"Did God really say you can't eat from that tree?" He put doubt in her mind and also told her if she did eat the fruit, she would be wise like God. We know the rest of the story. She ate the fruit and offered some to Adam, and he also ate. As a result, they were sent out of the garden (east of Eden) and were each given a curse.

Here is what is said in Genesis 3:14–19:

> So the Lord God said to the serpent, "Because you have done this, "Cursed are you above all livestock and all wild animals! You will crawl on your belly and you will eat dust all the days of your life. [He did not start out as a snake.] And I will put enmity between you and the woman, and between your offspring[a] and hers; he will crush[b] your head, and you will strike his heel." [Her offspring was Jesus, who crushed Satan on the cross.] To the woman he said, "I will make your pains in childbearing very severe; with painful labor you will give birth to children. Your desire will be for your husband, and he will rule over you." [Childbirth became painful, and husband-wife relations…well…] To Adam he said, "Because you listened to your wife and ate fruit from the tree about which I commanded you, 'You must not eat from it,' "Cursed is the ground because of you; through painful toil you will eat food from it all the days of your life. It will produce thorns and thistles for you, and you will eat the plants of the field. By the sweat of your brow you will eat your food until you return to the ground, since from it you were taken; for dust you are and to dust you will return." [Bodily death would happen and work would be a curse.]

Now, why would I bother to quote all this scripture in my book? Because it frames the entire Bible and the entire story of life on earth!

At the beginning of Genesis 1:1–3, here is what is said about creation: "In the beginning God created the heavens and the earth. Now the earth was formless and empty, darkness was over the surface of the deep, and the Spirit of God was hovering over the waters. And God said, 'Let there be light,' and there was light." From darkness to light. Day 1. Amazing.

When Jesus was born, people who walked in darkness saw a great light, but they preferred darkness (to hide their sin). Light shines on such things! The light will guide your feet into the way of peace, but only if you follow the Prince of Peace (Jesus). People were sitting in darkness until they saw a great light; upon them light dawned. Isn't it interesting that time itself is based on the birth of Jesus? Dates are either BC (before Christ) or AD (anno domini, Latin for "in the year of the Lord," referring specifically to the birth of Jesus Christ). It was the turning point of all time on earth.

Paul told the people living in Corinth, "The one who has shone in our hearts to give the light of knowledge of the glory of God in the face of Christ." Jesus came to change hearts. He told His apostles, "If you know Me, then you know the Father. We are one." The apostle Peter told the followers of Christ, "You are a chosen race, a royal priesthood, a holy nation, a people for God's own possession, so you may proclaim the excellencies of Him who has called you out of darkness into His marvelous light!" We can choose to move from living in darkness to light.

Paul told the people in Ephesus, "You were formerly darkness, but now you are light in the Lord. Walk as children of light!" At the end of the book of Acts, the prayer for the believers who were going out into the world to open their eyes so that they may turn from darkness to light and from the dominion of Satan to God to receive the forgiveness of sins and an inheritance among those have been sanctified by faith. Matthew said, "Proclaim it from the housetops!" What a call to action for all Christians! It is all about turning our lives around and walking in the light of Jesus. We need to shout it to the world! There is no such thing as a "meek believer."

The reason I had to include this chapter is that it is so important. So many people think they can straddle the line between light and darkness, but that is not what Jesus taught. It is so interesting that in the final book of the Bible, Revelation, the Lord begins by talking to John about the seven churches and where they went wrong or right (yes, churches!). Here is a summary of what he said to each church (source www.christianity.com):

1. Ephesus, the church that has abandoned its love for Christ and His teachings (Rev. 2:1–7). The lesson in the letter to Ephesus teaches that truth and love must go hand in hand. A church that upholds doctrinal purity at the expense of showing love is just as flawed as a church that upholds congregational harmony at the expense of truthful teachings. Instead, Jesus reveals that a church fashioned in His image must teach God's truth in love.

2. Smyrna, the church that remains faithful amid persecution (Rev. 2:8–11). Like the church in Smyrna, Christians are persecuted worldwide in obvious and insidious ways. This letter warns all Christians that although we may suffer greatly, the length of tribulation will be short compared to the promise of eternal life.

3. Pergamum, the church that compromises its beliefs (Rev. 2:12–17). Like the Christians in Pergamum, it's easy to normalize the non-Christian behavior of those around us and allow that behavior to dilute our values (1 Cor. 15:33). But the Bible urges us to "not conform to the pattern of this world" but be transformed by the renewal of our mind in accordance with God's Word (Rom. 12:2).

4. Thyatira, the church that follows false prophets (Rev. 2:18–29). Just as some in Thyatira's church were led astray by a false prophet, Christians today fall prey to cult leaders, occult practices, and other false teachings. To share in Christ's victory, we are to avoid these so-called deep secrets of Satan (Rev. 2:24) and hold firm to Christ's teachings.

5. Sardis, the church that is spiritually dead (Rev. 3:1–6). Today, Christians can fall into the trap that ensnared the church in Sardis if we merely go through the motions of

practicing our faith without really feeding our spirit. We can avoid becoming "the living dead" by engaging in our faith through Bible study, prayer, and fellowship.

6. Philadelphia, the church that patiently endured despite weaknesses (Rev. 3:7–13). The message to Philadelphia shows us the blessings that come when we maintain our faith despite life's tribulations. In fact, those who persevere despite weaknesses will stand strong as pillars in heaven. (Isn't it cool that our Declaration of Independence was signed in a city called Philadelphia? Our Christian Founding Fathers knew the Bible and created one nation under God starting in this very city.)

7. Laodicea, the church with a lukewarm faith (Rev. 3:14–22). Like the church in Laodicea, it's easy to become complacent in our faith during times of abundance. Christ warns us in this revelation that He will "spit out" lukewarm disciples. Instead, Jesus urges us to keep seeking the Lord's face even after His hand has bestowed riches in our lives.

Light versus darkness? A most important concept to understand and to share. I thank God that He revealed this to me as part of my manna along the way. It is like taking off rose-colored glasses and seeing things as they really are, as seen by our Creator and Lord. There is so much darkness in the world today. We need to be able to discern the dark forces from those who bring light and abide in the light.

CHAPTER M

Mary (A Roommate, an Aunt, a Saint)

There is no other female name more revered in the Catholic Church than Mary. She was the mother of Jesus. The Catholic Church teaches that she was born sinless (immaculate conception) and is holy as Jesus is holy. The Bible does not teach this. In fact, when the apostles started teaching the good news after Pentecost and new believers would kneel before them, they would say, "Get up! There is no one holy but God [Jesus]." Nonetheless, it is a beautiful name with a lot of meaning.

We are introduced to Mary, the mother of Jesus, in the book of Luke when the archangel appears to her to let her know she will bear a son, the holy one of God, and to name Him Jesus. As a young teenage virgin who is engaged to Joseph, she must have been overwhelmed, but she was so gracious to say to the angel, "I am a servant of the Lord." See Luke 1:26–38:

> In the sixth month of Elizabeth's pregnancy, God sent the angel Gabriel to Nazareth, a town in Galilee, to a virgin pledged to be married to a man named Joseph, a descendant of David. The virgin's name was Mary. The angel went to her and said, "Greetings, you who are highly favored! The Lord is with you." Mary was greatly troubled at his words and wondered what kind of greeting this might be. But the angel said to her, "Do not

be afraid, Mary; you have found favor with God. You will conceive and give birth to a son, and you are to call him Jesus. He will be great and will be called the Son of the Most High. The Lord God will give him the throne of his father David, and he will reign over Jacob's descendants forever; his kingdom will never end." "How will this be," Mary asked the angel, "since I am a virgin?" The angel answered, "The Holy Spirit will come on you, and the power of the Most High will over-shadow you. So the holy one to be born will be called[a] the Son of God. Even Elizabeth, your relative is going to have a child in her old age, and she who was said to be unable to conceive is in her sixth month. For no word from God will ever fail." "I am the Lord's servant," Mary answered. "May your word to me be fulfilled." Then the angel left her.

Wow. What mature faith for such a young lady! As we know, the same angel went to Joseph and told him it was okay to get married to Mary since she was to bear the Son of God. Then Mary went to visit her cousin Elizabeth, who was also with child as a result of the Holy Spirit blessing her womb in old age. When Mary approached her, the baby in her womb (John the Baptist) leapt for joy! Since the prayer Hail Mary is such a part of the Catholic faith, I was amazed to read that the first part of this prayer was very biblical (good). But the second part was completely added on by the church (bad). One thing I know is that you should *never* add a single word to the Bible; it is the perfect, inspired Word of God. Here is the first part from Luke 1:42: "In a loud voice she exclaimed: 'Blessed are you among women, and blessed is the child you will bear!'" There are no words to say, "Holy Mary, mother of God, pray for us sinners now and at the hour of our death. Amen."

I do not bring this up as a criticism of members of the Catholic faith who love this prayer and also love praying the rosary (five decades of the Hail Mary with the Our Father in between) but rather as a point of enlightenment about what the Bible really says. This prayer creates a picture of Jesus at the right hand of God and Mary at His right hand. By praying to her, she will talk to her Son and offer prayers for the sinners saying the prayer. This is so false. Saints might be honored for their good life, and especially martyrs who died for their faith, but you cannot invoke their help with your problems or any help to be granted salvation. Faith in the Lord Jesus the Christ (Savior) is one of a personal relationship with Him alone. When He died on the cross, He gave us direct access to God forever. We no longer need to go through a priest to access almighty God. The temple curtain was torn in half from top to bottom (Matt. 27:51). We can now access God directly. Jesus reconnected heaven to earth. Hallelujah!

So what does the name Mary mean? According to www. behindthename.com, the usual English form of Maria, the meaning is not known for certain, but there are several theories, including "sea of bitterness," "rebelliousness," and "wished-for child." However, it was most likely originally an Egyptian name, perhaps derived in part from my "beloved" or my "love." Wow. Those are really different meanings for this name! According to Wikipedia, there are several women named Mary in the Bible. A common Protestant tradition holds that there are six women named as Mary in the New Testament: Mary, mother of Jesus; Mary Magdalene; Mary of Bethany; Mary, mother of James the Younger; Mary, mother of John Mark; and Mary of Rome. A common Roman Catholic tradition includes six New Testament saints called Mary: Mary, mother of Jesus; Mary Magdalene; Mary, mother of James and John; (Mary) Salome (who is also identified as the mother of the sons of Zebedee); Mary of Clopas; Mary of Bethany, sister of Martha and Lazarus. And there are other variations. In most traditions, at least three Marys are present at the crucifixion and at the resurrection, but again traditions differ as to the identities of these three and as to whether they are the same three at these two events.

The important thing in all these writings is the word *tradition*. According to *Webster's Dictionary* definition of *tradition*: "1a: an inherited, established, or customary pattern of thought, action, or behavior (such as a religious practice or a social custom); b: a belief or story or a body of beliefs or stories relating to the past that are commonly accepted as historical though not verifiable." These are things passed on from one generation to another, often by verbal stories. So what you believe about any biblical person named Mary is usually a matter of your tradition.

When I entered college in the fall of 1972, I chose to live in a dorm on campus. As such, I was assigned my first roommate. She was a very quiet young lady named Penny. We did not do much together, but I did make other female friends as a freshman, including those of us who were chosen to be the hockey cheerleaders for a new thing on this Catholic campus—a boys' hockey team! Among this group, I met a new friend named Mary, and she and I have remained lifetime friends. During our sophomore year, we were roommates and had such fun together. We would often go out on weekends to dances at the campus next door, the University of Minnesota–Duluth (UMD). That was where she met her future husband, Lanny. Her soul mate.

While I came from a large family (seven children), she only had one brother, and her dad had died years earlier. So I got to know her mom, Marie. Another derivative of the name Mary! She was a grand old lady with a lot of spirit! I "shared" my dad with Mary, and he came to think of her as a daughter. It was a sweet relationship in every way. At one point, Mary and Lanny were going to break up, but I convinced them to work it out because I could tell they were madly in love. They did. Mary chose to go to a college in Michigan for her last two years of school, but after our junior year, they got married, and I had the great joy to be in their wedding. I don't think all marriages involve marrying your soul mate, but such was the case for Mary and Lanny. Precious.

When my dad retired (1985), he had a heart attack and then open-heart surgery performed in Minneapolis in January 1986. Since I lived in California and it was short notice, I could not fly back to be with him before surgery, so I called Mary and asked if she would go and see him for me. Since she lived in the Twin Cities, she agreed.

That was special for me and my dad. One thing we shared was a love of dancing. When we were in college, Mary loved slow songs and called them "belly-rubbing tunes" (BRT). How sweet is that? To this day, I picture my time in heaven dancing with Jesus, a BRT, because it creates such a special connection with someone you love. Dear Lanny was diagnosed with cancer in his leg/knee and seemed to have it beat, but when it came back, he had to have an above-the-knee amputation. I recall the Christmas letter in 2018 written by Lanny when he revealed his tender story. He is now getting used to prosthetic devices that have to be adjusted/changed regularly. My prayer for both of them is that they will never stop dancing. That was how they met. That is part of their love story.

I also had an aunt named Mary Louise. She was in nursing school with my mom at the same college that we all attended. She also fell madly in love and got married after her junior year of college. The difference is that she dropped out of college. She went on to have six live-born children, but then tragedy struck and her husband dropped dead of a heart attack when her children were all young. So she raised six children on her own—what a feat! She did go back to our college and get her teaching credential and ended up working as an elementary teacher. She had such a heart for kids. When her mom became a widow (another heart attack), she stayed close to her and Grandma moved to her town and worked in the church rectory, taking care of the local priest. I know this was special for both of them.

Mary Louise was my dad's older sister, and she was the only one the family could afford to send to college. My dad took some classes at the local community college, but I know he was always a little resentful that he was not able to go to college. So when I went to that same college, he would come down for visits and reminisce about his fond memories of courting my mom there. Isn't that sweet? He could still recall the nuns he liked the best—ha!

In old age, Mary Louise ended up in a senior apartment on the campus of our college, part of the Benedictine Health Center. As her health deteriorated, she was moved to their skilled nursing facility in the same building. She made it to age ninety-one and died on the campus where she met her loving husband, also at a dance. Her life was filled with so many challenges, including the death of her son (Fred) while in the Army in Germany (on the autobahn). She lived to enjoy many grandchildren and great-grandchildren. She had a wicked sense of humor, and we sure enjoyed time at the lake with Aunt Mary Louise.

When my own mom started falling and breaking bones and we had to put her into assisted living, I had hoped she would end up back on our college campus in the Benedictine Center. Instead, she went from one facility to another, and her final years in memory care were not very pretty. She died in a home-based unit called Home Sweet Home that was very close to the hospital where she worked for years. Her final treatment was good. Yet I could not have helped but think, What if she could have been cared for in the Benedictine setting where she met my dad? She would say, "That's too expensive," but in the end, there would have been a way to make it work. So the name Mary will always remind me of the College of Saint Scholastica in Duluth, Minnesota. One more shout-out to my junior-year roommate from Tennessee named Marybelle—what great fun we had! She was really a Southern belle. We have stayed in touch, and I have gone to visit her several times. Mary was also my confirmation name. So yes, Mary is a very special name to me!

Michael (A Brother, Boyfriend, and Great Angel)

The two most famous archangels mentioned in the Bible are Gabriel and Michael, so this is another pretty special name. My own brother Michael was number 5 in our family—my mom had a boy, girl, boy, girl, boy, girl, then boy. The first three of us were one year apart, and the youngest three were two years apart. What set him apart was that at age three, he spiked a fever and got encephalitis that fried his brain. He was diagnosed with mental retardation and epilepsy, so he was the "special" kid in our family. In those days, there was not much in education for special needs children, so he was sent away to a children's home and we only got to see him during summers. He came back during third grade and did that year with sister Joan. Dear

Michael. We learned how cruel kids can be, saying "retard," and we learned how to defend our brother as well.

So what does the name Michael mean? According to www. behndthename.com, the name Michael is a Hebrew baby name meaning "Who is like God, gift from God." Michael is one of the archangels in Hebrew tradition and the only one identified as an archangel in the Bible. In the book of Daniel in the Old Testament, he is named as a protector of Israel. In the book of Revelation in the New Testament, he is portrayed as the leader of heaven's armies in the war against Satan and is thus considered the patron saint of soldiers in Christianity. Wow, that is one powerful name!

There was a time when my poor dad was marrying off a child every summer: 1978, 1979, 1980, 1981. And Michael watched as all his siblings found someone to spend their life with. He longed to have the same thing. While at a program called Homes Incorporated, he met a gal named Pauline, also with mental retardation. He asked our parents if they could get married, so the parents came together and agreed that these two could take care of each other, but not children. So Mike had a vasectomy and we had one more wedding in 1985—just one year before my dad died. I think the Lord made sure this happened before my mom became a widow, or she might have promoted letting Michael live with her the rest of his life.

They have now been married over thirty-five years and live independently in a two-bedroom apartment with their little dog. They both work part-time to add to their Social Security Disability income and are quite the success story, one I love to share. Every time I go home to Minnesota for a visit, I am sure to spend time and at least one meal with Mike and Pauline. She does cross-stitch on dish towels (for each day of the week), and I buy a couple sets every year and give them away as Christmas gifts. I always add a label, "Made by Pauline with love, despite her disability." They have become cherished by so many recipients. Michael got a driver's license and owned a car until recently, when his seizures returned and he had to forfeit that privilege. But they use local transportation and do quite well. They live a sweet, simple life.

I have to salute my sister Sue, who has the power of attorney to help them handle their finances and all their medical needs and housing issues. She is a gem! My sister Joan also helps with their needs, and both make sure Mike and Pauline always have a place to go during all holidays. Michael used to fish along the Mississippi River and caught a large walleye from a dock once. Pauline's dad took it to a taxidermist to hang on his wall. During a visit after this event, I asked Mike where his prize fish was. He proudly took me to his garage and showed me where it was hanging. I asked, Why there? He said when people come home from work and go into their garages, he can show off his fish. How smart is that? Dear Michael.

So who was my boyfriend named Michael? During the time after my divorce, I bought my own condo and joined the HOA board. This group of folks became my friends, and they invited me to join the local ski club, so I did. During one of the first meetings, they were planning a learn-to-ski week at Lake Tahoe (January 1986), and I signed up to join them. On the bus ride to the mountain, there was a pesty fellow from my church trying to get my attention, so I spotted a single guy (handsome with a black beard) and asked if I could sit with him? He agreed. He saved me. My archangel. We learned to ski together. We then started dating.

I came to find out that he was going through a divorce. His wife had left him and their two children. She was tired of marriage and being a wife and mother. How sad. He was an engineer by occupation and was an intelligent fellow, and we had good fun together. Skiing. Golf. Outdoor theater events. Racquetball. Sports. Although he had no faith of his own, he respected my Catholic values. We never spent a night together. He actually preferred that for his children, as well as my choice. When I took a new job in Arizona in 1987 and had to vacate my condo, which had been sold, I spent my last night in California at his home (different bedrooms). He then admitted that he had fallen in love with me. Oh dear. So much for "fun dating only." I believe he did reconcile with his wife and finished raising his children, but I have to thank him for being such an important "first relationship" after divorce. A true gentleman. A sweet relationship for sure.

274

Our family had such high regard for our brother Michael that several nephews were given that name. So Michael is a pretty special name to me and my family. We love our Michaels!

Minnesota (The Place of My Upbringing)

You may say, Why did I not say Minnesota is the place I was born and raised? It is because I was the only one of my siblings to not be born in Minnesota. That was due to the Korean War. My dad was in the US Army when he and my mom married. They spent their first year on the West Coast, in Monterey, California, before they got transferred to the East Coast, in the Washington, DC, area. He was in Army language school on both coasts. It was December 1952 (one year after their marriage) that my mom was due to give birth to their first child, so she went home to Saint Cloud, Minnesota, to deliver her son. They would move east in 1953.

They settled in Fort Belvoir, Virginia, where there was an Army base and an Army hospital. I was born in that hospital in January 1954. I was my mom's only child to come early. She had an ear infection and was hospitalized and gave birth during that time. When diarrhea broke out in the nursery, they had to take me home early despite my small size, around five pounds. My dad said I was so small I would fit in a shoebox. By 1955, his Army enlistment was over, and they moved back to northern Minnesota. My next brother would be born in July 1955, and all other siblings after that would also be born in Hibbing General Hospital. So I was the "unique" child from early on in our family. Yet Minnesota will always be home to me.

We lived in a three-bedroom, one-bath ranch home in a rural town called Pengilly. It was full of bunk beds! A boys' room, a girls' room, and a very small bedroom for Mom and Dad. (No such thing as a master bedroom in those days!) We lived next to a nine-hole golf course, and my dad would buy a family membership each summer for about $100 so we all got to play golf for free! I never knew what a green fee was until after college! Swan Lake was located in our small town, so in summers we could walk to the beach to swim. The only other establishments in town were a couple of churches, gas stations, a Laundromat, a small store, a post office, and of course, a bar and liquor store. We either walked or rode our bikes everywhere we went. We were considered middle class and rarely shopped for new clothes. My grandma Schmid would make us new dresses to start the school year and for Easter Sunday. The eldest boy got basic clothes, and after that, it was pretty much hand-me-downs. My dad worked full-time during the week in the iron mines (as did most dads), and my mom was an RN who went back to work when my youngest brother started kindergarten. My dad also worked part-time on weekends for the local sheriff as a dispatcher. There were a lot of mouths to feed!

So what was it like growing up in the land of ten thousand lakes? Pretty simple. We lived in one of seven different small towns on the iron range, and a bus picked us up for school every day. We had a local elementary school, then joined all the other towns' kids for junior high (grades 7–9) and high school (grades 10–12) about twelve miles away. The most common thing I can remember hearing my mom say is, "Go outside and play!" I think that was to get us out of her hair, but we liked the outdoors, climbing trees and playing outside until dusk with the other neighborhood kids.

Many years later, a California friend told me about a book called *Lake Wobegon Days*. Here is how it is described by Wikipedia: *Lake Wobegon Days* is a novel by Garrison Keillor, first published in hard-cover by Viking in 1985. Based on material from his radio show *A Prairie Home Companion*, the book brought Keillor's work to a much wider audience and achieved international success, selling over one million copies. Like some of Keillor's other books, it is unusual in that it could be said that the audiobook preceded the publication in written form.

The work is a humorous account of life in fictitious Lake Wobegon, Minnesota, a heartland small town. Its early chapters are written in the form and style of a history of the town, and later ones chronicle the lives, concerns, and activities of its inhabitants, with intergenerational tensions and relationships forming a major theme. Most of the latter material was originally delivered on radio in the form of monologues. Due to the nature of the original material, the second half of the novel has many recurring characters but little in the way of plot, resembling an incompletely integrated group of short stories.

When I listened to this book on tape, I thought it quite accurately depicted growing up in small-town Minnesota. From church potlucks to all the neighbors knowing everything about one another to good old-fashioned kindness, we all knew one another's nationality of origin (long before 23andMe), and no one found any disdain in being known as an Italian (Wop) or German or Swedish or Irish— it was just part of our heritage. I must say we did pick on the Finlanders the most—my dad knew a ton of Finlander jokes! (No offense to my brother-in-law Ross, who is Finnish. He did grow up with an outdoor sauna and no indoor plumbing! But that made him Minnesota hearty!) Many years later, when I made a trip back to the home of my grandparents (Avon), it was now located off a new interstate highway (I-94), and the exit to Avon said, "Lake Wobegon Trail." How about that? I actually spent my summers in the Lake Wobegon area (a fictitious name) and did not even know it. I always knew that summers in Avon were extra special. My grandparents had a corner lot surrounded by a white picket fence, a two-story home, a cottage, a playhouse, a carport, and Grandpa's candy shed, with a lake and dock right there so we could fish and swim all we wanted. It was heavenly!

As I said in my chapter on educational systems, we had a very good public education. Minnesota was one of the best since the mining companies wanted their kids to have a good education. There were several sections of Minnesota that had distinct names and characters. We grew up in northern Minnesota on the Iron Range, so we were called rangers. The biggest population was Minneapolis–Saint Paul, called the Twin Cities. We just called them the cities kids. Duluth was the second biggest population and was located on Lake Superior. We just called it cold! The wind "lake effect" made it quite chilly in the winter. Hockey was the biggest sport, and we had an indoor arena. Our little high school made it to the Minnesota state hockey championship a couple of times—quite a feat! Back in those days, we had to play the large high schools from the cities. Now they have different divisions by school size. Like I said, it was all one big Minnesota tradition to go to hockey finals. Many years later, when the United States Olympic team beat the Russians in hockey, that coach was from the University of Minnesota. It made us Minnesota proud! Newcomers say, "Minnesota nice."

We also loved Minnesota Viking Football. We would watch it on TV every weekend, and that was when I learned to yell at the TV when they played! Those were the good old days of rivalries with the Green Bay Packers, Chicago Bears, and the Detroit Lions—Upper Midwest teams. Many years later, when I got to go to UCLA football, I was so excited to see big games in person. I still knew how to yell at players, coaches, and referees! We also followed the Minnesota Twins baseball team, and I did get to go to a few games with Grandma and Grandpa. But most summer evenings, we would just sit outside in a large two-sided wooden swing and listen to the games by radio. Yes, that was what you did in Minnesota on summer evenings—until the mosquitoes came out and started biting. Time to go inside!

I remember the first time I took my husband, Bill, back to Minnesota for a July 4 vacation. He could not believe how a small town of five hundred people (Nashwauk) would swell into five thousand people, including many young blond children! Towheads! There was an old-fashioned parade where my brother Michael would proudly dress as Uncle Sam and ride his unicycle. There were local fireworks as well, and it was good fun! Bill also enjoyed the big barbecues that were held. Our family had a big spit and roasted whole pigs or a side of beef or a leg of lamb or all these! That Minnesota tradition was started by my dad with the help of his Serbian friends. Remember that Army language school he attended? He learned to read, write, and speak Serbian. They know the best way to season and barbecue meat for sure!

Going to Minnesota is always best if you can stay on a lake. The extended family of my sister Sue built a nice cabin on a nearby lake, and we are able to enjoy cabin time nearly every summer—they shared with all the extended families! Bill loves to take boat rides on the lake and see bald eagles and the loons in late evening with their unique voice. We have fires by the beach and listen to good music and enjoy family time. In fact, I grew up in Itasca County, which has over one thousand lakes, including Lake Itasca, the headwaters for the Mississippi River! I took Bill to see this as well. He also got to enjoy the riverboat shows in Grand Rapids that were held on the banks of the Mississippi. Yes, Minnesota has some pretty special and unique qualities, and I am always proud to say that is where I am from!

A note about Minneapolis riots in June 2020: This is so unusual for Minnesota. Now my home state has a scar on it caused by one death of a black man at the hands of one policeman. Protests were okay, but riots, looting, and fires were not. This all happened in a small section of Minneapolis, but nevertheless, it has become a sad thing that some may think that "Minnesota nice" has ended. The police and first responders were told to stand down by local officials, and then the "defund the police" effort began. I do hope that peace and law and order will be re-established in all the Twin Cities. I was pleased that three business leaders from northern Minnesota (mines and forestry) were included in the Republican National Convention this year. I suspect my old state may vote Trump (conservative) this year. That would be a turn for the best. I pray my dear home state becomes "normal" again very soon. Minnesota nice.

Missions (The Great Commandment)

When I was growing up, we never knew anyone who went into mission work. I do remember my grandma Schmid supporting the Maryknoll missionaries, but this was the only case I knew. It was not until I started attending Protestant churches that I learned the concept of people dedicating their lives to missions work, both in America and abroad, often raising their own support on which to live. Every church we have attended has supported several such individuals and organizations. We now love being a part of missions work being done all over the world! As Jesus said, go and tell the world the good news!

Our first such outreach was being a host family to foreign students who were living and going to school in the USA. The first couple I was assigned to were from Egypt; he came over to the USA to teach in a Christian school, and during that time, his wife got pregnant. Since I worked in a hospital, I helped her get through childbirth classes and get ready for the delivery. The first English word I taught her was *epidural!* They were so appreciative of my help and friendship they gave me some beautiful wall hangings for my home. They are still on our walls!

The second person we were assigned (now as a married couple) was a young college student from Japan. He was quite shy, but he loved to play golf, so we would take him out on Friday late afternoon for twilight golf—all the holes you could play until it got dark! When he returned home the following year, some Cal Lutheran students told us it was the best part of his American experience. How sweet is that? As I mentioned in the chapter for my son Josiah, we hosted another Japanese high school student one year (Yo), so we sure enjoyed learning more about that country! Bill has also traveled to the Philippines twice to help with missions work there through our connection to Grace Brethren Church. Ted and Viv just retired this year and are back in the States, but I know this place and these people hold a special place in Bill's heart. So someday when we get to visit Asia, we will try to visit our friends in these nations.

In 1997, we were assigned to a college freshman from Tanzania named Gabriel (see extended story in his chapter). We were his American family for all four years of his college experience and eventually met his own parents and even traveled to Tanzania to stay with them on a special adventure that included fun (safaris) as well as missions work to visit orphans with AIDS. In fact, when we landed in this sub-Saharan country, the notices were all over the airport about this disease and warnings, but it was also home to Mt. Kilimanjaro, which was near where Gabriel grew up. We have helped Gabe financially along the way, as needed, and now call each other family. He works in Washington, DC, for the UN, and we are very proud of him!

In 2005, we met Sharon Barlow, whose dad had started a missions outreach just after WWII to the people of Ethiopia. He was a doctor treating jungle diseases and came across a condition called mossy foot that was much like elephantiasis (see chapter E). We visited that country in 2008 and continue to keep in touch with Pastor Zewdie, who is a local preacher in the south part of this country. It is such an honor to help him and his work and his family—they live in a very poor area of the country. We also sit on the board of an organization called Renewed Hope, which helps the orphans in Zimbabwe. We sure hope to get back to Africa someday to help in person with this mission work! Ironically, Kathy's high school boyfriend was from Rhodesia—now called Zimbabwe—so we consider this another God connection. Oh, to do His work!

We were also mission sponsors to a World Vision child in Tanzania until they would not let us visit our child when we traveled to Africa. So we changed to Compassion International and now support another young lady in Tanzania. It is such a joy to get her regular letters, and we hope to go and visit her someday. We also supported a couple who went to Mozambique, but they had to come home for medical reasons. But such great work they did, and they loved the people there. Yes, another Africa trip is on our list!

When I got involved with Moms in Prayer International, I was able to make a mission trip to Romania in 2009 to help moms set up prayer groups and also do outreach through an organization called E3 Partners. We also supported a couple who moved to Holland and lived north of Amsterdam. We got to visit them one year and see the home of Corrie ten Boom and get to meet the local people from this "dark north" country who were now being served by Greater Europe Missions, GEM, Chis and Terry. When they returned to the States, Chris lived with us while getting ready to buy a home in Colorado Springs. My friend Debbie (whose job I took at the school district) went to work for GEM and now lives in Germany. We also support a young family who live in Ukraine, working for Campus Crusade for Christ, and we hope to get back to Europe and visit all these folks in the coming years. World travel is sure more interesting and inspiring when you are meeting fellow Christian workers with a heart for the Lord.

Alphabetically, here are some other Christian organizations we support regularly:

- Christen Chaplains Service in Denver (prison ministry)
- Joni and Friends (international disability ministry)
- Ligonier Ministries (Bible teaching of Pastor R. C. Sproul)
- Navigators (Christian outreach on college campuses)
- Open-Door Ministry (helping the inner-city homeless of Denver)
- Samaritan's Purse (the annual shoebox ministry at Christmas)

We also support occasional needs as they come our way, including many areas of service at our local church, including the Good Samaritan Fund. It is not until we do our taxes every year that we actually have to come up with a list for our CPA—he cannot believe how long that list is! But as God has blessed us, we want to share with others. We are not sure if we will get involved in any one mission organization now that I am retired, but it is on our life list.

One more note about training for missions and the program called Perspectives. Kathy earned a certificate of training in May 2017 from Perspectives, and we hope to take more classes from this organization together. Perspectives on the World Christian Movement is a Christian education course designed to help believers learn more about God's heart for all nations and how believers worldwide can play an active role in the Great Commission. It is run locally, coordinated regionally, and supported behind the scenes by a national office. The focus is on working with the indigenous people to help them launch/lead Christian outreach in their nation. So we keep our passports up-to-date, in case we get a call to go and serve! We are open to whatever God wants to use us in the world. We are blessed that He has already used us in so many ways across the globe. God always provides the manna we need along the way.

Moms in Prayer (Praying for Kids and Schools)

During our time at the first church we attended in Castle Rock, there was a class for newcomers to the area. One of the speakers was a gal named Cheryl, who showed us a short video about an organization called Moms in Touch, later changed to Moms in Prayer. I listened intently since this effort was started in California and I had never heard of it. According to their website, Moms in Prayer International influences children and schools worldwide for Christ by gathering mothers to pray. Moms meet once a week (usually at someone's home) and spend one hour in prayer, using preprinted sheets with the attributes of God and using a four steps of prayer for each attribute and praying your children into Scripture. Here is an example, for God is able.

1. *Praise.* Praise God for who He is, His attributes, His name, and His character. The attribute definition is listed (i.e., God is able, one who has sufficient power, ability, resources). Scriptures listed (to look up and read aloud): 2 Corinthians 9:8; Ephesians 3:20–23; Hebrew 7:25.

2. *Confession.* Silently confessing your sins to the God who forgives, for cleansing. If we confess our sins, He is faithful and righteous to forgive us our sins and to cleanse us from all unrighteousness (1 John 1:9). This is the second step we use.

3. *Thanksgiving.* Thanking God for what he has done. In everything, give thanks, for this is God's will for you in Christ Jesus (1 Thess. 5:18). This is a fun third step! We keep track of these thanks, and at the end of the year, we read aloud how God has done great things for us! These are often answers to previous prayers. I love this part of the hour of prayer!

4. *Intercession.* Coming to God on behalf of others. We do this for four groups:

    a. *Our own children.* Each mom chooses one child, first praying the child into the Scripture and then adding any special requests (i.e., able—God, may ____ know that You are able to bless him/her abundantly, so that in all things at all times, having all that ____ needs, he/she will abound in every good work [2 Cor. 9:8]).

b. *Teachers/staff.* We can use the verse below or the verse for your child: Open ____ eyes and turn him/her from darkness to light and from the power of Satan to God, so that he/she may receive forgiveness of sins and a place among those who are sanctified by faith in Jesus (Acts 26:18). We also add any specific prayers for any specific teachers that we know are going through a challenge, such as a health issue.

c. *School concerns.* We pray for revival and spiritual awakening at the school(s), for protection over the staff and students, or for any other concerns. I would often pray for modesty at school dances—now that's a cry for a miracle!

d. *Moms in Prayer concerns.* We pray that every school worldwide would be covered in prayer, for protection over the ministry, to keep it pure and undefiled, and to pray for donors to partner with the ministry in equipping groups and reaching nations.

What is prayed in the group stays in the group!

I started my first Moms in Prayer (MIP) group in the spring of 2007 with a group of moms meeting at my home for our local elementary school. As those kids grew up, we stayed together and rotated homes where to pray, usually to help the mom with any pre-school-aged children. These women became some of my best local friends and Christian sisters. I went on to become an area coordinator for our region and also joined the state team for a while. While recruiting moms to join MIP, I would stress it is easy, no preparation or homework; just come with an open heart to be led by Holy Spirit prayer!

The reason I include Moms in Prayer in my book is that I believe it is one of the most life-changing ministries I have ever had the privilege to join. The power of moms praying for their kids! I was blessed to go to Romania on an MIP trip in the summer of 2009, and I helped local women start groups in the capital city of Bucharest. I also came to find out one of the key pastors I had met in Ethiopia was instrumental in helping form MIP groups there. Women would walk for days to join a group of moms, often carrying one cup of rice to share with others. In this case, I know they spent a lot longer than one hour praying for their kids!

Here is what the founder, Fern Nichols, has to say about how she got started in 1984. When they were starting junior high in 1984, Fern knew that her two eldest children were about to be faced with their greatest test. Her heart was heavy and burdened with concern as she thought about their upcoming challenges to resist immoral values, vulgar language, peer pressure, and philosophies that could undermine their faith. She cried out to the Lord, praying for Him to protect her children. Praying that He would enable them to see clearly the difference between right and wrong and to make good decisions.

She found one other woman to pray with her, and the rest is history. The ministry is now international and includes groups in every state in the USA and in more than 140 countries. Talk about a *big* prayer that was answered. There is always more work to do. When the Columbine tragedy struck in Colorado in 1999, there were established MIP groups surrounding that school, and all the families affected in prayer. Talk about "for such a time as this." Check it out—you will be blessed if you do. So much manna.

Motherhood (A Godly Role—Not for Everyone)

When I was growing up, I had friends who had one ambition: to marry the man of their dreams and start a family, have lots of kids! I remember one such friend named Lucy who did just that. She got married just out of high school and had her first baby boy the following year. Then another came along twelve months later. And by year 3, she had triplets—all boys! So when they came to our church on

Sunday morning, there were the five of them waddling in together. Amazing! Perhaps because I was raised in a big family and saw it as such "dashed dreams" for my mom, I did not share this ambition. Ironically, she did get her college degree before getting married and starting a family, but everything changed so fast for her. Some girls went to college to get their "Mrs. degree"—find a husband! Not me. I wanted to see the world first before ever settling down. I never gave much thought to becoming a mom.

I was always good at planning things. First, I got my degree. Second, I found a good job in a beautiful area to live. Third, I found a handsome guy to marry and settle down. Fourth, we bought our first home and settled into our professional careers. Fifth, we could now start about starting a family. Or so I thought. I suggested to my husband that I stop taking birth control pills and try to get pregnant, and he freaked out! It was then that I learned about his affair, and by the time of the divorce, I was grateful we did not have any children together. Thank You, Lord! So I spent the next eleven years as a single professional woman. I thought this might satisfy me, but it did not, and I yearned to have a family of my own. But my biological clock was ticking; any woman who has her first pregnancy after age thirty-five is considered an elderly primigravida. I did not want to be one of those!

It's funny how the things you never wanted as a young lady in your twenties become extremely important in your late thirties. Such was the case for me and motherhood. My mom had over twenty grandchildren and great-grandchildren, so I was the favorite, Aunt Kathy. It was certainly a fun role to play, but not the same as being a mom. I often volunteered to work in the nursery at several churches that we joined and had a good way with babies—the Lord gave me a peaceful presence that seemed to soothe the young ones. I had more than one parent say, "How did you ever get our baby to go to sleep?" I would smile and say, "Gentleness." God was watching me.

So by the time Bill and I got married, I was forty-one years of age and certainly a candidate for a high-risk pregnancy if we were able to conceive. No such luck. So we decided to adopt children and ended up with two small boys to make our family (see chapter on adoption). I seemed to be able to balance working full-time and rais-ing boys, but I can see where my high energy helped out. Since we adopted our boys from foster care, their birth moms were somewhat crazy. I always thought I would ask Jesus when I get to heaven, "Why did You let such messed-up women have babies?" I then thought I already knew the answer. For folks like me to adopt and love.

The Bible is full of stories about women who yearned to have a child and could not get pregnant. They used to say their womb was cursed—how sad. Yet these women became close to my heart because God answered many of their prayers by giving them children. First there was Abraham's wife, Sarah. She was ninety years old before she had her first and only son! Her grandson, Jacob, had two wives, and the one he loved the most (Rachel) could not have children until God opened her womb and she brought forth Joseph and Benjamin. Of course, Joseph happens to be one of my favorite heroes of the faith, so that is such a sweet story to me.

Then there was Hannah. She went years as a barren woman, and when the Lord opened her womb, she gave birth to Samuel. She dedicated him to the Lord, and he went on to become one of the greatest prophets of all time. He was the one the Lord sent to find a young man to replace King Saul, who had fallen from grace. This young man was King David. Poor Samuel had to break the bad news to King Saul, but he must have loved watching the young shepherd grow into a man after God's own heart. It all started when God opened the womb of Hannah, a strong woman of prayer. It is said that Hannah went on to have many more children and was able to raise a beautiful family of her own.

In the New Testament, we are introduced to Elizabeth, who was barren in her old age. When the angel Gabriel came to give her hus-band the good news that she would have a son "born of the spirit" and to name him John (John the Baptist), he had doubts but she had joy. This baby in her womb leapt for joy when her young cousin Mary came to visit her, also bearing a child that was born of the Holy Spirit, Jesus. I never knew all these stories when I was growing up, because we never studied the Bible. I am so glad that God took spe-cial pleasure in allowing women to become mothers. I know He val-

ued motherhood. I know I do. God seems to talk more about parents, but I know He has a special place in His heart for moms. More manna for me.

Movies (Learning As We Watch!)

As I said in earlier chapters, I did not grow up reading a lot of books, but I always enjoyed going to the movies. In time, I would really like those that were true stories. When folks would say, "Did you read the book?" I would usually have to say no, but I came to love these stories that played out on the big screen. Many prompted me to learn more and to read more. So please bear with me as I list a few such movies and let you know how they spoke to me. Ten of my favorites in alphabetical order (of course!)

Movie Title	The True Story	Key Characters	Things I Learned
Amazing Grace	John Newton, a slave trader, repents of his role in this practice and becomes a pastor; he writes *Amazing Grace* and works with William Wilberforce to take the cause to the British Parliament in the last 1700s.	John Newton, a slave trader who becomes a pastor and the fight to end slavery; his friend, William Wilberforce, who took the fight to Parliament and won.	When a cause is righteous, such as ending slavery, never give up the fight! Cover your work in prayer and have the right colleagues to help in the fight; it's never too late to repent of your sins.
Argo	The true story of the CIA rescue of Americans in Tehran during the 1979 hostage crisis.	A CIA agent named Tony Mendez sneaks into Iran and spirited away six American diplomats who were hiding with Canadians.	American military covert operations are often classified and not released until many years later, here 1980 to 1997; truth can be quite a surprise.

Beyond the Gates of Splendor	This movie chronicles the events leading up to and following Operation Auca, an attempt to contact the Huaorani tribe of Ecuador, in which five American missionaries were killed.	Jim Elliott is a brave missionary who brings the gospel to a remote tribe in South America and ends up losing his life for it.	Losing your life for sharing your faith in Jesus as Savior is a beautiful thing— your entry into heaven is beyond the gates of splendor.
Luther	A German Catholic priest who turns the world upside down by challenging the practices of the Roman Catholic Church (the papacy) and translating the Bible into the language of the people.	Martin Luther, a Catholic monk who writes a thesis to challenge the pope and gets excommunicated; he wanted to "reform" the church but instead created a firestorm, including the translation of the Bible into the language of the people.	The Word of God is more important than the word of the pope. You need to study the Bible and listen to what it teaches and use that as your guide; you need to have the courage of your convictions to stand up for what is right and fight corruption at every level, and then tell the world. Man is not saved by works but by faith in Jesus as Lord and the grace of God.

Mr. Holland's Opus	*Mr. Holland's Opus* began with a movie, based on a true story, of a composer and reluctant music teacher who, over the course of his career, touched the lives of generations of students. Did he make a difference?	Glenn Holland, a music teacher in Portland, Oregon, from 1965 to 1995.	Teachers can have a huge impact on the lives of the students that they teach. Never give up! Use every tool you have to make learning fun!
Rudy	*Rudy* tells the true story of football player Daniel "Rudy" Ruettiger, who was, by all accounts, way too small to play football at the collegiate level. He not only overcame his shortcomings but also went on to play for the prestigious Notre Dame University.	Rudy is a young man with a great ambition to one day play football at Notre Dame; he achieves this goal despite all odds and using all his heart.	Never give up! Don't let others define what you can or cannot be based upon your physical attributes or intelligence— go for it! Give it all you have!
Temple Grandin	Temple Grandin is an autistic woman whose innovations revolutionized practices for the humane handling of livestock on cattle ranches and slaughterhouses.	Temple Grandin, an autistic child whose mom never gives up on her; her brain goes where normal ones can't venture, and she gives a voice to the world of autism.	Parents, never give up on your special needs child—they may have true genius to share with the world! A good "squeeze" is good for everyone.

The Imitation Game	*The Imitation Game* was largely based on the biography of Alan Turing, the Enigma, the story of breaking Hitler's code by creating a machine that would become the first computer.	Alan Turing, a brilliant mathematician who had to learn how to work with a team to break the Enigma code used by Hitler; also a gay man in an era in England when it was illegal to be gay—price paid.	You can be the smartest person in the world, but if you cannot work with others, your brilliant ideas may never amount to anything. To have one loving friend who understands you can make all the difference.
The King's Speech	King George VI suffered from a severe stutter yet made tremendous strides in his speech and in giving a speech that helped inspire England and all her colonies at the beginning of WWII.	King George (Bertie) is helped by a speech therapist (Lionel) to overcome his stutter and lead the world as king of England; his daughter becomes Queen Elizabeth II.	With the right teacher and coach, you can overcome anything, including a severe stutter. Don't be a parent who shames their child to do anything; it creates huge emotional issues. Class difference can be overcome by true friendship.
The Sound of Music	Von Trapp family singers led by a governess who becomes a mom; WWII escape from Austria then onto USA.	Maria, who thought she wanted to become a nun then fell in love.	Your plans may not match up with God's plans, so listen to your heart; there are all kinds of vocations.

The Theory of Everything	In the 1960s, Cambridge University student and future physicist Stephen Hawking fell in love with fellow collegian Jane Wilde. At twenty-one, Hawking learns that he has motor neuron disease. Despite this, and with Jane at his side, he begins an ambitious study of time, of which he has very little left, according to his doctor. He and Jane defy terrible odds and break new ground in the fields of medicine and science, achieving more than either could hope to imagine.	Stephen Hawking, a man with a serious motor neuron disease (ALS), was given two years to live, but he overcomes all odds with the help of a loving wife and becomes a very important scientist.	When you are diagnosed with a very serious disease and are told you have limited time left to live, don't give up! Keep going! Have a partner who will be at your side to help.

As you can see, there are several themes from these movies that I find inspiring:

- When a cause is righteous, never give up the fight!
- Don't believe everything the government tells you.
- Losing your life for your faith will be rewarded in heaven.
- The Word of God is more important than that of any ruler on earth.
- Teachers can have a huge impact on their students—keep going.
- Don't let others define what you can do. Go for it!

- Never give up on a special needs child; they may be a genius.
- Learn to work with others as a team. Your brilliance is best shared.
- With the right coach, you can overcome anything—keep trying.
- God has great plans for you. Listen to Him in your heart.
- A diagnosis of a terminal disease cannot stop you. Go forward!
- In all things, believe in yourself and persevere.

So if you have the chance to see a movie or read a book that is a true story, go for it. You will be amazed how you can be inspired in so many ways. Books are often better than movies, but learn from both. Always be a lifelong learner.

CHAPTER N

New Jersey (East Coast and My Jewish Family)

We all tend to remember firsts in our lives. For me, the summer after my first year of college included many firsts for me, including (1) my first time on a jet, (2) my first time traveling on trains and subways, (3) my first time working out of state, (4) my first time acting as a governess, (5) my first time being part of a Jewish family, (6) my first time to explore the East Coast of the USA, and (7) my first time seeing the ocean! Since all these occurred in the state of New Jersey, I just had to include a chapter about this state.

According to the official website for the state of New Jersey, Abraham Browning of Camden is given credit for giving New Jersey the nickname the Garden State. Browning called New Jersey the Garden State while speaking at the Philadelphia Centennial exhibition on New Jersey Day (August 24, 1876). Browning said that our Garden State is an immense barrel filled with good things to eat and open at both ends, with Pennsylvanians grabbing from one end and New Yorkers from the other. The name stuck ever since. Benjamin Franklin is credited with a similar comparison of New Jersey to a barrel tapped at both ends! So it's a garden filled with good things to eat and drink. On December 25, 1776, General George Washington and a small army of 2,400 men crossed the Delaware River at MacConkey's Ferry, in Bucks County, Pennsylvania, on their way to successfully attack a Hessian garrison of 1,500 at Trenton, New Jersey. So our early American history is tied to the capital of this state.

I flew from Duluth to Philadelphia to Trenton upon my first arrival in this state as well. Hello, New Jersey!

My Jewish family lived in a prosperous suburb called Lawrenceville, and I learned that they were not far from the Ivy League campus of Princeton University. According to www.princeton.edu, it's common knowledge that Princeton University was founded by proponents of the great revival movement, often called the Great Awakening, that swept the American colonies about 1725. The word *revival* refers to the quickening of the human heart to hear and receive the gospel in a decisive way. Wow. This gem of the Ivy League has historic Christian roots.

We did spend a month on the Jersey Shore, in a large home with a walkway to the beach—it was beautiful! I was amazed at the sand dunes and the flowers that grew there (hydrangeas). Jumping into the Atlantic Ocean was sure different from jumping into a freshwater lake—the tide! But I enjoyed playing in the waves with the kids and experiencing the taste of salt water—ha! Years later, while living on the other coast (California), I noticed the beaches had sand that was not as sugary as the East Coast's, and the Pacific Ocean was actually cooler. Awe for firsts!

As I said in chapter J (Jewish governess), I did make a trip to Atlantic City and the famous boardwalk. That was quite a thrill, including eating saltwater taffy and eating seafood for lunch. Years later, when I saw the movie *Beaches*, it reminded me of the sights and sounds of Atlantic City. I have not been back since they added all the casinos and rebuilt the city, but I think I got to see the best of this town in its simpler days. According to www.unusalfacts.com, New Jersey is the most densely populated state in the country; it is considered the diner capital of the country, with 525 diners, and has the longest boardwalk in the world. It is also home to the New York Giants football team—go figure. Quite the interesting state, for sure!

New Zealand (Honeymoon 1995—Beautiful!)

So if we were to leave Trenton, New Jersey, and fly to Auckland, New Zealand, we would travel over 8,700 miles! Yes, it is on the other side of the world! I never knew much about this beautiful country consisting of two rather-small islands until we started to plan our honeymoon to follow our February 1995 wedding. My British friends Brian and Janet told me one of their favorite places to visit was New Zealand (she had a sister who lived there), so I suggested this for our first two-week trip together. Bill agreed, and we contacted a friend who was a travel agent and started making plans. It was a new venture for all of us. We decided to stay at B&Bs during the entire trip (rather than hotels) and were so glad we did.

Here is some of what Wikipedia says about the history of this country. The history of New Zealand (Aotearoa) dates back approximately seven hundred years to when it was discovered and settled by Polynesians, who developed a distinct Māori culture. Like other Pacific cultures, Māori society was centered on kinship links and connection with the land, but unlike them, it was adapted to a cool, temperate environment rather than a warm, tropical one. The first European explorer known to sight New Zealand was Dutch navigator Abel Tasman on December 13, 1642. In 1643, he charted the west coast of the north island; his expedition then sailed back to Batavia without setting foot on New Zealand soil. British explorer James Cook, who reached New Zealand in October 1769 on the first of his three voyages, was the first European to circumnavigate and map New Zealand. From the late eighteenth century, the country was regularly visited by explorers and other sailors, missionaries, traders, and adventurers.

We had to cross the international date line to travel from California to New Zealand, leaving LA on a Sunday night and arriving on Tuesday morning—yes, we lost an entire day! New Zealand is so far south of the equator that it does have a cool temperate climate, and it is the closest jumping-off point to the South Pole (Antarctica)! So we traveled farther south than the tip of South America and came to love these two islands. We spent one week on the north island (warmer, closer to the equator) and one week on the south island (cooler and includes the Southern Alps!). We rented a car in Auckland and began to drive on the wrong side of the road. We both drove and ended up giving each other hand signals (right or left) since our brains were not wired to "hear" the right course—ha!

Our first stop was called a homestay in Auckland. This was similar to a B&B but not only included breakfast but also a gourmet evening meal—it was wonderful! Our hosts were Louisa and Cliff, and we got to meet some other travelers over our meals. It was so special. As God would have it, one of Bill's best PK friends (John) had parents who had moved from Rhodesia to the east coast of New Zealand, so we got to go and visit them for lunch one day. They were amazed that a couple on their honeymoon would take time to visit some old missionaries like them, but it was our honor and great pleasure.

We then headed north to the Bay of Islands and a small town called Russell. The beaches reminded us of Hawaii. It was simply beautiful. This was one city where our travel agent had booked a hotel, but after one look, we decided to find our own B&B. As God would have it, we went to a phone book and found the home of Ray—he had built an extra guesthouse next to his home for his own family. He also raised grapes and made his own wine. We struck it rich! We could see the entire bay with small sailboats and spent two days exploring the area. When we got home, Ray would have a little private wine-tasting time for both of us. It was great fun! We got to take a boat ride around the beautiful harbor and a cruise through a hole in the rock. We enjoyed a picnic lunch each day, usually a fresh loaf of bread, some cheese, wine, and fruit. We loved our picnics! There were so few people around that we felt like we had the island to ourselves. Since their seasons were opposite to ours, we were enjoying late summer and saw more birds than people—perfect! (Apparently, that is true, a land of more birds than people.) We also discovered excellent cuisine at modest prices.

We then traveled south to the area of Rotorua, where the Maori Indians lived. We stayed near beautiful Lake Taupo, where Bill got to do some trout fishing. We had lunch by the waterfalls, and by evening, we got to enjoy the show put on by the Maori Indians—they were very entertaining! They stick out their tongues a lot, but it is not out of disrespect. We watched Maori women dance, large Polynesian gals who could shake it up! The Maori feast was much like a luau in Hawaii, with pork cooked underground. We also visited thermal geysers and beautiful botanical gardens and traveled along Lake Rotorua.

We then took a ferry to the south island and stayed at a beautiful B&B in Queenstown, at the base of the Southern Alps. I thought I was back in Geneva, Switzerland! While staying there, we took a day trip west to the Milford Sound, an area filled with beautiful glaciers and waterfalls. Now it felt like we were in Norway. We took a bus ride out to catch a boat to cruise around the sound—it was so gorgeous. We then flew back to Queenstown on a small plane and got to see all the beauty from above. Wow! Our B&B hosts, Grant and Deborah, were very kind. We met other newlyweds at breakfast, and he was surprising her with the awesome foursome. What?

New Zealand is the home of adventure for all types, from bungee jumping to jumping off cliffs and hang gliding to riding on jet boats down roaring rivers. So what is the awesome foursome? According to www.NewZealand.com, the awesome foursome is adventure, with some of the best things to do in Queenstown, the adventure capital of the world! You can choose either the Kawarau Bridge Bungy Jump (the original) or the Nevis Bungy Jump (the biggest in New Zealand at 134 meters) and combine it with the famous Shot over Jet and a Heli-Rafting trip all in one day. It's nonstop, action-packed adrenaline activity! The new bride was pretty scared. We would be too. We did go and observe some of these adventures but did not do all of them.

We took a gondola up the mountain and, after hiking, stopped for one of our wine-and-cheese picnics. We then went down the mountain and got onto jet boats—pure fun! We did stop and enjoy many beautiful coves along the way with sparkling clear water. When we got back to our B&B, we drank sherry to warm up. Yes, we used sweatshirts on many of our adventures! We also enjoyed a pub lunch in Queenstown and thought we were back in England—so fun! We did go and watch bungee cord jumpers at this old historic bridge—lots of crazy people like to hang upside down, I guess!

We then traveled onto the Hermitage Lodge at Mount Cook, the highest point in New Zealand. We had beautiful accommodations, a real cozy suite. We took a four-wheel-drive tour of a glacier and had dinner at the lodge restaurant. Such amazing food (fresh fish) and desserts filled with fresh fruit. Bill got to talking to the waiter about trout fishing, and would you believe it, that guy took him to his favorite fishing place the next day. What a friendly country, indeed!

I took a hike in the rocky areas while Bill fished, and we joined up for lunch afterward. Then we took a ride on another boat across the glaciers. We could touch the icebergs! We did enjoy another glacier picnic of wine and cheese one more day before heading to the southern part of the southern island, Christchurch. Now we thought for sure we were back in London!

We took a city bus tour on a red double-decker bus and then took a walking tour of this charming place. We punted on the Avon River (like a gondola) and spent time at the Cathedral at the town center. We stayed at Eliza's B&B and enjoyed our first king-size bed and more wonderful meals. We made it to an exhibit at the International Antarctic Center—what an interesting exhibit. We also discovered the beautiful music of pan flutes at the local park. Christchurch was clearly a very quaint place.

It was then time to get back on Air New Zealand and get on our flight home. With headwinds, we had to make a stop on the Fiji Islands as well as Hawaii, but we gained that day back that we had lost two weeks earlier, so it was the longest day of our life! But it was so worth it. We plan to go back someday. As God would have it, we were recently in a Breaking Bread Together (BBT) group dinner at our home, and one of the couples brought a good friend visiting from out of town. You know where he was from? New Zealand! So now we have another new friend to go and visit. God is so good. So much manna. So much of his beautiful creation to enjoy.

Numbers (They Mean Something to God)

I have heard that certain numbers have a special meaning to God, such as 7 being the perfect number, such as seven days in a week, the time for all of creation. But during a recent women's Bible study, I heard the teacher say that many numbers have a great meaning to God, so I decided to do some research. After all, I do have a degree in math and an interest in mathematics and numbers. I have heard 666 is Satan's number, but what about other numbers? Here are some fun findings from www.bible study.org. Consider this chapter just for fun. Here are just some examples.

The number 1 is only divisible by itself. It is independent of any other numerals yet composes them all. It symbolizes in the Bible the unity and primacy, and the oneness of the Godhead. What is known as the Shema (or Shema Yisrael), a quote of verse 4 in Deuteronomy 6:4 that is often used in Jewish prayer services, attests to this fact. The number 1 also represents the unity between God the Father and His Son, Jesus (John 10:30). Jesus, by His singular sacrifice, has made possible the forgiveness of all our sins. He is the one Mediator and Shepherd (1 Tim. 2:5; John 10:16) in the life of a Christian.

The number 2 conveys the meaning of a union, division, or the verification of facts by witnesses. A man and woman, though two in number, are made one in marriage (Gen. 2:23–24). There is also the union between Christ and the church (see 1 Corinthians 12). The testimony of God is divided into Old and New Testaments. His agreements with mankind are divided into old and new covenants. And though 2 in number, God the Father and God the Son (Jesus Christ) compose a single Godhead. The first man, Adam, sinned and brought death and destruction into the world. Jesus, however, as the second (or last) Adam, brings the hope of the resurrection and eternal life (1 Cor. 15:21–22, 45–49).

The number 3 is used 467 times in the Bible. It pictures completeness, though to a lesser degree than 7. The meaning of this number derives from the fact that it is the first of four spiritually perfect numerals (the others being 7, 10, and 12). The three righteous patriarchs before the flood were Abel, Enoch, and Noah. After the deluge, there were the righteous fathers, Abraham, Isaac, and Jacob (later renamed Israel). There are twenty-seven books in the New Testament, which is 3 x 3 x 3, or completeness to the third power. Jesus prayed three times in the garden of Gethsemane before His arrest. He was placed on the cross at the third hour of the day (9:00 a.m.) and died at the ninth hour (3:00 p.m.). There were three hours of darkness that covered the land while Jesus was suffering on the cross from the sixth hour to the ninth hour. Three is the number of resurrection. Christ rose on the third day: Friday, day 1; Saturday, day 2; Sunday, day 3.

The number 4 derives its meaning from creation. On the fourth day of what is called creation week, God completed the material universe. On this day He brought into existence our sun, the moon, and all the stars (Gen. 1:14–19). Their purpose was not only to give off light but also to divide the day from the night on earth, thus becoming a basic demarcation of time. They were also made to be a type of signal that would mark off the days, years, and seasons. Interestingly, the Hebrew word for *seasons* in Genesis 1:14 is *moed* (Strong's Concordance #H4150), which literally translated is "appointed times" (divine appointments) in reference to God's festivals. This is the earliest known allusion to what would later be called the holy (or feast) days (periods) of worship, which are seven in number. The fourth of the Ten Commandments is to remember and keep God's holy Sabbath day (Exod. 20:9–11). The Sabbath day is tied directly to the creation week. God Himself made the period between Friday sunset and Saturday sunset extra special when He rested on it after bringing everything into existence the previous six days (Gen. 2:1–3; Exod. 20:11).

The number 5 symbolizes God's grace, goodness, and favor toward humans and is mentioned 318 times in Scripture; 5 is the number of grace, and multiplied by itself, which is 25, is grace upon grace (John 1:16). The Ten Commandments contains two sets of five commandments. The first five commandments are related to our treatment and relationship with God, and the last five concern our relationship with other humans. (Now I beg to differ with this one, since commandment 5 is "Honor your father and mother," a human relationship.)

The number 6 symbolizes man and human weakness, the evils of Satan, and the manifestation of sin. Man was created on the sixth day. Men are appointed six days to labor. A Hebrew slave was to serve six years and be released in the seventh year. Six years were appointed for the land to be sown and harvested. The number 6 is also associated with Satan in his temptation of Jesus. The bringing together of three 6s is the number and mark of the end-time beast of Revelation. As such, it represents the very best system of governance that mankind can produce without God and under the constant influence of his chief adversary.

Used 735 times (54 times in the book of Revelation alone), the number 7 is the foundation of God's Word. If we include with this count how many times *sevenfold* (6) and *seventh* (119) are used, our total jumps to 860 references. Seven is the number of completeness and perfection (both physical and spiritual). It derives much of its meaning from being tied directly to God's creation of all things. According to some Jewish traditions, the creation of Adam occurred on September 26, 3760 BC (or the first day of Tishri, which is the seventh month on the Hebrew calendar). The word *created* is used seven times describing God's creative work (Gen. 1:1, 21, 27, three times; 2:3; 2:4). There are seven days in a week, and God's Sabbath is on the seventh day. The Bible, as a whole, was originally divided into seven major divisions. They are (1) the Law; (2) the Prophets; (3) the Writings, or Psalms; (4) the Gospels and Acts; (5) the General Epistles; (6) the Epistles of Paul; and (7) the book of Revelation. The total number of originally inspired books was forty-nine, or 7 x 7, demonstrating the absolute perfection of the Word of God.

The number 8 in the Bible represents a new beginning, meaning a new order or creation, and man's true born-again event when he is resurrected from the dead into eternal life. Like the Old Testament Passover lamb, Jesus was selected as the Lamb to take away man's sins on the Hebrew day of Nisan 10 (April 1, AD 30; John 12:28–29). He was crucified on Nisan 14 (Wednesday, April 5 in AD 30). His resurrection occurred, exactly as he stated, three days and three nights after He was buried, which was at the end of the weekly Sabbath day that fell on Nisan 17 (seventeen symbolizes victory). Nisan 17 was also the eighth day, counting inclusively from the time Christ was selected as man's sacrificial Lamb. All this bears a record of Jesus's perfect sacrifice and His complete victory over death.

Used forty-nine times in Scripture, the number 9 symbolizes divine completeness or conveys the meaning of finality. Christ died at the ninth hour of the day, or 3:00 p.m., to make the way of salvation open to everyone. The Day of Atonement (Yom Kippur) is the only one of God's annual feast days of worship that requires believers to fast for one day. This special day, considered by many Jews to be the holiest of the year, begins at sunset on day 9 of the seventh Hebrew month (Lev. 23:32). The number 9 also represents the fruits of God's Holy Spirit, which are faithfulness, gentleness, goodness, joy, kindness, long-suffering, love, peace, and self-control (Gal. 5:22–23).

In the Bible, the number 10 is used 242 times. The designation *tenth* is used 79 times. Ten is also viewed as a complete and perfect number, as is 3, 7, and 12. It is made up of 4, the number of the physical creation, and 6, the number of men. As such, 10 signifies testimony, law, responsibility, and the completeness of order. In Genesis 1 we find the phrase "God said" ten times, which is a testimony of His creative power. God gave the Ten Commandments to man. Ten, therefore, represents man's responsibility to keep the commandments. A tithe is a tenth of our earnings and is a testimony of our faith in the Lord. The Passover lamb was selected on day 10 of the first month (Exod. 12:3), as was Jesus, the Lamb that takes away the sins of the world (John 12:28–29; 1 Cor. 5:7). Day 10 of the seventh month is also the holy day known as the Day of Atonement. This unique day of fasting pictures the removal of Satan, the author of sin, before the millennial reign of Jesus begins (Rev. 20:1–2).

The number 12 can be found in 187 places in God's Word. Revelation alone has twenty-two occurrences of the number. The meaning of 12, which is considered a perfect number, is that it symbolizes God's power and authority, as well as serving as a perfect governmental foundation. It can also symbolize completeness of the nation of Israel as a whole. For example, Jacob (Israel) had twelve sons, each of which represented a tribe begun by a prince, for twelve princes total. Ishmael, who was born to Abraham through Hagar, also had twelve princes. God specified that twelve unleavened cakes of bread be placed every week in the temple with frankincense next to each of the two piles that were to be made. The priests were commanded to change the bread every Sabbath day (Lev. 24).

These are just a few examples. I do *not* believe in numerology, which is defined in Wikipedia as any belief in the divine or mystical relationship between a number and one or more coinciding events. It is also the study of the numerical value of the letters in words, names, and ideas. It is often associated with the paranormal, alongside astrology and similar divinatory arts. There is certainly a spiritual battle going on in the world, but I believe that such things as your horoscope are evil and should not be used for any guidance in one's life. Flee. This is metaphysical science. It is often part of the occult.

I have heard Nancy Reagan would go to a numerologist to predict the future of what was going to happen to her husband, Ronald Reagan. How sad. I have also read that after Ronald Reagan had his near-death experience in April 1981 (only three months after taking office), he told the Lord he would dedicate the rest of his presidency to Him if He saved his life. He was saved. There are many such great stories by his son Michael Reagan in his book *Twice Adopted*. Michael was adopted into the Reagan family and also into the family of God, so he considered himself to be "twice adopted." He has quite a testimony to share. I would recommend this good read.

Satan is such a copycat. I think because he knows that numbers have meaning to God, he also wanted to use numbers in a metaphysical way to mislead people. I once had such a spiritual person tell me a lot about my fall in life that happened to be true. I met her through a Methodist pastor who thought she was real but then realized she was evil. Yes, even the Bible says the demons knew who Jesus was, and they shuddered. We must be aware of such twisted use of God's Word and never forget what Satan spoke in the garden of Eden. Did God really say? Chilling.

CHAPTER P

Patrick (A Great Friend, a Saint)

In the Catholic world, especially among the Irish Catholics (lots of priests come from there), Saint Patrick is a highly revered saint. Here is what Wikipedia has to say about him. Saint Patrick was a fifth-century Romano-British Christian missionary and bishop in Ireland. Known as the apostle of Ireland, he is the primary patron saint of Ireland. When Patrick was sixteen years old, he was captured by Irish pirates. They brought him to Ireland, where he was sold into slavery in Dalriada. There his job was to tend sheep, which he did for the next six years. (So that may be where the Pittsburgh Pirates got their name?)

According to www.Irish-geneology.com, during this period, he became increasingly religious. He considered his kidnapping and imprisonment as a punishment for his lack of faith and spent a lot of time in prayer. After a vision led him to stow away on a boat bound for Britain, Patrick escaped back to his family. There he had a dream that the Irish were calling him back to Ireland to tell them about God. This inspired him to return to Ireland as a priest, but not immediately. At this point he didn't feel adequately prepared for a life as a missionary. His studies took him to France, where he was trained in a monastery, and he dedicated this period of his life to learning. It was some twelve years before he returned to Irish shores as a bishop sent with the pope's blessing. From this time on, he became beloved as the bishop of Ireland.

KATHY KRAMER

As we all know, Saint Patrick's Day is celebrated every March 17 in America, the date of Saint Patrick's death. The holiday has evolved into a celebration of Irish culture with parades, special foods, music, dancing, drinking, and a whole lot of green. So how did all this tradition start? According to www.history.com, here are seven fun facts about Saint Patrick's Day.

1. The real Saint Patrick was born in Britain. As stated above, he was captured by pirates and brought to Ireland at age sixteen. (But he did spend most of his life in Ireland.)
2. There were no snakes around for Saint Patrick to banish from Ireland; early history shows that the region was covered in ice and would have been too cold for the reptiles. (So much for myths.)
3. Leprechauns are likely based on Celtic fairies, the red-haired, green-clothed gents and ladies. The original Irish name for these figures is lubricin, meaning "small-bodied fellow." The Celtic belief was that these were tiny men and women who could use their magical powers to serve good or evil. In Celtic folktales, leprechauns were cranky souls responsible for mending the shoes of the other fairies (oh, dear).
4. The Shamrock was considered a sacred plant. The shamrock, a three-leaf clover, has been associated with Ireland for centuries. It was called the "seamroy" by the Celts and was considered a sacred plant that symbolized the arrival of spring. According to legend, Saint Patrick used the plant as a visual guide when explaining the Holy Trinity. By the seventeenth century, the shamrock had become a symbol of emerging Irish nationalism. (How special!)
5. The first Saint Patrick's Day Parade was held in America in 1601 in the area of Saint Augustine, Florida. The parade and a Saint Patrick's Day celebration a year earlier were organized by the Spanish Colonies Irish vicar Ricardo Artur. More than a century later, homesick Irish soldiers serving in the English military marched in Boston in 1737

and in New York City on March 17. Enthusiasm for the Saint Patrick's Day parades in New York City, Boston, and other early American cities only grew from there. (Those Irish soldiers don't know what they started!)

6. The Irish were once scorned in America. While Irish Americans are now proud to showcase their heritage, the Irish were not always celebrated by fellow Americans. Beginning in 1845, a devastating potato blight caused widespread hunger throughout Ireland. While approximately one million perished, another two million abandoned their land in the largest single population movement of the nineteenth century. Most of the exiles, nearly a quarter of the Irish nation, came to the shores of the United States. Once they arrived, the Irish refugees were looked down upon as disease-ridden, unskilled, and a drain on welfare budgets. (So sad.)

7. Corned beef and cabbage was an American innovation. The meal that became a Saint Patrick's Day staple across the country—corned beef and cabbage—was an American innovation. While ham and cabbage were eaten in Ireland, corned beef offered a cheaper substitute for impoverished immigrants. Irish Americans living in the slums of Lower Manhattan in the late nineteenth and early twentieth century purchased leftover corned beef from ships returning from the tea trade in China. The Irish would boil the beef three times, the last time with cabbage, to remove some of the brine. (Yuck!)

So why do I list all these fun facts about the second biggest drinking holiday in America (only surpassed by New Year's Eve)? I don't even have any Irish blood in me, but I do love the fun that the Irish folk have added to our country! After my dad died, my mom started drinking and ended up in alcohol rehab and AA. It was a perfect family irony that she died on Saint Patrick's Day! Her brother (also in AA) preceded her in death on what day? You guessed it, New

Year's Eve! So who says God does not have a sense of humor? (Maybe He is partly Irish?)

I met *my* Patrick in the summer of 1977 when I moved to Santa Barbara. The fellow I started dating and eventually married worked for the district attorney's office, and Patrick was the assistant DA. He was the heart of many a party and does have a wicked sense of humor! He originally came from Pittsburgh, where he attended Duquesne University (good Catholic boy), and he thought all Pittsburgh teams were the best. I would humor him and cheer for his teams as long as the Steelers weren't playing the Vikings or the Pirates going against my Minnesota Twins. I even bought him a homer hankie the year the Twins won the World Series!

My ex-husband asked Patrick to be in our Minnesota wedding, so he flew back to my home state and he loved meeting the rest of my family. He knew that one of his idols, Bob Dylan, came from Hibbing, Minnesota, so we found the place he was raised and toasted to him at the Northern Lights Bar. That was Patrick—let's go to a bar and have some fun! When my parents would come to California, he would always have them over for dinner. They got a kick out of him. To know Patrick is to love him—a generous, kind soul.

When my marriage fell apart and we sold our home, it took me three weekends to move into the condo I had bought (bank delays). The first one to get all my items into the garage at our home that had sold, the second one to move to the condo garage, and finally, the third to move everything from my condo garage up to my new penthouse location. He and several other DA office friends were there to help me. I stayed at their home during all this—they were so good to me. Many of these folks were my first and best California friends, and I am forever grateful for that.

When my job in Scottsdale fell apart, he called and urged me to sell my home and move back to California and stay with them for a while, until I got my feet on the ground. Since I was "frozen" in a state of anxiety and depression, I would not make that move for another thirteen months, when my sister Sue conceived a plan with Patrick to come and get me and take me back to Santa Barbara. God bless them both. That was pure manna from God at a time I did not know if I could ever recover. But I did, and I have Pat and Esther to thank for that first big step.

When my new husband, Bill, met Patrick, he immediately liked him very much! We enjoyed so many parties and dinner at his home and also loved to pick avocados from his large crop of trees and other fruit and vegetables he grew (such a farmer at heart). So you can see why the name Patrick has such a special place in my heart. God put him into my life for such a time as this on more than one occasion. So I celebrate this holiday every year with great gusto! Thank you to my dear friend Patrick.

Paul (My Brother, a Great Saint)

Paul was the firstborn child in our family, and I was second born. When I started reading the Bible, I could not help but draw the comparison to the first two children born to Adam and Eve, Cain and Abel. Here is a summary of what the book of Genesis says about this rivalry (from Wikipedia). In the biblical book of Genesis, Cain and Abel are the first two sons of Adam and Eve. Cain, the firstborn, was a farmer, and his brother Abel was a shepherd. The brothers made sacrifices to Yahweh, each of his own produce, but Yahweh favored Abel's sacrifice instead of Cain's. Cain then murdered Abel, where-upon Yahweh punished Cain by condemning him to a life of wandering. Cain then dwelt in the land of Nod (wandering), where he built a city and fathered the line of descendants beginning with Enoch. After Cain murdered Abel and God came looking for him, his response to God was, "I am not my brother's keeper." Ouch. Such lack of reverence for God.

So what does the name Paul mean? According to www.sheknows.com, the biblical meaning of the name Paul is "small; little." Ouch. If Paul ever knew that was the meaning of his name, I am sure he would have one more reason to hate my dad. Yet according to www.behindthename.com, Paul was an important leader of the early Christian church. According to Acts in the New Testament, he was a Jewish Roman citizen who converted to Christianity after the resurrected Jesus appeared to him. After this, he traveled the Eastern Mediterranean as a missionary. His original Hebrew name was Saul. Many of the epistles in the New Testament were authored by him. Due to the renown of Saint Paul, the name became common among early Christians. It was borne by a number of other early saints and six popes. In England it was relatively rare during the Middle Ages but became more frequent beginning in the seventeenth century. A notable bearer was the American Revolutionary War figure Paul Revere (1735–1818), who warned of the advance of the British Army. It is borne by British musician Paul McCartney (1942–). This is also the name of the legendary American lumberjack Paul Bunyan. Now, that makes it a great Minnesota name!

I can only imagine how many times my brother Paul wanted to kill me. He was firstborn but never the favored one by our father. Paul has asked that I not include his story in my book, so I will honor that request. We have not met his current wife (Diane) yet but hope to make a trip to Idaho, where he now lives his life. Her name means "luminous and perfect." We sure hope it fits!

My Bible verse for Paul: "Therefore, if anyone is in Christ, he is a new creation. The old has passed away" (2 Cor. 5:17). Go forward in joy and make every day count. May this part of your life be the best one—truly blessed.

Prayer (God's Special Bowl in Heaven)

When you grow up in a large Catholic family, you are taught prayers to memorize, but not much about prayer as a way to talk one-on-one to God. We learned the Our Father, the Hail Mary, the Glory Be, the Apostles' Creed, and our nighttime prayer, "Now I lay me down to sleep, I pray the Lord my soul to keep; if I should die before I wake, pray the Lord my soul to take. Amen." These types of prayers don't tend to bring one closer to Jesus, but they do count as a check-off of the things you do to get to heaven—part of the expected works of the church.

When I was in college, I was part of a Christian retreat team that offered teen retreats at a place owned by the Catholic diocese called the Welch Center. It was during this experience that our team would often pray before and after our weekends together that I seemed to learn more about spontaneous prayer. I liked it. Many years, while studying the book of Revelation, I found out an interesting thing. When the earth is destroyed by God, who creates a new heaven and a new earth, one thing remains in a bowl in heaven: the prayers of God's chosen ones. Wow.

According to Revelation 5:9 (NIV), "And when he had taken it, the four living creatures and the twenty-four elders fell down before the Lamb. Each one had a harp and they were holding golden bowls full of incense, which are the prayers of God's people." Wow. There are bowls of incense in heaven that are our prayers and all those around these bowls sing, "Worthy is the Lamb!" Jesus Himself was the best example of "going away to a private place each day to spend time with his Father." Oh, that we adopted members of his family would do the same! I do talk to Jesus throughout every day, but I can always improve my prayer life. Who can't?

When I joined Moms in Prayer in 2007, I learned what "praying in one accord" means. According to www.MomsInPrayer.org, one-accord prayer is praying as a conversation where we become more aware of the other person; we take turns and only one person talks, and everyone stays on the same subject. One-accord prayer is spirit-directed prayer. The Holy Spirit within us moves in our hearts, initiates our requests, and leads us in how we should pray. Therefore, the focus is on God and not on the approval of others. This is based upon Acts 1:14. All these with one accord were devoting themselves to prayer, together with the women and Mary, the mother of Jesus, and His brothers (Acts 1:14 ESV).

One-accord prayer is praying one subject at a time. If a mom starts to pray on a particular subject, the other moms need to be keenly aware of her request. Hear her, hear. Then, when she is finished, other moms may feel free to pray on the subject as well. One mom can pray on more than one subject if the Holy Spirit leads her, but after her subject is exhausted, the Holy Spirit will lead another mom to pray for a new subject.

One-accord prayer is brief, honest, and to the point. Prayers should only be a few sentences, remembering that good conversation is letting someone else have a chance. It is also spoken in conversational language. You speak to the Lord with the simplicity of a child talking to her father. The more natural the prayer, the more personal He becomes to you. So why pray together like this? Here are some reasons noted in scripture.

- Matthew 18:20 (ESV): "For where two or three are gathered in my name, there am I among them." God promises He will be present with you.
- Galatians 6:2 (ESV): "Bear one another's burdens, and so fulfill the law of Christ." Burdens shared become lighter.
- Matthew 18:19 (ESV): "Again I say to you, if two of you agree on earth about anything they ask, it will be done for them by my Father in heaven." When there is agreement in what is asked, no room is left for doubt or wavering.
- 1 Thessalonians 5:11 (AMP): "Therefore encourage and comfort one another and build up one another, just as you are doing." As we pray with other moms, trust develops, and we become more transparent in our prayers. Meeting together will build each other up in faith. I love this passage so much. When I led a small group for moms with disabled children, I used this verse for our ministry.

Many say they don't have the words to say, but the Bible says the Spirit knows how to pray on our behalf. According to Romans 8:26 (NIV), in the same way, the Spirit helps us in our weakness. We do not know what we ought to pray for, but the Spirit Himself intercedes for us through wordless groans. "For we do not know what to pray for as we ought, but the Spirit himself intercedes for us with groanings too deep for words." So we don't need all the right words. God knows. His Spirit knows. His Son listens. Isn't that special? I have heard some say they prayed for many years for someone in their family to be saved and it was not until their deathbed that it happened. So never give up! Prayer is so important. I know many folks were praying for me during my time of depression in Scottdale. I truly believe it made all the difference. So never give up on prayer. You could save someone's life!

I have to add a PS about one of my all-time favorite movies. It is about "answered prayer." At the beginning of the movie, there is an angel in heaven that notices a lot of people are praying for a guy named George. I will paraphrase some of their prayers. "Dear Lord, please help my husband, George. He is a good man, but he is in trouble." "Dear God, please help our daddy. He is gone, and we need to find him because we love him." "Dear Lord, please help my son George through whatever is happening to him. He needs your help." "Dear God, please help our friend George." Do you remember this movie too? *It's a Wonderful Life*. George Bailey has an eccentric uncle who accidentally misplaces a big deposit while at the bank. George finds out and says, "We are ruined!" He gets so upset he goes to the local bridge in town and plans to jump off and take his life. Then an angel named Clarence jumps in first, and George jumps in to save him and shows him what the world would have been like if he had never been born.

It shows how our life affects so many others around us. A brother who would have died as a child in a winter sledding accident instead of saving a ship of soldiers as a military pilot. A pharmacist who would have gone to prison for adding poison to a prescription that kills a person in town instead of being stopped by young George. An uncle who loses his mind when his actions lead to the bankruptcy of the Bailey Building and Loan—he goes to an insane asylum instead of keeping the Building and Loan going. Bailey Park of lovely little homes for the working class is never built, so folks are left to live in the slums of Mr. Potter, the evil rich man in the story. And his wife, Mary, never gets married but ends up as a spinster who is now the lonely town librarian. And so many more. George finds you; he really did have a wonderful life, and he should never have considered ending his "miserable life." Such is the power of prayer! The movie ends with "Hark! The Herald Angels Sing." What a great Christmas story. Answered prayer.

CHAPTER R

Rebecca (A Friend and a Biblical Wife)

Don't you love stories of love at first sight? Such is the case for one couple in the book of Genesis—Isaac and Rebecca. Issacs's dad (Abraham) sends a trusted servant to go back to his home to find his son a proper wife. According to www.theisrealbible.com, here is the story of this moment in the Old Testament:

> After burying his own wife, Abraham turns his attention to finding a wife for their son, Isaac. Knowing as he does that Isaac is meant to be his spiritual heir, not just any woman will do. Nor may Isaac leave the Holy Land for any reason. Therefore, Abraham charges his trusty servant to select a wife for Isaac from among Abraham's own kin back in Aram-naharaim. If the woman the servant finds refuses to come, Abraham assures him he has at least done his duty. The servant swears to uphold Abraham's requests and he sets off, with ten camels and an array of gifts in tow. When the servant arrives at the well on the outskirts of town, he turns to God for direction. He sets a sign for himself: the woman who not only offers him water, but his camels, too, is the right one for Isaac. Before he even completes his prayer, the servant spies young Rebecca,

daughter of Bethuel and granddaughter of Abraham's brother, Nahor. He asks her for water, and she replies by giving it to him, then watering all his camels. Watching her work, the servant becomes convinced that this woman is destined to marry his master's son, and he brings forth the jewelry which he carried for that purpose. He asks who her family is and if they will take him in overnight. She confirms her identity and invites him to stay with her family. The servant responds by thanking God for bringing him to the right place. (Gen. 24:1–27)

Rebecca goes back to the land given to Abraham, and when she meets Isaac, it is love at first sight for both of them. Sweet.

The Israel Bible discusses the significance of the caravan which the servant brought with him. The Hebrew word for camel, gamal, also means 'to be independent'. It is used throughout the Bible to describe weaning children or ripening fruit (see Genesis 21:8, Numbers 17:23). According to Rabbi Natan Slifkin, the camel earned this name because it is "able to survive in the absence of water for many months." How fitting that this symbol of independence carried back Rebecca, who made an independent choice to join Isaac in the Holy Land of Israel!

According to Wikipedia, Isaac was forty years old when he married Rebecca. Twenty years elapsed before they had children; throughout that time, both Isaac and Rebecca prayed fervently to God for offspring. God eventually answered Isaac's prayers, and Rebecca conceived. The Bible states that Isaac was sixty years old when the twin boys, named Esau and Jacob, were born. Rebecca favored the second born (Jacob), and so did God. According to www.enterthebible.org

(Gen. 25:21–27), "Isaac prayed to the Lord for his wife, because she was barren; and the Lord granted his prayer, and his wife Rebekah conceived. The children struggled together within her; and she said, 'If it is to be this way, why do I live?" So she went to inquire of the Lord. And the Lord said to her, 'Two nations are in your womb, and two peoples born of you shall be divided; one shall be stronger than the other, the elder shall serve the younger.' When her time to give birth was at hand, there were twins in her womb. The first came out red, all his body like a hairy mantle; so they named him Esau. Afterwards his brother came out, with his hand grabbing Esau's heel; so he was named Jacob." Isaac was sixty years old when she bore them. When the boys grew up, Esau was a skillful hunter, a man of the field, while Jacob was a quiet man living in tents. Isaac loved Esau, because he was fond of games, but Rebekah loved Jacob. Oh no, another story of the second born being favored over the firstborn!

As Isaac grew older, his sight was failing, and Rebecca devised a scheme whereby Jacob could trick his dad into giving him the first blessing. While Esau hunted, she made stew from wild meat and had Jacob put on his brother's clothes. He brought the stew to Isaac and claimed to be Esau so Jacob blessed him. When the real Esau returned from hunting, he was furious! So was Isaac, but he could not take back the blessing. Hence, the "heal-grabber" and "deceiver" named Jacob would become the son of the blessing and the one who had twelve sons who would become the twelve tribes of Israel. Sometimes God's plans seem so strange. So unfair. But He is God. I often thought Rebecca was a bad mom for her role in this story, but she was doing the will of God, which was to bless the younger son, the one who would rule over his older brother. Sounds like the story of Ishmael and Isaac—the second born gets the blessing. But God is in charge.

When I moved back to California in the spring of 1990, I started to attend the church where Bill and I met. He had been part of a singles group in that church, which included many people who have remained some of our lifelong friends. Among them was a couple named Paul and Becky. Paul was older than Becky, and they, too, could not have children. After we adopted our two boys from foster care, they were inspired to do the same, and they adopted a foster child named Austin. He will graduate from high school in 2021. It has been a parenting challenge for both of them, but they have worked through all the bumps. When I found out Becky was from my home state of Minnesota, we became very good friends. To this day, we stay in close touch, and I treasure the "Rebecca" in my life.

I have one other Becky in my life who hosts a Moms in Prayer college and career group. She is such a servant of the Lord! I have joined this group as often as possible and have been blessed by her warm hospitality. She raised a boy and a girl with her son (Michael) ending up in a wheelchair. She has been a loving, supportive mom during his journey in life. She told me about his love of sled hockey. I grew up in a state where hockey reigned, but I never heard of such a thing. So I went to watch a sled hockey tournament. Amazing!

According to www.disabledsportsusa.org, *sled hockey* (sledge hockey in Canada and Europe) is a sit-down version of ice hockey for players whose disability prevents them from playing stand-up hockey. How is it played? There is little difference in sled hockey and stand-up hockey. The goal is still to put the puck in the net. The players just do it from their sleds! The teams sit on the sides of the rink and are called in and out to sub for one another, just like in regular hockey. I must share this with my friend Joni Eareckson Tada someday! So exciting.

As it turns out, this friend Becky did marry a Brit from South Africa, so we have another thing in common—falling in love with one of those charming gentlemen from Great Britain. We still need to have tea and share stories. In the meantime, I want to do a shout-out to my MIP friend Becky, who has the gift of hospitality and has the joy of the Lord!

So what does the name Rebecca mean? According to www.urbandictionary.com, Rebecca is the name reserved only for the genuine and best women on earth. They are cute, beautiful, very smart, driven, have a wonderful and playful personality, and have this cute awkwardness about them. They are fun-loving, adventurous, and silly. Rebecca has the most amazing eyes ever. She always makes people laugh. It's hard to get close to Rebecca at first because they choose their friends wisely. This is a good thing, though, because if they talk to you, they really mean everything they say and are very straightforward about their feelings toward someone. Rebeccas severely underestimate everything about themselves, so you need to constantly prove to them that they are much better than they think. It's impossible to be actually mad at a Rebecca, no matter what they do, because they are so lovable.

According to www.behindthename.com, the name Rebecca comes from the Hebrew name Rivqah, from an unattested root probably meaning "join, tie, snare." This is the name of the wife of Isaac and the mother of Esau and Jacob in the Old Testament. It came into use as a Christian name after the Protestant Reformation, and it was popular with the Puritans in the seventeenth century. And don't forget the book *Rebecca of Sunnybrook Farm*. *Rebecca of Sunnybrook Farm* is a classic 1903 American children's novel by Kate Douglas Wiggin that tells the story of Rebecca Rowena Randall and her aunts, one stern and one kind, in the fictional village of Riverboro, Maine (Wikipedia). Lord, thank You for bringing several Beckys into my life!

Religion versus Relationship (What Jesus Taught)

There are many religions in the world, including several denominations of Christians (i.e., Catholics, Evangelicals, Baptists, Methodists, Lutherans, etc.), as well as other world religions, such as the Jewish faith, the Mormon faith, the Muslim faith, the Buddhist faith, the Hindu faith. These are all man-made institutions! When someone says to us, "You are the religious ones in the family," we say, "Oh, please don't say that." The Pharisees were religious, and Jesus soundly denounced them! We have a personal relationship with Jesus as our Lord and Savior. So what's the difference?

In a religion, you follow rules and traditions established by that faith, and the prize is that you get to go to heaven (or some type of eternal paradise). Really? I think Jesus looks down from heaven and sheds many tears over what we have made from what He intended when the world was formed and human beings were created in the likeness of God. Since I now attend a Presbyterian Church, I will share the primary belief of this faith. Presbyterian theology typically emphasizes the sovereignty of God, the authority of the Scripture, and the necessity of grace through faith in Christ. The chief end of man is to glorify God and love Him forever. Wow. This is so different from the list of rules I was taught to follow in the Catholic Church.

When Jesus was getting ready to leave this world and go back to heaven, He prayed a high priestly prayer over His disciples. I think it is well worth seeing his emphasis.

In John chapter 17 (ESV), here is what Jesus said:

> When Jesus had spoken these words, he lifted up his eyes to heaven, and said, "Father, the hour has come; glorify your Son that the Son may glorify you, since you have given him authority over all flesh, to give eternal life to all whom you have given him. And this is eternal life, that they know you, the only true God, and Jesus Christ whom you have sent. I glorified you on earth, having accomplished the work that you gave me to do. And now, Father, glorify me in your own presence with the glory that I had with you before the world existed.
>
> "I have manifested your name to the people whom you gave me out of the world. Yours they were, and you gave them to me, and they have kept your word. Now they know that everything that you have given me is from you. For I have given them the words that you gave me, and they have received them and have come to know in truth that I came from you; and they have believed that you sent me. I am praying for them. I am not praying for the world but for those whom you have given me, for they are yours. All mine are yours, and yours are mine, and I am

glorified in them. And I am no longer in the world, but they are in the world, and I am coming to you. Holy Father, keep them in your name, which you have given me, that they may be one, even as we are one. While I was with them, I kept them in your name, which you have given me. I have guarded them, and not one of them has been lost except the son of destruction, that the Scripture might be fulfilled. But now I am coming to you, and these things I speak in the world, that they may have my joy fulfilled in themselves. I have given them your word, and the world has hated them because they are not of the world, just as I am not of the world. I do not ask that you take them out of the world, but that you keep them from the evil one. They are not of the world, just as I am not of the world. Sanctify them in the truth; your word is truth. As you sent me into the world, so I have sent them into the world. And for their sake I consecrate myself, that they also may be sanctified in truth.

I do not ask for these only, but also for those who will believe in me through their word, that they may all be one, just as you, Father, are in me, and I in you, that they also may be in us, so that the world may believe that you have sent me. The glory that you have given me I have given to them, that they may be one even as we are one, I in them and you in me, that they may become perfectly one, so that the world may know that you sent me and loved them even as you loved me. Father, I desire that they also, whom you have given me, may be with me where I am, to see my glory that you have given me because you loved me before the foundation of the world. O righteous Father, even though the world does not know you, I know you, and these know that you have sent me. I made known to them your name, and I will continue to make it known, that the love with which you have loved me may be in them, and I in them."

This prayer is all about the relationship Jesus had with God the Father—they were one. He prayed that we would have this same type of relationship! When people spend their lives following rules, it will never change their heart, and that is what Jesus is all about—a change in our heart so that we are born again and filled with the Holy Spirit, who guides us.

Some might ask, Then why did God give us the Ten Commandments? I think Wikipedia gives us the most succinct summary. The Ten Commandments are a summary of the requirements of a works covenant (called the old covenant), given on Mount Sinai to the nascent nation of Israel. The old covenant came to an end at the cross and is therefore not in effect. They do reflect the eternal character of God and serve as a paragon of morality. The other good summary I have read is to show us our sin nature and guidelines for a holy life. It is interesting that these commandments are the foundation of many of our current legal codes (laws). People still need a code of conduct to follow to live a good, moral life.

When laws are broken, there are consequences (both criminal and civil penalties), and such is the same at the end of this age. Jesus will be the judge of our life and how we have lived. Those who have a personal relationship with Him will enter into heaven because we followed Him and He paid the price for our sins. Those who don't know Him will be cast into hell. Wow. That is one of the things God has shown me along the way in my life. It took me off a rule-following life to one of obedience to Jesus and knowing Him personally. This is contrary to what the world teaches, but so important. God does provide if we ask Him into our heart and let Him be the Lord of our lives. Thank You, Jesus! More manna. More provision along the way.

Richard (My Dad and a Later Lustful Attraction)

How does one write a chapter on the influence of one's dad on their life? My dad was named Richard Francis, and he only lived to age fifty-six. He fathered seven children and was a big force in the community where he lived, including a leadership role in the American Legion and a leader in our local Catholic Church. There is a saying, "Like father, like daughter," and I often wonder which of his characteristics I have inherited.

So what does the name Richard mean? Here is what Wikipedia has to say. The Germanic first or given name Richard derives from the old Germanic words *ric* ("ruler, leader, king") and *hard* ("strong, brave, hardy"), and it therefore means "strong in rule." Nicknames include Richey, Dick, Dickon, Dickie, Rich, Richie, Rick, Rico, Ricky, and others. My dad went by the name Dick. Yes, he was a hard ruler in our home for sure. Sadly, he often ruled with a great Italian temper.

Of all famous Richards in history, my favorite is Richard I of England. He was called Richard the Lionhearted. Richard is known as Richard Cœur de Lion (Norman French), or Richard the Lionheart, because of his reputation as a great military leader and warrior. Most of his life as king was spent on Crusade, in captivity, or actively defending his lands in France (Wikipedia). My dad was half-Italian (his dad's side of the family) and half-French (his mom was French Canadian), so this historical figure seems to lean French. My dad's middle name was Francis, and this name means "French man." Saint Francis is the patron saint of Italy. It all seems to fit!

So what impact did this first Richard have on my life? My dad was so proud of everything that I did—how can you not enjoy that? When I graduated from high school (number 1 in my class), there was one award given by the American Legion for the most outstanding student. I clearly remember our principal saying it was a hard choice since our class had so many excellent students. He then said one still stood above the rest, and he announced my name. My dad started to cry. I think it was out of sheer pride but also because it was the American Legion, and he was very active in that organization.

When I graduated number 1 in my college class, I know he found great pride in seeing my name first on the list of students (by GPA). I graduated summa cum laude, which means with the highest distinction. Again, the buttons on his jacket were bursting. Similar feelings arose when he attended my graduation from USC earning my master's degree, again number 1 in my class; ironically, it would be the last time I would see him alive.

The problem with all these accolades is that you can get puffed up while your brothers and sisters feel like blowing you up—ha! After all, I was the first in our family to graduate from college with a full-ride scholarship, and many of the teachers along the way would say to these siblings, "Your sister was always our favorite." Darn. More nails in the coffin of sibling rivalry. Yet it was my dad who seemed to rub it in and brag about it more than I ever could do. I wish I would have known then how damaging this is to childhood relationships. Really, Dad? I wish you had read the Bible story about Jacob and Joseph—maybe it would have taught you something.

My dad also had a horrible Italian temper. I have heard that he disciplined his sons the same way his dad had done—with his belt. This was fairly common in our growing-up era. There was no talk about child or spousal abuse back then. It was just the way it was. I remember my aunt Dottie said she loved her husband (my dad's youngest brother) but really had a hard time when he disciplined their kids in the same way. We never shared such information when we were growing up. It just wasn't done. My sister Sue said many years later that she found out we were known as one of the poor families in town. Really? Maybe because my dad had to work two jobs to feed so many mouths and our family took up an entire pew at every Sunday Mass, often wearing hand-me-downs. Gratefully, we girls learned how to sew and could make some of our clothes. We always got three meals a day and a bed to sleep in and clothes on our back, so we never gave it much thought. I wonder if my dad did. He was a proud man.

Yet my dad had a big heart and showed so much more emotion than my mom. I remember when they celebrated their twenty-fifth wedding anniversary (just after I graduated from college), we kids all got together and had a family portrait done to surprise them. He cried. I don't think my mom showed any emotion at all. My mom told me that her mom (my grandma) told her if she did not pay more attention to her husband, she would lose him. He was a gregarious guy! He never did anything halfway—you might say he had a gusto for life! No wonder he was so excited to be offered the role of Tevye for the play *Fiddler on the Roof* his last year of life. He had that same kind of strong spirit! At his wake and funeral, I stood at the door and greeted folks and thanked them for coming. My aunt Mary Louise (his sister) came up to me and said, "You are so much like your dad. He would be proud." What? It seemed like the natural thing to do.

It was the summer before my senior year of college, while I was working in the Philadelphia area, that I got the call from my siblings to say I needed to come home for a family meeting. Why? Because Dad had admitted to having an affair with another woman, and we needed to help decide what to do. My siblings all rallied around my mom (the victim), and although I did feel sorry for her, my support went to my dad. I had rarely, if ever, seen any signs of affection between my mom and dad, and I somehow sensed his need for affection. After all, I was his "date" on many occasions when Mom was too tired or just not interested in attending some event with him. I know that might sound odd, and it was not "wrong" in any moral way, but it was just what happened. In fact, in retrospect, I believe the affair started when I went off to college and he lost his date. Ironically, the other woman lived in the city where I attended school, and I later found out that when he came down to see me, he also saw her. How convenient and sad.

My brother with children said if Dad decided to leave his marriage, he would not see his grandchildren again. That sealed the deal. He stayed with Mom and broke off the other relationships (we hoped). He would live just eleven more years. During that time, he seemed to be sad at times and more mellow. I am sure he was resigned to live his life as that good Catholic dad to all those kids, or so everyone thought. When he was fifty-five years old, he retired from his job of thirty years and began to let himself go. That winter was when he had his first heart attack.

He was driving on winter roads and felt an ache in his arm and chest, but he was able to drive himself to the local hospital ER, where he was admitted with a heart attack. After tests were run, it was discovered he had blockage in four arteries of his heart and he would need an open-heart bypass surgery. This was done in January 1986 in Minneapolis, and my sister Joan said it was a time of the family all coming together (I could not make it from California). He was faithful in his cardiac rehab, and this near-death experience led him to confess all his life sins to our parish priest. At his funeral, Father Noel told me he had made amends with God and my mom, and the last six months of his life, he was a different (better) man. God gave him that time to travel in his new van to visit all his children and grandchildren and have fun. He did not drop dead of his second major heart attack until he got home. That final period of time was a true gift from God.

When my sister gave birth to her third son, she named him Richard Joseph, after his two grandparents—he became RJ. When we adopted our sons, we let them both keep their first names (from birth) but changed their middle names. James became James William (after Bill), and Josiah became Josiah Richard, after my dad. I just had to honor my dad in some way, and that seemed like the best way to do it. I only have one regret about not sharing one thing—one person I dated with my dad. He was a high-ranking officer with the US Army in the Eighty-Second Airborne. Since my dad was also in the US Army and I was born in an Army hospital, I think they would have liked meeting each other. This was my "other Bill" (see chapter W for "William"), and his schedule was so erratic such a meeting probably would have been impossible, but I think my dad would have been excited.

So what about the other Richard in my life? I struggled as to how to describe him and our relationship, so I shall just call him my lustful attraction. It was the spring of 1987, and I attended a Catholic retreat at the old mission in Santa Barbara with my friend Jean—just a weekend to get away and reflect on life. Mind you, I had made many such retreats in my life, so I had no expectations for what was going to happen. It is, after all, a beautiful place to spend a weekend, for sure! Ah, yes, I had met my British high school boyfriend at a retreat too.

The first night in our large group session, a couple walked in, Richard and Candace. I would come to find out that they were engaged to be married. They did seem very much in love. Yet I felt a strong attraction to this man (not one I acted on; after all, he was engaged), but nonetheless, the attraction was the strongest I had ever felt. About a month after the retreat, many of the retreat members gathered for a hike in Santa Barbara, and he was there. Alone. Come to find out they had broken off their engagement. What? My emotions went wild.

It was shortly before Memorial Day weekend, during which I flew to Arizona to go camping with my sister and her family. When I got home, the red blinking light was going off on my answering machine (you remember those old machines that came before voice mail), so I listened to the message. Sure enough, it was Richard asking me if I would like to go to lunch, so I accepted. As luck would have it, his office was just a few blocks away from the hospital where I worked. So he picked me up at the front driveway and we had a very pleasant time together. I can't remember what I ate, but I do remember feeling dizzy when I got back to my office. He told me he felt the same way. But no follow-up. What? No summer romance. Just lunch.

We did enjoy a couple lunch dates together, but that was it. In September of that year, I got the job officer to move to Scottsdale, Arizona, and told him all about it. He said, "Go for it!" So I did. It was not until our final lunch date the week before I left that he told me if we spent any time together, we would fall madly in love and have to spend the rest of our life together. What? That sounded wonderful to me, yet it was not what he wanted. He liked being single and having control of his life. He told me he had been married once to another gal named Kathy and it ended up in dashed dreams for him. Never again. But I had my confirmation that the pheromones between us were pretty strong. During my first day on the job in Scottsdale, he sent me red roses. My new colleagues said, "Why are you here if he is there?" I could not provide an answer.

Even though we did not spend much time together, he seemed to know me so well. Before starting the Scottdale job, I flew to North Carolina to visit the Army officer who had proposed to me the day after my divorce in 1984. It was way too soon to say yes to such an offer, but we did stay in touch and he wanted to see me before I left for Arizona, so I went. It was good fun. Later, Richard would say to me, "That is not who you are, in relationships with multiple interested fellows at one time." He was right. My ego was out of control, and I had three guys who seemed very attracted to me, so why not? In retrospect, Richard was right, and I was wrong. Yet how did he seem to know me so well?

It reminded me of the Bible story where Jesus encounters a Samaritan woman at the well (John 4:1–42) and He asks her for a drink of water and then tells her that He has everlasting water to share with her. He goes on in verses 16–26 to ask her about her husband:

> He told her, "Go, call your husband and come back." "I have no husband," she replied. Jesus said to her, "You are right when you say you have no husband. The fact is, you have had five husbands, and the man you now have is not your husband. What you have just said is quite true." "Sir," the woman said, "I can see that you are a prophet. Our ancestors worshiped on this mountain, but you Jews claim that the place where we must worship is in Jerusalem."
>
> "Woman," Jesus replied, "believe me, a time is coming when you will worship the Father neither on this mountain nor in Jerusalem. You Samaritans worship what you do not know; we worship what we do know, for salvation is from the Jews. Yet a time is coming and has now come when the true worshipers will worship the Father in the Spirit and in truth, for they are the kind of

worshipers the Father seeks. God is spirit, and his worshipers must worship in the Spirit and in truth." The woman said, "I know that Messiah" (called Christ) "is coming. When he comes, he will explain everything to us." Then Jesus declared, "I, the one speaking to you—I am he."

So the woman goes back to her village and says to everyone, "He knew everything about me." Clearly, Jesus is God, so He does know everything about us. But did you ever think of those from the spirit world in our midst? The demons know who Jesus is, and they shudder. My pastor friend Maria introduced me to a gal who told me everything about me, including having it all and then losing it all. How did she know that? I then thought those in the spirit world know such things and they are evil. That is why one should never go to a fortune-teller—they may know things, but their way of knowing is quite evil. I learned much later that Richard was part of such a cult in a local hippie area of our county near Ojai, California. I had no idea about such things.

By the end of January in 1988, I was flying back to California to attend a Superbowl party at the home of my good friends Pat and Esther and to see other friends. Once again, Richard and I fit in a lunch date, and that turned into my first visit to his home. What a romantic afternoon! (No, I do not kiss and tell.) When Valentine's Day came two weeks later, so did a dozen red roses in a satin-lined box from Richard. Talk about mixed messages! I was falling in love with someone who did not want a committed relationship. But I told myself, "Even if it does not amount to anything, I know I am in love, and it sure feels good." Then came months of nothing.

By the fall of that year, I could feel my body was falling into depression (like the one I had experienced during my divorce), and I called Richard. Once again, I flew to California for a weekend in December and we had a lovely afternoon together. By the beginning of January, it was getting close to my birthday, and once again he sent a huge bouquet of flowers to my office to say all would be well. Yet when we talked, he had to remind me we would never get married. I think my emotions fell apart. So did I. (For that and many other losses in my life.) I spent that birthday in a psych hospital and brought those beautiful flowers with me. As they seemed to fade away, so did our relationship. My counselor at that time said I had two Richards in my life (my dad and this guy) who were both not dependable in terms of the unconditional love that I needed. Maybe she was right.

I did not see Richard again until I returned to Santa Barbara in the spring of 1990, while staying with my friends. Again, another lovely afternoon, but I was still very depressed, and probably the last thing I needed was to see him, but fools rush in. By that summer, when I began dating Don, I talked to Richard and he said, "You should marry him and make babies," but that was not to be. It almost felt like he wanted me to be okay. To be happy. To be loved. Just he could not be the one. After I wrecked my knee skiing and started into my year of knee surgeries and Don and I had parted, I did end up having lunch with Richard to catch up. It always felt like we had never been apart. So odd.

I can remember during one dinner date in the city where I was working, we were sitting next to each other at a table in the restaurant, getting ready to order. When the waiter came by, he said, "I know what you want, lettuce alone." *Let us alone.* I guess we looked like starstruck lovers. If he only knew it was all pheromones and no real love story. Or was it? I must have been crazy to even agree to see him, knowing the limitations of our love, yet the attraction was profound.

Once I started dating Bill, Richard once again said, "You need to marry him and start a family," so I said yes to Bill's proposal and goodbye to Richard. We did stay in touch (as friends) for a while, but I did not see him in person again, in a one-on-one situation. I kept him on my Christmas card list for a while, and he did respond once, "When I see how your life has developed so sweetly, I almost decided to change my own life and find what you have." But I don't know if he ever did. I made a vow to myself to completely break off our friendship once I moved out of California—that was a wise thing to do. I often wonder if anyone else ever has this kind of whimsical love affair without it really being an affair. The stuff novels are made of. God protected me and let me move on. Knowing someone really stuck with me as I grew closer to Jesus; only this time it would require spending time together. Jesus already knows me.

I must digress for a minute and reflect on an old movie called *An Affair to Remember*. This was a 1957 American romance film starring Cary Grant and Deborah Kerr. It is considered one of the most romantic films of all time (Wikipedia). One guy and one gal meet on a cruise across the Atlantic, both involved in other relationships, but they fall madly in love after she meets his grandmother on an island where they stop and she sees him in a new light. (He is a playboy that has to change his ways.) They agree to reunite at the top of the Empire State Building in six months' time if they have succeeded in ending their relationships and starting new careers. They both get to the Empire State Building, but as she looks up to the top (where they are to meet), she gets hit by a car and ends up in a wheelchair. She never lets him know what happened, so it is not until the end of the movie when he finds her on Christmas Eve and they reunite. He asks, "Why did you not let me know?" She says she wants to be whole for him, happily ever after.

The reason I give this example is that they spent very little time together. I am not sure they even shared a kiss. But they were drawn to each other in such a strong way that nothing could seem to keep them apart. This was my story with Richard, but the ending was not happily ever after for me—he did not want to change his ways or his life. Yet he always seemed to care about me in a very deep way. I know many of you may say I was just being a romantic fool. Perhaps. But now I understand the expression "Crazy in love," because our hormones have overtaken our brains and our actions don't seem to make sense to even us. I remember the one and only time he met a good friend of mine (Darcy) that she told me he was smitten with me. Really? I knew my feelings were strong but did not see how obvious our chemistry was. So what did I learn? You will not die if you don't get to marry the person that appears to be perfect for you. God knows better. So many times in the Bible it talks about lust of the flesh, but I always thought that primarily referred to men and not women. I now know differently. So Go protected me in a big way. Thank You, Lord. Manna.

CHAPTER S

Sarah (Biblical Wife, Niece, and Friend)

When I studied the book of Genesis, I was intrigued by all the true characters that made big mistakes but were still chosen by God for a very big role. Such was the case for the wife of Abraham, Sarah. The Bible says she was quite beautiful. They married early in life, and she devoutly followed him wherever the Lord sent him. In many ways, despite their wealth, she spent her life not living in a palace but in a tent. She was barren and not able to give Abraham a child until her womb was opened by God in her nineties and she gave birth to the son of the promise, Isaac.

She traveled to Egypt with Abraham, and he tried to pass her off as his sister so the king would leave him alone. According to Genesis 20:2–3, there Abraham said of his wife Sarah, "She is my sister." Then Abimelech, king of Gerar, sent for Sarah and took her. But God came to Abimelech in a dream one night and said to him, "You are as good as dead because of the woman you have taken. She is a married woman." So the king let them both go to avoid harm from God. Why would Abraham do this? Why would she go along? We are all weak.

Sarah had been barren for a long time and sought a way to fulfill God's promise to Abraham that Abraham would be father of many nations, especially since they were getting older, so she offered her maidservant, Hagar, to Abraham as a second wife. Hagar became pregnant, and Sarah got jealous, so she asked Abraham to get rid of this woman! What a mess she made! Hagar was sent out of the camp because Sarah was trying to get ahead of God. Really? How often do we get impatient with His promises?

As God would have it, Hagar became the first woman to be visited by an angel of the Lord while alone in the desert. Here is the story from Genesis 16:7–13 (NIV):

> The angel of the Lord found Hagar near a spring in the desert; it was the spring that is beside the road to Shur. And he said, "Hagar, slave of Sarai, where have you come from, and where are you going? "I'm running away from my mistress Sarai," she answered. Then the angel of the Lord told her, "Go back to your mistress and submit to her." The angel added, "I will increase your descendants so much that they will be too numerous to count." The angel of the Lord also said to her: "You are now pregnant and you will give birth to a son. You shall name him Ishmael for the Lord has heard of your misery. He will be a wild donkey of a man, his hand will be against everyone and everyone's hand against him, and he will live in hostility toward all his brothers. She gave this name to the Lord who spoke to her: "You are the God who sees me," for she said, "I have now seen the One who sees me."

How good is our God? He sees us in our troubles.

The Lord appeared to Abraham through three men (angels) who told him, "One year from now, your wife, Sarah, will have a son." Sarah heard it from her tent, and she laughed. Can you imagine laughing at news from God? Despite this act, she did give birth to Isaac one year later. The child of the promise. As he grew up, Ishmael was not nice to him, so Sarah once again told Abraham to send Hagar and Ishmael away, so he did. The Lord rescued them in the desert with water, and they lived. Ishmael did go on to have twelve sons— the twelve Arab tribes. Isaac had twin sons (Jacob and Esau), and

Jacob had twelve sons, the twelve tribes of Israel. These two sets of tribes have been fighting ever since in the Middle East. Look at what a mess Sarah created! So why did I choose Sarah for my book? She completely blew it but was still blessed by God. She is even mentioned in Hebrews 11, Hall of Faith. Amazing.

So what does the name Sarah mean? According to www.sheknows.com, in biblical names, the meaning of the name Sarah is "lady; princess; princess of the multitude." Wow. That is quite a blessing for any woman. This certainly happened for Sarah since she was the princess of the multitude of the nation of Israel. By the time they went to Egypt (during the famine) and ended up enslaved there for four hundred years, it is said they increased greatly...but the Israelites were exceedingly fruitful; they multiplied greatly, increased in numbers, and became so numerous that the land was filled with them (Exodus 1:7). It's quite amazing to think it all started with a barren woman who did not have her first child until she was ninety! Nothing is impossible with God.

I have a niece named Sarah. She was firstborn to my sister Sue. She went to college, then the Peace Corps, then to school to become a naturopath, so by the time she got married, she was in her mid-thirties. She married another naturopath, and they tried to have children for several years before she would carry a baby to term. But God was good and blessed her with a little boy, whom she named Leonidas. According to www.babynames.com, the name Leonidas means "lion-like" and is of Greek origin. The line of Sarah in the Bible eventually led to the birth of Jesus, called the Lion of Judah. How sweet that my niece Sarah got a lion of her own!

My niece Sarah can be as strong-willed as Sarah in Genesis. She spent summers on a hot-shot crew to fight fires—one of the only females. She spent two years in Morocco while in the Peace Corps, and during her daily jog, she had to run from wild dogs! She tried to get equal rights for women in a Muslim culture, where men dominate. No one can say she never tried to save the world! She did, however, attend a liberal college in the Twin Cities and developed a warped worldview from all the liberal professors. She is a victim of our system. I pray for her.

I have another friend named Sarah who is ten years older than me. We met when she was referred to my Moms in Prayer group praying for Douglas County High School. My son James was attending at the same time her grandson Andrew was at the school, so we prayed for both of them nearly every week of the school year for two years. Sarah is quite an interesting lady. She had her one baby (a daughter) when she was just a teenager, but that relationship did not last. That daughter ended up getting married, and her son was the Andrew that we prayed for.

Sarah would remarry many years later to her boss (an executive in Detroit named Bill), and they had a good life together, including a lot of travel. When he got sick, Sarah had to care for him until he died. Most of their wealth was gone, so she ended up in a two-bedroom apartment near the high school, living off her Social Security income. She loved her grandson, but since her daughter got divorced and remarried, it was a challenging relationship with both male spouses in Andrew's life—a lot of coming and going from home to home.

But Sarah taught me a lot about prayer. She is an amazing, bold prayer warrior! No matter where we go, she will stop a waiter/waitress or grocery clerk at a store to ask if we can pray for them. They usually say yes. She seems to have a sense of who needs prayer. What a gift! We sort of adopted her into our family and included her during holidays, and she was so grateful she would sometimes say it was like Christmas in a Norman Rockwell painting. She always had a way to make every occasion seem special. She knew her art, books, and movies too.

After we introduced her to our new church, she became a member. She had lived in our area so long that she knew a lot about all the local churches and pastors and stories. Shortly after our induction as new members, she fell on ice in her parking lot, just before we picked her up for church. That broken femur led to several hospitalizations and time in rehab centers, followed by a cancer diagnosis with more of the same. Poor Sarah. Finally, one discharge planner said she could not live alone any longer, so she got on a list for a senior apartment in Denver and was finally accepted around 2018. We now go and visit her at her new home, where everything is provided for her—a lovely place. God certainly provided for her along the way.

Sarah also knows a lot about the Bible. Since the Moms in Prayer format includes praying our kids into Scripture, she always had her take on every verse and what it meant. She seems to be able to discern good from evil forces around her, and her intelligence and wit are quite fun to enjoy. She has a bright, loving spirit, and it is my honor to call her my sister in the Lord.

So if you have the name Sarah, who knows what will happen to you? It certainly had different endings for these three ladies, but God always provided manna along their path in life.

Socialism: Anarchy (Trouble Facing the USA)

Now that's quite a left turn in the conversation, you may say. Indeed. But this is an alphabetical book, and I had to fit in a chapter about all that is happening in our country as I write this book. The year 2020 has turned into one crazy year. First the coronavirus pandemic, then a police shooting in Minneapolis that started many protests across the country, saying we are a racist nation and blacks are mistreated, especially by police; these turned into riots and burning and pure anarchy on the streets of many of our cities. What happened?

So I went to the *Webster* dictionary to find a definition of *socialism*: "1: any of various economic and political theories advocating collective or governmental ownership and administration of the means of production and distribution of goods. 2a: a system of society or group living in which there is no private property." In essence, the government controls everything supposedly for the common good, and our freedoms are lost. So much for the words from the preamble to our Declaration of Independence: "We hold these truths to be self-evident, that all men are created equal, that they are endowed by their Creator with certain unalienable rights, that among these are life, liberty, and the pursuit of happiness." We had to memorize the words to this document as students. How could our country get so far away from our foundations?

So I went to Wikipedia to find out about the history of social-ism in America. Here is some of what I found (that I never knew). The socialist political movement includes a set of political philoso-phies that originated in the revolutionary movements of the mid to late eighteenth century and out of concern for the social problems that were associated with capitalism. By the late nineteenth century, after the work of Karl Marx and his collaborator, Friedrich Engels, socialism had come to signify opposition to capitalism and advocacy for a postcapitalist system based on some form of social ownership of the means of production. By the 1920s, communism and social democracy had become the two dominant political tendencies within the international socialist movement, with socialism itself becoming the most influential secular movement of the twentieth century. Socialist parties and ideas remain a political force with varying degrees of power and influence on all continents, heading national govern-ments in many countries around the world. Today, many socialists have also adopted the causes of other social movements, such as envi-ronmentalism, feminism, and progressivism.

I never studied much of this in school, but apparently it is widely taught in our colleges and universities, where capitalism is taught as wrong, with too many people having all the wealth, while socialism is taught as more fair, including the distribution of wealth as an overall goal. No wonder why Bernie Sanders is so popular with young people! And no wonder that the liberal Democratic Party has embraced environmentalism, feminism, and progressivism. This is not the party of Hubert Humphrey or John F. Kennedy. It is now full of anarchists who are bent on remaking America into something the Founding Fathers never intended. The pure economics of giving everything away is staggering lunacy. It is so sad to watch.

I don't think this is a question of right versus left, but rather right versus wrong. I believe that it is wrong to allow rioters to loot and burn buildings and break the law with no repercussions. I believe it is wrong for those elected to protect and defend our citizens to stop keeping this pledge and turn the other way and let lawbreaking become okay. I believe it is wrong that when you hold a different viewpoint, you are harassed and may lose your job or your life. Just plain wrong. I cannot understand how American citizens and leaders can see it as right. So crazy.

When I graduated from high school as class valedictorian, I had to give a commencement speech, and I can still remember the opening line: "To see what is right and not do it is want of courage" (Confucius). This was the era as the Vietnam War was ending, and there were a lot of angry young people protesting the war and the government. Freedom of speech, yes. But not freedom to destroy anyone who does not think like you and lead riots and destroy property. Where are our leaders with the courage to do what is right and necessary? They seem to be in hiding. Martin Luther King must be turning over in his grave. I recently read that Rosa Parks, a black woman, refused to give up her seat on a bus to a white woman. She did not burn the bus. Neither would Martin Luther King.

I can't help but think of the words of Jesus, who said He came to seek and save the lost. Boy, do we have a lot of lost people in our country! There are so many young people that have been taught revisionist history to make our founders look bad. Hence, our country is bad. So sad. In the last few years, I have found some leaders who give accurate information about the foundation of America. One is a history teacher named David Barton, who started an organization called Wall Builders. Go find his work and you will be amazed. Yes, he is a strong Christian (as were our Founding Fathers), but his opponents hate his Christian perspective.

The other is Dinesh D'Souza, who is an Indian-born American author and filmmaker. He was born in the same month as me (January 1954) and does excellent research before producing his books or documentaries. According to Wikipedia, D'Souza has written over a dozen books, several of which have been New York Times best sellers. In 2012, D'Souza released the documentary film *2016: Obama's America*, based on his 2010 book *The Roots of Obama's Rage*; it earned $33 million, making it the highest-grossing conservative documentary of all time and one of the highest-grossing documentaries of any kind. He has since released three other documentary films: *America: Imagine the World Without Her* (2014), *Hillary's America* (2016), and *Death of a Nation* (2018). His opponents see him as one filled with conspiracy theories, but I believe he does a good job presenting both sides of most every story he tells. I would strongly recommend watching these films, then judge for yourself. The next one to be released soon is *Trump Card*, and I plan to watch it and form my own opinions. The more I can learn, the better!

I must digress about the adjectives and nouns that are used to define people in online resources such as Wikipedia (left-leaning encyclopedia). I did not realize this until recently when I heard someone being interviewed about how they were described on Wikipedia—it was incomplete and inaccurate, much taken out of context. From the two examples above, here are the complete definitions of each man according to Wikipedia.

David Barton is an evangelical Christian political activist and author. He is the founder of Wall Builders LLC, a Texas-based organization that promotes unorthodox theories about the religious basis of the United States. Wikipedia What? David finds original sources (books) and takes his information from these sources. He does not make quotes from books written about our Founding Fathers but rather written *by* our Founding Fathers.

Dinesh Joseph D'Souza is an Indian-born American far-right political provocateur, author, filmmaker, and conspiracy theorist. Born in Bombay, D'Souza moved to the United States as an exchange student and graduated from Dartmouth College. He became a naturalized citizen in 1991. Wikipedia. Once again, Dinesh uses authentic sources and not secondary ones. He provides both sides of a story in his documentaries and books. It is of note, when he writes about Barack Obama, he can clearly compare their lives since they both moved to the USA from another country around the same time (Obama from Kenya), and they both went to Ivy League schools (Obama, Harvard), yet they ended up with completely different views of America. Dinesh is eternally grateful to live in the land of the free and home of the brave, while Obama did an apology tour to offer apologies for all the "wrongs" done by America. Really? No nation is perfect, but I would hope if you rise to the highest office in the land and you are the commander in chief, you should be proud of your country. I find this very striking.

The reason I include this chapter in my book is to stress that ignorance is not bliss. When you get to the end of your life, it will not be okay to say, "I just didn't know." Just ask the Germans who allowed Hitler to do all his evil; it is important for us to search for the truth every day. To pray for discernment. To be willing to stand up for what is right. To seek to understand others and not just push your own agenda. And to never confuse right versus left with right versus wrong. Some things are just plain wrong. Satan is a liar, and the truth is not in him. His forces have a lot of control in our world. Be careful how you listen and to whom. It can make all the difference. Thank goodness we know who wins in the end. The author of truth, Jesus.

Stanley (An Uncle and Other Famous Ones)

When my dad was growing up, he had one older sister (Mary Louise) and two younger brothers, Fred and Stanley. Since Stan was sixteen years younger than my dad but only ten years older than me, he felt like an older brother at times. During my first trip to the East Coast in the summer of 1973, I would travel to the Boston area and see where he lived and raised his family. On most every trip to our eastern shores after that summer, I would take the time to go and visit Stan, who was named after his dad.

So what does the name Stanley mean? According to www.baby-namewizard.com, Stanley is a Christian boy name, and it is an English-originated name with multiple meanings. The name Stanley means a stony meadow, and the associated lucky number is 6. Now that is not very interesting at all. So I looked at famous people named Stanley, and one stood out to me because of his last name, Stanley Kramer. According to Wikipedia, Stanley Earl Kramer was an American film director and producer responsible for making many of Hollywood's most famous "message films." As an independent producer and director, he brought attention to topical social issues that most studios avoided. As producer and director: *Not as a Stranger* (1955), *The Pride and the Passion* (1957), *The Defiant Ones* (1958), *On the Beach* (1959), *Inherit the Wind* (1960), *Judgment at Nuremberg*

(1961), *It's a Mad, Mad, Mad, Mad World* (1963), and *Ship of Fools* (1965). Interesting!

So what about my uncle Stan? After high school, he enlisted in the US Army and ended up guarding the eternal flame at the gravesite of John F. Kennedy in Arlington National Cemetery. It was during his time in our nation's capital that he met Dottie (from Delaware), and they were married in the 1960s. He did bring her to Minnesota for a few summer trips during times of family reunions or weddings. During the years I lived in California and they were in Massachusetts, we would meet in the middle of the country in Minnesota and catch up, often comparing our current living situations to life on the Iron Range. I laugh the first time we tried to find a good bottle of wine at a local liquor store; we could only find large jugs of wine with screw-off tops (such as Gallo), but certainly no fine wines. After all, most folks in Minnesota back then drank beer! Now, those of you in the Midwest, I do not say this as a point of criticism, just one of fact: beer served from kegs was the norm at most parties in northern Minnesota.

Stan had a small home in an area just outside Boston with a big swimming pool in the backyard. (At that time, it seemed very big since we did not know anyone with a pool!) He was very good to his mom (my grandmother), and she would often go to visit and stay with them and spend hours on a float in the pool while being served cold beverages. She loved spending time with her youngest son. He was also very good to his sister (Mary Louise) and his brother (Fred), who would come to visit, sometimes with all their kids! Now that is a loving uncle (and aunt). I believe the only time my mom and dad went to visit him was one summer when my first husband and I met them at Stan's home to see fall colors. We all slept in the basement with sleeping bags on cots, which was fine, except for my dad's horrible snoring! We did manage to go out for lobster, and that was always a favorite thing to do, since I had my first lobster while visiting them in Boston in 1973. Yum!

After losing his long-term job, Stan and Dottie opted to move to Florida, where her sister was living, and start a new life. They still live in Lakeland (halfway between Tampa and Orlando), and it is always such a pleasure to go and visit. I went to his daughter's wedding and liked her dress so much that I borrowed it years later for my own wedding, during which he walked me down the aisle, since my dad had died. Bill and I went there on our first anniversary and again on our twenty-fifth anniversary and enjoyed both visits. His youngest son ended up moving to Tampa and now lives there with his wife and two children, so Grandpa Stan is not too far from some of his grandchildren. His other daughter, Debbie, had one daughter who also moved to the Lakeland area, so he is now close to family.

So why did I include Stanley in my book? Because he was always a favorite uncle to me, and I always told him that I was his favorite niece! He had the same temperament as my dad but also the same great sense of humor, so he was fun to be around. Several years ago, he was diagnosed with lupus, an autoimmune disease, as well as COPD. As such, he can't fly anymore and stays home so he can take his medications and do his inhalation treatments.

According to www.medlineplus.gov, lupus, also called SLE, systemic lupus erythematosus, is an inflammatory disease caused when the immune system attacks its own tissues. Lupus (SLE) can affect the joints, skin, kidneys, blood cells, brain, heart, and lungs. Symptoms vary but can include fatigue, joint pain, rash, and fever. These can periodically get worse (flare up) and then improve. While there's no cure for lupus, current treatments focus on improving quality of life through controlling symptoms and minimizing flare-ups. This begins with lifestyle modifications, including sun protection and diet. Further disease management includes medications, such as anti-inflammatories and steroids. One such medicine is the same one used to treat COVID-19, hydroxychloroquine. During our most recent visit in March 2020, the coronavirus was just being recognized as a possible pandemic. We were sad to think that this made him fearful of our visit (getting the virus), but gratefully, we did not have the virus. Clearly, it is sad to see my once-vigorous uncle so weak and unhappy. We love you, Uncle Stan, and we pray for you.

Steven (A Boyfriend, a Boss, a Martyr)

Do you remember that twelve-week trip I made to Europe after I graduated from college? It was during this adventure that I met other recent college graduates from various states, but some of my best friends came from Georgia. One of them was a sweet guy named Steve. He had just graduated from Georgia Tech, where he played both football and rugby. Yes, he was part of the rambling wreck from Georgia Tech!

So what does the name Steven mean? According to www.sheknows.com, in English baby names, the meaning of the name Stephen is "crown; wreath." In the Bible, Stephen was the first Christian martyr. Wow, the name seems fitting for a king! In the case of the first martyr, Stephen, his crown was in heaven. According to www.biography.com, Saint Stephen is a recognized saint in many Christian theologies and is considered to be the first Christian martyr. According to the fifth book of the Bible's New Testament, the Acts of the Apostles, Stephen was denounced for blasphemy after a dispute with members of a Jewish synagogue circa the year 36. According to chapters 6 and 7 of the book of Acts, he was condemned and stoned to death—the scene of which was depicted in Dutch artist Rembrandt's *The Stoning of Saint Stephen*. Today, Western Christians annually celebrate Saint Stephen's Day on December 26. I know they have this holiday in England. He certainly was a special man of the early church. The thing I love best about this saint is that while he was being stoned, he quoted Jesus's words from the cross, "God, forgive them, for they know not what they do." Oh, to have such compassion for the lost!

My Georgia Tech Steve was a sweet, handsome Southern gentleman. There were a group of about eight of us (guys and gals) who always went a little further to have a little bit more fun in every place we visited! Mind you, everything we did was legal, moral, good fun, but it created a bond between us. I can remember climbing the Alps with him in Switzerland as well as dancing on the tables in Florence, Italy, for the Fourth of July. Our brave group went skinny-dipping one night at midnight while on the Greek islands, and we found the

Rathskeller in Berlin to drink fine white wine. We also drank beer from a boot in Heidelberg, where the last one who finished the boot had to turn it upside down on the table for one minute. If it formed a ring, they had to buy the next boot. Good fun! I must admit, he became a favorite guy for me on our trip.

When the group was heading back to the USA and I was staying one more week in England (with Brian) Steve told me to please come to Georgia to visit him if I ever got the chance. So after the romance with Brian seemed to die, as he was aghast at all our American fun, he wanted to stay in England while I wanted to go home to America. So when I saw a job opening in Atlanta with the CDC, I interviewed and got the job. It was then I reconnected with Steve.

At that time, he took me to my first rugby game, and I got to meet his guy friends, who taught me some pretty funny rugby songs! That came in handy many years later, when I took the ferry from Liverpool, England, to Dublin, Ireland—an all-night crossing where I met some guys from northern England who also taught me rugby songs as we drank Guinness! I loved the concept of having a scrum of teammates you could count on as you carried one another down the field. Certainly not like American football! Steve gave me a Georgia Tech Rugby shirt, and I think I wore it out!

Steve was an only child, and his dad had died years earlier, but he did introduce me to his mom, who was a very sweet Southern lady. She taught me how to make real sweet ice tea! She and I talked, and she wondered why Steve had never settled down with a nice young lady (like me), and I must admit, I wondered the same. Steve began training for a triathlon, so I also got to experience watching my first ever triathlon including a big pasta meal the night before. Since our CDC team was flying in and out of Atlanta as we traveled up and down the East Coast, I would see him when we were in town.

I also met with a friend from the trip (Judy) who told me that she and her new husband (David) were so surprised to see Steve coming out of a gay bar one night when they were out. So now I knew why he was not settling down with a nice young lady. What a shame—he was a really good kisser! But life moves on. God's protection from getting too involved in a relationship that had no future. A year later, Steve did make a trip to California and we did spend one day in Solvang, north of Santa Barbara, a place known as Little Copenhagen. We reminisced about our time in this capital city of Denmark and enjoyed some sweet pastries together. I never heard from him again. I do hope his life turned out well. Such a sweet friend for a special time.

The other Steven in my life was my IB boss. He had a PhD in philosophy and was a very kind, caring teacher. In fact, during the spring, when I was being trained, he was selected by the student body to give the commencement address at a high school graduation. He is a very intelligent guy, with a dry wit but ever caring heart. We were so different that we made a good pair. He was the philosopher, and I was the one who took care of all the details of the day-to-day work. I was blessed to call him my boss for my two years working at our local high school. When the movie *Iron Man* came out, I thought my role resembled that of Pepper Potts, assistant to Tony Stark. What would he have done without her? (If you don't get this, go see the movie.) She was very smart and very well organized and understood exactly what her boss needed. Just like me, I think. (who wouldn't want to be compared to Gwyneth Paltrow—ha!)

During those two years, I was also in a Moms in Prayer group, and we prayed for our kids and schools, including teachers and parents. We had three Stevens that we regularly prayed for: my boss (the intellectual teacher), Deb's son (the student with brains but no job), and the husband of Pamela, a retired doctor who was dad to their three daughters (not part of any church). We enjoyed exchanging our prayers for these three special fellows. I think God has a special place in His kingdom for guys named Stephen—at least the ones I knew.

Susan (My Sister and a Warrior)

As I said earlier, my mom had seven children—the three oldest, the three youngest, and one in the middle. That was my sister Sue. On my birthday (born January 1954), we are five years apart in age. By her birthday (born September 1958), we are four years apart. As such, our high school years never overlapped, nor did a lot of the rough years in our home. She is still the one in the middle, who seems to hold us all together at times. She is very special! Such a heart!

So what does the name Susan mean? Here is what Wikipedia has to say. Susan is a feminine given name, from Persian *lily flower*; from Egyptian *ssn* and Coptic *shoshen*, meaning "lotus flower"; from Hebrew *Shoshana*, meaning "lily" (in modern Hebrew, this also means "rose" and a flower in general); from Greek *Sousanna*; from Latin *Susanna*; from Old French *Susanne*. A beautiful flower—yep, that is my sister Sue!

Since we were all named after saints, I had to look up Saint Susanna. Since she is still a devout Catholic, I thought I'd search www.Catholic.org, and here is what it says. The beautiful daughter of Gabinius, a priest, and niece of Pope Caius, Susanna refused the emperor's Diocletian request that she marry his son-in-law Maximian and converted two of her uncles (Maximums and Claudius) to Christianity. Diocletian was so enraged by what she had done that he sent one of his favorites, Julian, to deal with the matter. Julian had Maximus, Claudius, burned to death at Cumae, and then had Susanna and her father beheaded. Yes, she became a martyr. I do think my sister would be willing to die for her faith as well.

When any of my husband's friends say that I am strong-willed (in a good way), I just say you have never met my sisters Sue and Joan—ha! They are the strong women in my family! Shortly after Sue married her high school sweetheart (Jeff), they moved to Globe, Arizona, where he got his first job as a mining engineer in the copper mines there. That was around 1981. She had her first child in 1983 (Sarah), then a boy in 1985 (Mat), and another boy in 1987 (RJ), and a final boy in 1989 (Sammy)—yes, she was pretty pregnant for many years! The good news for me was that I got to be the favorite Aunt Kathy to these kids—a role I cherished.

The year I took the job in Santa Barbara (1977) was the year she graduated from high school. She drove with me in my Chevy Malibu to California to help with the driving, and we had a fun road trip together. I still remember the first time we went to a beach at the

Pacific ocean and how the guys paid attention to her—she was always pretty, playful and friendly. After her marriage, during the time of her first pregnancy, I found out my husband was cheating on me and she flew to California to be with me for a few days to make sure I was okay. At that point she was nearly six months pregnant, but she came nonetheless. What a great sister, always there to help!

While living in California, I often flew to Arizona to spend holidays with Sue and Jeff and their kids—those were such special times. It was one of the reasons I took the job in Scottsdale in 1987, to be closer to them, and then it was most weekends. I have especially fond memories of going camping together, including a trip to the North Rim of the Grand Canyon when Sarah was just a baby and Sue was pregnant with Mat. I got to go on the mule ride along the edge of the canyon with Jeff—now that is an experience everyone should have. Scary! Their Arizona friends all treated me as one of the gang, and I even learned to play poker during those visits. Fun!

What was not fun was when I fell into a deep depression after losing that job and those visits to their home in Globe. I was a mess! She put up with me for nine months until she was pregnant with her final child, who was born in March 1989, the very month my life fell apart. She always told me to remember that God never closes a door without opening a window. She was right. Yet it was really hard to not see them January to April of 1990. She gave me a big time-out. She did scheme behind my back to get my friend Patrick to come and get me from Scottsdale and take me back to California. She and Jeff packed up my house and put all my belongings in storage. We were able to rent that home, and I was able to recover within a few months. God. Manna.

By the time I met Bill, she was delighted that I had found about the nicest guy she had ever met to be my life mate. She was the maid of honor in our wedding, and *all* those kids were in our wedding— what an amazing day! I still remember how all the nieces and nephews jumped into the limousine taking us from the church to the reception—what a first for all of us! Now they are all grown up and married, with three of the four having children of their own. Her second born (Mat) is my godson, and he is just getting married this year. He had to travel the world first (just like his aunt Kathy), but I could not be happier for anyone. So just like you toasted us at our wedding, Sue, I now toast you for being such a dear sister and friend. Bill and I love our time together with both you and Jeff. We both retired this year, so here's to many more!

One final note, my sister wonders why I left the faith of our family, and I hope this book will help clarify my journey through the Bible and my expanded Christiane faith. I honor her faith and hope we can both chat more when we get to heaven. I am looking forward to it! My Bible verse for Sue, Proverbs 7:4, "Love wisdom like a sister; make insight a beloved member of your family." You are beloved and wise.

Suicide (Up Close and Personal)

It was the spring of 1982. My husband, Gary, and I had flown to Arizona for the Memorial Day weekend to be with my sister Sue and Jeff. Upon our return to LAX, his mom picked us up and brought us back to their home in the South Bay, about fifteen minutes away. Upon our arrival at the house, all the doors were locked, which was very odd. We could hear their two big dogs barking outside in the backyard, and we rushed back there to see what was going on. We found his dad in a pool of blood. He had shot himself in the head. We called 911, and he died en route to the hospital. This was something none of us had ever had to deal with. Shocking.

His dad suffered from Parkinson's disease and diabetes and had recently had a pacemaker put in to help his heart. He had such a fear that he would end up dying in a hospital (like their teen daughter had done years earlier due to kidney failure) that he could not take it. As most folks who commit or think about taking their life, I do not believe he was in his right mind. He did leave a note to this effect: "I know I may die soon and don't want it to be in a hospital." Clearly, it sent Gary and his mom into a deep period of grief.

I immediately called my mom and dad, and they took the next plane out to California. In my dad's leadership role with the American

Legion, he had to arrange for many funerals of veterans. I was not sure if he had ever dealt with this type of funeral, but I did know he would add a calming presence to Gary and his mom, who had no other family. He did just that. Funny how my dad could rise to the occasion for big life challenges (like a death) but would lose it if the mashed potatoes and gravy weren't done at the same time for Thanksgiving dinner.

But I digress. Suicide has a huge shame factor associated with it—no one wants to talk about it. No one knows what to say. Such was the case during this event. Gary hoped the coroner would change the cause of death to heart attack. After all, his dad had a recent hospitalization for heart problems. My dad and I had to gently let him know this was not possible. Gary's mom was the organist at their small church in Torrance, and she never even told the pastor or her closest neighbors the whole truth about his death. So the small graveside service was even sadder, thinking they could not get the counseling they needed for such a death and for such unique grief that often leaves one saying, "Why didn't I see it coming?"

According to the National Institute for Mental Health (www.nimh.org), suicide is a major public health concern. Suicide is among the leading causes of death in the United States. Based on recent nationwide surveys, suicide in some populations is on the rise.

- *Suicide* is defined as death caused by self-directed injurious behavior with intent to die as a result of the behavior.
- A suicide attempt is a nonfatal, self-directed, potentially injurious behavior with intent to die as a result of the behavior. A suicide attempt might not result in injury.
- Suicidal ideation refers to thinking about, considering, or planning suicide.

In the late 1990s, I would get a call from my family in Minnesota saying that our cousin (Charlie) had committed suicide. I could not make it back for the funeral, but I did go to one of our senior pastors (Mike) and asked if he had any materials on coping with suicide. He gave me some great handouts, and I mailed them to my uncle Fred and his new wife. He would later tell me that this helped them a great deal—they did not know how to cope. No one does.

Our youngest son (Josiah) was very much a loner in high school. He had very low self-esteem and started listening to dark music, which made him more depressed. He started writing in his notebooks at school some very dark thoughts (which sounded like suicidal ideation), so his counselor called me one day in the 2012–2013 school year to say I needed to come to school and bring him to the local ER to be put on suicide watch. I did. We went. He was released within a few hours when it was determined he had not made a plan to kill himself and therefore was not felt to be a danger to himself. At that time, we noticed he had been cutting himself and were told that it was not a suicide attempt—it was just a cry for help. A way to get attention. A way to soothe the anger and sadness and loneliness going on inside. We did not know what to do.

By the 2013–2014 school year, he was enrolled in the alternative high school in our area. At first, it was hard, but as time went on, it became a great place for him to be. He got a lot of the one-on-one attention that he needed. He could not hide in the crowd like he had during his time at the much bigger high school in our area. He now had a girlfriend (Krystal) who became a great support to him, and he was also working full-time at Walmart. Life seemed stable for him. When he graduated from high school, Krystal broke off their relationship, and he was once again very sad. He moved out to live in an apartment with two other female friends, and one of them called one day to say she thought he was going over the edge, so we met at the local ER and sat together once again. We went through a lot of therapy with Josiah to work on all this. It was never easy to understand, especially since we had adopted him and he was a drug baby, and we were not sure how much damage that had done to the portion of his brain responsible for executive function. We later found that it was the primary area of injury for such children.

As God would have it, during the 2011–2012 school year, I was actively involved in Moms in Prayer in our county, one big school district. We had a very big problem with teens committing suicide. I think over ten such cases in the first semester. So we planned a prayer siege against suicide on Leap Year Day (February 29, 2012), just two weeks after I started my first job with the school district. We had prayer groups in three different geographic locations in our county, in churches, and it was an amazing time of prayer. Suicides did start to go down. By the springtime, I was heading to a national Moms in Prayer event in Branson, Missouri, and women from across the country were praying for our school district. God was working through me. It made me shudder.

Since the COVID epidemic started in our country and around the world in March 2020, there has been a huge jump in depression and suicide among teens. When you isolate people and make them stay home, with not much to do, and remove their normal social interactions, such things will happen. According to the CDC Morbidity and Mortality Report in early summer, during June 24–30, 2020, US adults reported considerably elevated adverse mental health conditions associated with COVID-19. Younger adults, racial/ethnic minorities, essential workers, and unpaid adult caregivers reported having experienced disproportionately worse mental health outcomes, increased substance use, and elevated suicidal ideation. It has also been reported in the news that suicide rates have nearly doubled since a year ago and are likely to continue to increase as shutdowns and school closures continue. So the topic of suicide is one that everyone will have to become familiar with; it is now all around us.

I know personally, when you suddenly lose your job, you feel like a complete failure and don't know if you will ever be able to work again. (That's depression speaking to your brain.) Clearly, many of our soldiers returning home from battle face this dilemma every day. It is a sad way to die. It is often even more difficult for those left behind, who keep asking, "Why did I not see the signs?"

After going through all my knee surgeries in 1991, I decided I needed to get away for a while in 1992, and I went to visit my former college roommate from Tennessee, now living in Atlanta. She was so thrilled to see me. Her husband said he clearly remembers the day that I called Mary during my time of deepest depression while in

Scottsdale. She hung up the phone and was ashen gray. She told her husband she thought I was going to kill myself.

I never considered killing myself, but I did have a passive desire to die. If only a truck would run me over and put me out of my pain. Perhaps my Catholic roots were screaming at me that anyone who kills themself cannot go to heaven. I clearly don't believe that at all anymore. But I do believe that depression is often a tool of the devil to push us into a place of complete despondency and hopelessness. So why would we want to live? Those would never be the worlds of our Lord and Savior, Jesus Christ.

I remember a scene in the movie *Luther* where a despondent young child hung himself from the local bridge, and as a Catholic priest, he was not allowed to give the family a Catholic burial Mass. He did, however, personally dig the grave for this young child in the church cemetery and defied all the rules of the church. It was just one more thing that the pope had decreed that made no sense to him. Hooray for Martin Luther! Hooray for other Catholic priests who will do the same. With the cloud of shame hanging over such families, why should we add to their grief? If you ever can help anyone who is affected in this way, please do. It is very important.

Another movie that came out in August 2010, called *To Save a Life*, deals with the subject of teen suicide on high school campuses. According to www.pluggedin.com, the movie deals with suicide. Sex. Teen pregnancy. Divorce. Drugs. Cutting. Hypocrisy. That's a lot of issues. We're asked to grapple with this daunting laundry list of problems through the eyes of Jake, a likable bloke who's finally beginning to wonder whether there's more to life than just basketball, beer pong, and popularity. Through the gentle guidance of a Christian youth pastor, Jake tries to come to grips with Roger's suicide. Maybe it wasn't his fault that Roger killed himself, he concludes. But he might've still prevented it had he taken the time. It's the beginning of a life transformed. Jake stops drinking and starts going to church. He takes Jonny, a shy, hurting student, under his wing. When girlfriend Amy asks Jake to choose between her and his new, church-filled life, he breaks up with her, only to rally to her side when she admits she's pregnant with their baby. You need to see the movie to hear the rest of the story.

The point of the movie and my point is that we have to stop ignoring these issues that face our young people every day. We have to come alongside them and offer hope and a plan to save another life any way that we can. Take small steps. Reach out to those around you who are the marginal kids. The lost souls. Make safe talk a part of your life—make it safe to talk about the things deep down inside. Just as it says in 2 Corinthians 1:3–4, praise be to the God and Father of our Lord Jesus Christ, the Father of compassion and the God of all comfort, who comforts us in all our troubles so that we can comfort those in any trouble with the comfort we ourselves receive from God. I know that a word of encouragement can be such a comfort in those low times. I have been there. I want to help others in similar spots. That is one of the reasons I write these true stories in my book. To bring comfort and hope to others. Manna.

CHAPTER T

Tanzania (A Place for Missions—Extended Family)

As God would have it, in January 1997, we were introduced to a foreign student at our local college named Gabriel from Tanzania, a country in sub-Saharan Africa about which we knew very little. When we had a chance to sponsor a child through World Vision, we chose a little girl from Tanzania. Eleven years later (2008), we were able to visit Tanzania for seventeen days and got to stay with Gabriel's parents and meet the rest of his family. We were not allowed to visit our World Vision child no matter how hard we tried to make it happen. Apparently, our completed/approved background check as foster parents was not good enough to make it "safe" for us to visit. So sad. But we did venture to East Africa in May–June 2008 and discovered the amazing country of Tanzania. We later changed to sponsoring a girl in Tanzania through Compassion International, who strongly encourage visits to your sponsored children.

According to www.countriesaroundtheworld.com, Tanzania is the thirteenth largest country in Africa and is situated in East Africa. It is actually a combination of two regions/states: the mainland, formerly known as Tanganyika, and Zanzibar island. Tanzania is bordered by Uganda and Kenya to its north; Zambia, Malawi, and Mozambique to its south; Rwanda, Burundi, and the Democratic Republic of the Congo to its west; and the Indian Ocean to its east. The capital of Tanzania is the city of Dar es Salaam. It is home to Mount Kilimanjaro, as well as Lake Victoria. (But Uganda will argue it is their lake!) The official languages spoken in Tanzania are Swahili and English. Like most sub-Saharan countries, the country is made up of strong Christian and Muslim elements and a small minority of people who follow other religions or none at all.

When we flew into Arusha (as the base of Mount Kilimanjaro, where Gabriel grew up), we were greeted with many warnings that we were in an area of the AIDS epidemic. As such, in our pretravel plans, we had to have our travel vaccines done. This included medicine for malaria that we had to take before, during, and after our trip, so we knew we were heading to a unique area of the world. Mount Kilimanjaro is called the rooftop of Africa—it's highest peak, at an elevation of 19,341 feet. Three times higher than the mile-high city of Denver! Cool.

Our trip had three primary purposes: to meet and get to know Gabriel's family, to visit local mission organizations that helped the poor, and to go on a few safaris! When we packed to visit a country located just below the equator, we thought we could be hot all the time. Wrong. We ended up being cold much of the time. I guess it was the high elevation? Gabriel's parents, Gabriel Sr. and Mama Flora, could not have been kinder to us. They raised their children in the Lutheran Church, and that was when Gabriel met a Lutheran teacher/missionary from the state of Washington named Ruth. We had met her twice in the USA, at Gabe's college and graduate school graduations. Sadly, during our stay, we got a call that she had been rushed to the hospital for a rupture in her abdomen and did not survive the surgery. So sad.

Papa Laizer invited all the neighbors over to meet Gabriel's' new/only American family, the Kramers. We felt so honored. We heard stories about all seven children they had raised. Gabe was the second oldest (just like both of us). One sister would study to become a doctor, and sadly, years later, she died in a tragic large truck / small bus accident along the treacherous African roads. We know how much that hurt the family, but they hung together. The community of friends and family around them was very strong. Another sibling had two small children, including a little girl that took a liking to me. It was so fun to have her sit on my lap and play. Gratefully, they all spoke English, so we did not have to learn any Swahili! Flora also loves chai tea like me.

Another schoolteacher from Washington State had retired and moved to Tanzania to run a travel agency, with a specialty in booking safaris. So we were able to enjoy several such adventures and were amazed by the Serengeti! The animals. The sunsets. The overall surroundings. On one trip, we asked our guide (David) to come and sit with us for dinner. He was pleasantly surprised. He told us such wonderful stories about the native tribes, including the Maasai, the tribe for the Laizer family. According to www.easytravel.co.tz, here is a snapshot of what you can experience in the country of Tanzania.

You are walking through a Tanzanian marketplace bustling with colors and sounds. The sweet smell of cloves hits your nostrils just as several Maasai craftswomen wave you over to look at their intricate beading, art, and textiles. Never have you seen such beauty. You are hiking up Mount Kilimanjaro, part of a weeklong trek along the Machame Route to Africa's tallest peak. You strike up a conversation with a porter: he's a young Chagga man who carries a large bag on his shoulders and smiles. Never have you been so humbled.

Some say a journey to Tanzania is like going to the beginning, like traveling to ground zero. But what you'll find here aren't tribes stuck in the past. No, you'll discover more than 120 different tribal groups living very much in the present, a human tapestry weaving traditional with modern, rural with urban. Nowhere else in Africa can you find this level of tribal diversity. In fact, Tanzania is the only African nation whose tribes represent all four of the continent's major ethnolinguistic groups—Bantu, Cushitic, Nilotic, and Khoisan. How cool is that? As for travel, any adventure to Tanzania can include world-class safaris, hiking, and beachcombing, but it also offers some of the most unique opportunities on the planet to learn about our shared human story, past and present. The diverse intersection of tribes, of languages, folktales, and music converges in Tanzania and invites you into its swirl of celebration. Our trip did include some time on the island of Zanzibar (part of Tanzania), and we learned all about the many spices grown on the island as well as very old turtles. What an adventure!

How cool is that? The very first young man we met from Africa happened to be from this amazing African country. We have so much more of the continent of Africa to explore, but I am happy our journey began when we met a freshman college student from this country, one brought to the USA by a Lutheran missionary, one who now lives with his own family in Washington, DC, while he works for the United Nations, with a focus on ending world hunger. He told us his dream is to someday be president of his home country—we hope he does! We will come for the inauguration!

Thomas Peter (A Brother, Apostles, Saints)

My brother Tom was third born in our family, one year behind me in school. I recently told him that he was the only one who was born in an odd year (1955), so that made him our odd brother in more ways than one! When he was young, he must have had a bit of dyslexia, since he would spell his name "Mot." He was our crazy brother, the one who did things like light his farts on fire as well as the pile of leaves in the neighbor's yard that almost set the neighborhood on fire! On the day of our mom's death, we went back to the house where we grew up, and sure enough, those neighbors were still there!

What fun to take a photo of several of us with the Marsh family. Everyone remembers Tom. I have to say he is my favorite brother.

So what does the name Thomas mean? According to www. behndthename.com, it means "twin." In the New Testament, this is the name of an apostle. When he heard that Jesus had risen from the dead, he initially doubted the story, until Jesus appeared before him and he examined His wounds himself. According to tradition, he was martyred in India. Due to his renown, the name came into general use in the Christian world. In England the name was introduced by the Normans and became very popular due to Saint Thomas Becket, a twelfth-century archbishop of Canterbury and martyr. Another notable saint by this name was the thirteenth-century Italian philosopher and theologian Thomas Aquinas, who is regarded as a doctor of the church. Other famous bearers include philosopher Thomas Hobbes (1588–1679), American president Thomas Jefferson (1743–1826), novelist Thomas Hardy (1840–1928), and inventor Thomas Edison (1847–1931).

Well, my brother was not a twin, but he sure followed in some pretty big footsteps—these men named Thomas were highly intelligent and very influential, especially in the faith of our family, the Roman Catholic Church. So I feel compelled to look at his middle name, Peter, the name he also gave to his youngest son. So what does Peter mean? Here is what is said in www.behindthename.com. Peter is derived from Greek (Petros) meaning "stone." This is a translation used in most versions of the New Testament of the name Cephas, meaning "stone" in Aramaic, which was given to the apostle Simon by Jesus. Simon Peter was the most prominent of the apostles during Jesus's ministry and is often considered the first pope.

Due to the renown of the apostle, this name became common throughout the Christian world (in various spellings). In England, the Normans introduced it in the Old French form Piers, which was gradually replaced by the spelling Peter starting in the fifteenth century. Besides the apostle, other saints by this name include the eleventh-century reformer Saint Peter Damian and the thirteenth-century preacher Saint Peter Martyr. It was also borne by rulers of Aragon, Portugal, and Russia, including the Russian czar Peter the

Great (1672–1725), who defeated Sweden in the Great Northern War. Famous fictional bearers include Peter Rabbit from Beatrix Potter's children's books, and Peter Pan, the boy who refused to grow up in J. M. Barrie's 1904 play. This late one fits!

During a big family reunion in the hometown of my mom's parents (the Schmids), our group did a tour of the local cemetery to see how many members of the family were buried in Avon. I was surprised to see that in the family plot for my grandpa and grandma (Ben and Lauretta), there was a small headstone for Thomas. This was apparently a stillborn child that she had given birth to. Perhaps, it was a beloved family name and that was where my brother got his name. One can only speculate. I bet it was special to my mom. My mom's brother Roger named his first child Tom, so I know it has family significance.

When my brother Tom was small, he had a big round head, like a pumpkin, with an ever-winning smile. I can remember during our summers at my grandparents' home in Avon, he was thought of fondly by a neighbor gal about to get married. As Tom would have it, he showed up at her wedding in his little Civil War soldier suit (Johnny Reb became Tommy Reb), and it made everyone laugh! He was always quite the little character. He was also well liked in school—a popular, fun kid. After high school, he spent two years at our local community college and then off to the University of North Dakota, where he got his degree in electrical engineering. He was good in math but often said he had the smartest roommate—that was his salvation.

During summer vacations, he worked part-time at a local place called the GI Club, where retired soldiers met for drinks nearly every day, usually after work, including our dad, who was very active in the American Legion. During these bartending times, he met Jayne and they fell in love, and she would become his bride in 1978. Then they started their family. Due to job changes, the first two sons were born in Minnesota and number 3 in Michigan. They then moved to Nebraska where they raised their family. All three boys went to the University of Nebraska (Lincoln), so Husker Red is a very popular color in that home!

Tom is probably the best golfer in our family, and he and my dad were good golfing buddies. Tom's brothers-in-law also golfed with him, and when my dad died, they created an annual golf tournament named after my dad, called the Saccy Best Ball. (Saccy is short for our last name.) I think Tom made it up to every one of those tournaments—he kept the Saccoman name going on our local golf course! This tournament was men only, so we three sisters were not happy about that. I do think my sister Sue crashed the event one year (good for her), but Tom would always kid us that this event was like men's night at the course—guys only! Really?

I loved visiting Tom and Jayne during my trips back to the Midwest, both to Michigan and to Omaha. I remember visiting them at the end of October 1984 (just after my divorce was finalized), and I happened to be there when Jayne delivered their third son (Peter), who was born two weeks late on Halloween! Tom and I took the little boys trick-or-treating before he headed to the hospital. It became a very easy birthday to remember——Peter, Peter, pumpkin eater, born on the big pumpkin day! In fact, I could almost picture my brother as a *Peanuts* comic strip character—maybe Charlie Brown? A big head with a big heart.

I loved to hear the stories of what special things he did for his boys during their growing-up years. He would decorate their birthday cakes; he read to them, played with them all the time, and even went up on the rooftop of their home to play Santa Claus at Christmas! Who wouldn't want a dad like Tom? I often wondered where he got this from (certainly not our dad), but I suspect part of it was the warmth he felt as part of Jayne's extended family. They were a close-knit group with many musical talents, including sitting around the piano and singing together. Jayne even taught piano lessons and had a beautiful voice. From a distance, I saw them as the ideal family.

But no family is ideal. His middle son, David, struggled in school, and both Tom and Jayne put on their teacher hats after work to help teach him in the evenings. When he graduated from high school, he started college and then he joined the Marine Corps and did his basic training at Camp Pendleton in California. I got to attend his induction ceremony and to also take him to dinner the night before he was deployed; it made me feel like a special part of the family. He would go on to graduate from the University of Nebraska and married Gina; they have a beautiful family and live close to Tom and Jayne in Omaha. The hard work paid off!

The other two boys ended up fathering babies out of wedlock, but they made great dads! I know it disappointed Jayne, but Tom still embraced his role as grandpa. Besides, we had four other such events in our family. They have a pool in their backyard, and it is a fun place to be on a hot summer day—the center of neighborhood fun when the boys were growing up. They were always gracious to us when we brought our boys for a visit. Our boys would say, "Uncle Tom is funny." As they got older, I would tell James to be sure to not let Uncle Tom get his mom (me) drunk—he could be quite the bartender!

So what did I learn from brother Tom? First, to have a great sense of humor. He certainly made my mom laugh a lot at our wedding, when he and my brother Paul gave out drink tickets to the guests for the bar. It was actually a cash bar, so when they would try to redeem their tickets, the bartender would be very confused and they would laugh hysterically at their table! My uncle Stan would say, "You have some pretty crazy brothers!" Secondly, to never give up. During my time of major depression, he would quote to me from the childhood book *The Little Engine That Could.* Third, to love your family deeply, no matter how you were raised yourself. Fourth, to be generous at all times and share what you have with others. He is always more than willing to pick up the tab for a dinner or special outing. Fifth, to have a tender heart about all that life has to throw at you and to be there for others when they need you.

During one evening of merriment at our home, Tom told me that he thought our mom favored her other grandchildren over his own boys. After all, when she came to visit, she would go to the store to get things for herself or her dog, but nothing for the boys. His children never had a generous, loving grandma. I then thought about a song that came out in 1970 called "The Tears of a Clown," by Smokey Robinson and the Miracles. Here are a few of the lyrics:

> Now if there's a smile on my face
> It's only there trying to fool the public
> But when it comes down to fooling you
> Now honey that's quite a different subject
> But don't let my glad expression
> Give you the wrong impression
> Really I'm sad, oh I'm sadder than sad
> You're gone and I'm hurting so bad
> Like a clown I appear to be glad (sad, sad, sad, sad)
> Now they're some sad things known to man
> But ain't too much sadder than
> The tears of a clown when there's no one around...

Now, one could say this song was about a boy who lost his girl and was sad. Yes, that is part of it, but I believe it reflects the hurt that all of us carry in our heart that we don't share with others. You can get "lost" in a big family and often feel alone. I know that firsthand. I spent years hiding my feelings until it ate me up—depression. They say depression is anger turned inward. I also think it can be sadness turned inward. Perhaps I have more in common with my little brother than I ever knew.

Tom recently told me that he could retire anytime (he has the funds saved up and is old enough for Medicare), but he does not know what to do with his time. What? I have so many things I want to do in retirement because I am so vested in so many things—our church, our local community, our neighborhood, many missionaries we support, local involvement in helping the poor and needy around us, travel (friends in so many places), and writing, hence this book. I love to read and write. I pray that he will find a retirement passion since he has so much to give. We know they won't come to Colorado to visit us—the elevation is too much for Jayne, who has trouble breathing. I just hope he will continue to open his home for our visits since we enjoy our time with them. God bless you, dear brother.

Mot. I pray that our Lord Jesus will show you His ultimate will in your life, one that brings pure joy. I must share my favorite Proverb with you. I have it on several plaques in our house.

> Trust in the Lord with all your heart, and lean not on your own understanding; in all your ways acknowledge him, and he will direct your paths [He will show you the way]. (Prov. 3:5–6)

I love you, dear brother, Mot.

Truth (Yes, There Is Such a Standard)

When we were at our first church in Castle Rock, they offered a thirteen-week program on Sunday nights called the Truth Project. Here is the definition from the website for Focus on the Family. The Truth Project is a groundbreaking small-group curriculum on the biblical worldview. This video-based home Bible study is the starting point for looking at life from a biblical perspective. Join Dr. Del Tackett as he takes you through thirteen engaging video lessons on the relevance and importance of living the biblical worldview in daily life, featuring insights from biblical experts like Ravi Zacharias, R. C. Sproul, Os Guinness, and Gordon Pennington.

The course included the following lessons:

1. Veritology: What Is Truth?
2. Philosophy and Ethics: Says Who?
3. Anthropology: Who Is Man?
4. Theology: Who Is God?
5. Science: What Is True?
6. History: Whose Story?
7. Sociology: The Divine Imprint
8. Unio Mystica: Am I Alone?
9. The State: Whose Law?
10. The American Experiment

11. Labor: Created to Create
12. Community and Involvement: God Cares; Do I?

The three months we spent watching these videos and having group discussions were really eye-opening to me. I can still remember the opening scene in the first video where Jesus is at the end of His life, being questioned by Pilate, who says, "What is truth?" And Jesus replies, "I am the way, the truth, and the life." Pilate is perplexed, but his wife has had dreams that this man is a great prophet and to leave Him alone. Pilate washed his hands of the matter and turned Him over to be crucified after He exclaimed, "I find no case against this man." Such lack of courage. Yet these very events were foretold many hundreds of years earlier, so it was just one more prophecy being fulfilled, so it was meant to be.

When I joined the IB department at our local high school, I found out they offered an annual symposium for IB students from across the Rocky Mountain region. The first one was held the year before I started, but I did see a video summary. The topic was, What is truth? As I heard speakers and students alike explain what they learned, it was clear the takeaway message was that everyone has their own truth. How sad. These students were not being given a compass that started with the Creator of the universe as the truth. My ex-husband used to say my biggest problem was that I saw many things in life as black-and-white while he believed there were often many shades of gray. Hence, our starting point was different, and so were our values. Truth is so important but so rarely taught, especially in colleges and universities. No wonder our world is in such a mess!

CHAPTER U

Underground (An Interesting Place to Be)

I must say that as I approached the end of the alphabet, I had to stretch to come up with a person, place, or thing for every letter. Such was the case for the letter *U*. I chose "underground" because I think that there are Christian movements that are completely underground because the country in which they are located considers such beliefs as a capital offense. As the Christians in our country are more and more maligned and Christian elements of key founding documents are removed, I wonder when and if we will have to go underground.

Back in the early 1980s, I was able to take a vacation up the West Coast of our country from California to Oregon and onto Washington State. This included some time in Seattle. I enjoyed my first fresh salmon dinner at the top of the Space Needle—that was exciting! The city was quite a unique place, and as we looked at interesting places to explore, we discovered a tour to see underground Seattle. In the early history of the city, it was burned to the ground and a new city was built on top of the old one. (I have come to find out this was common in the Middle East.) As our tour guide told us about old Seattle, it was interesting to think it had been so well preserved. I have since told others about this tour, and most all have never heard of it.

Part of the history of our country includes an underground railroad, a system for helping fugitive slaves escape into Canada or other places of safety. If you have never seen the 2019 movie *Harriet*, you should. According to www.imdb.com, it is described as the extraordinary tale of Harriet Tubman's escape from slavery and transformation into one of America's greatest heroes, whose courage, ingenuity, and tenacity freed hundreds of slaves and changed the course of history. Don't you just love these true stories? She had to go underground to help fellow slaves to escape to freedom.

I think of the early Christians in Rome who had to live and meet underground. If caught by crazy Emperor Nero, they might be tarred and set on fire as streetlamps. How gruesome! Yet this group of early Christians had tremendous unity of spirit and dedication to their faith. The apostles themselves went into hiding, for fear they might be the next one crucified for believing in Jesus as Christ, the Savior. It was only after they were empowered by the Holy Spirit on Pentecost (fifty days after Passover) that they found the courage to go and tell the world about the good news of Jesus as Savior.

If the Christian Church in America ever has to go underground, I pray that it will bring great unity of the body of Christ and great courage to stand up for a living faith in Jesus Christ.

CHAPTER V

Virginia (The Place of My Birth)

When I had to get my first passport in 1976, I had to get a copy of my birth certificate to submit to the Department of State. It was the first time that I noticed that the certificate said I was born in the Commonwealth of Virginia. Isn't that cool? It is a beautiful certificate, and it makes me feel a little proud that my life started in the same place as some of our Founding Fathers.

So what is the state of Virginia all about? According to www.history.com, Virginia is a southeastern US state that stretches from the Chesapeake Bay to the Appalachian Mountains, with a long Atlantic coastline. It's one of the thirteen original colonies, with historic landmarks including Monticello, Founding Father Thomas Jefferson's iconic Charlottesville plantation. The Jamestown Settlement and Colonial Williamsburg are living-history museums re-enacting Colonial- and Revolutionary-era life. I have had the pleasure of visiting Williamsburg, and it is a treat—with no modern cars, or dress, it truly feels like you are back in the 1700s. Our second oldest college is located there, the College of William and Mary. I'd love to go there!

According to www.encylopedia.org, Old Dominion is one of the best-known nicknames for Virginia, along with Mother of Presidents and Mother of States. The nickname probably derives from the fact that Virginia was the first, and therefore the oldest, of the overseas dominions of the kings and queens of England. How interesting is that? It appears that the British empire looked at Virginia as a special place in the colonies.

So what about Thomas Jefferson? According to www.biography. com, Thomas Jefferson was the primary draftsman of the US Declaration of Independence, the nation's first secretary of state, and the second vice president (under John Adams). As the third president of the United States, Jefferson stabilized the US economy and defeated pirates from North Africa during the Barbary War. He was responsible for doubling the size of the United States by successfully brokering the Louisiana Purchase. He also founded the University of Virginia. The Jefferson Monument in Washington, DC, is one of my favorites!

Yet many college students are taught that Jefferson was a bad man because it is told that he had slaves and made several babies with one. According to www.Monticello.com, years after his wife's death, Thomas Jefferson fathered at least six of Sally Hemings's children. Four survived to adulthood and are mentioned in Jefferson's planta-tion records: Beverly, Harriet, Madison, and Eston Hemings. Sally Hemings worked for two and a half years (1787–1789) in Paris as a domestic servant and maid in Jefferson's household. While in Paris, where she was free, she negotiated with Jefferson to return to enslave-ment at Monticello in exchange for "extraordinary privileges" for herself and freedom for her unborn children. Decades later, Jefferson freed all of Sally Hemings's children: Beverly and Harriet left Monticello in the early 1820s, while Madison and Eston were freed in his will and left Monticello in 1826.

So even with all his great accomplishments, this is what univer-sity professors choose to focus on? Can you imagine that at the end of your life, you were considered accomplished at many things but had one fault and the history books would look primarily at that fault? That is what our history professors seem to do—they teach the part of a story that fits their narrative. So if the narrative is that America is a bad country and many Founding Fathers had slaves, they want to paint a picture of this very thing. How sad. As I watch statues being torn down by radical leftist rioters, my heart aches to think how fast anarchy could come to our great country. All because young people have been so badly misled about our racist country, the very nation that gave freedom to slaves and is a land of opportunity for all people regardless of race.

I choose to look at the good in all people, and I think that Virginia as a state had a lot of good people in its history. According to www.thefamouspeople.com, here are some of the most notable people born in the state of Virginia (just for fun, in case you didn't know).

1. George Washington, our first president.
2. Thomas Jefferson, our third president.
3. Robert E. Lee, Confederate general in Civil War. (Interesting note: when the South lost the war, Robert E. Lee's property was confiscated, and the current location of Arlington National Cemetery was one of them.)
4. Zachary Taylor, twelfth president.
5. Woodrow Wilson, twenty-sixth president.
6. Booker T. Washington, dominant black leader/adviser to presidents.
7. Meriwether Lewis (of Lewis and Clark), explorer.

The younger generation would favor the following list: actors, TV, Music.

1. Chris Pratt
2. Sandra Bullock
3. Rob Lowe
4. Mackenzie Phillips
5. Shirley MacLaine
6. Katie Couric
7. Toby Mac

Sadly, some of the younger generation may not know all the names on the first list. We have made celebrities our heroes and our true American heroes as bad. That is so messed up. I still love Virginia and all its great history.

CHAPTER W

William (The General)

Yes, I dated another "Bill" in my life, but I decided to leave him for the end of my book since the story of our relationship is so unique. I noted above the names of some of the famous folks from the state of Virginia. My William is the only real famous person and only military officer that I ever dated. Just for the fun of it, I Googled his name and this was what Sam Houston State University had to say about this alumni.

William F. Garrison is a major general in the US Army, serving as commanding general of the John F. Kennedy Special Warfare School at Fort Bragg, North Carolina. Garrison graduated with a master of business administration from Sam Houston State University. Prior to that, he earned his bachelor of business administration from Pan American University. Garrison entered the US. He was a private in July 1966 and was commissioned as a second lieutenant in 1967 after graduating from officer candidate school. He was then promoted through the ranks as colonel, brigadier general, and major general as the youngest officer to hold those ranks.

Garrison has held various command positions, including recent assignments as deputy commanding general, US Army Special Operations Command at Fort Bragg; commander, First Special Forces Operational Detachment–Delta, at Fort Bragg; and deputy commander, US Army Intelligence Security Agency, US Army Intelligence and Security Command, in Washington, DC.

Garrison served two full tours in the Vietnam War, where he was awarded the Bronze Star Medal for valor with four Oak Leaf Clusters and the Purple Heart. He has also been awarded the Legion of Merit Defense Distinguished Service Medal, Defense Meritorious Service Medal, Air Medal and Meritorious Service Medal with three Oak Leaf Clusters. Most recently, he served as commander of the United Nations peace-keeping force on the Sinai Peninsula amid opposition from forces in the Near East. He also led a special forces group in an effort to capture Somali warlord Mohamed Farrah Aidid. Yes, *Black Hawk Down*.

Wow, quite the résumé. Here is what is added in his full résumé on Wikipedia. He is known for being the commander in charge of Task Force Ranger during Operation Gothic Serpent in Somalia. Garrison took full responsibility for the tactical setbacks experienced in Operation Gothic Serpent, which effectively ended his military career. Mark Bowden, the author of *Black Hawk Down: A Story of Modern War*, described Garrison as a military ascetic. According to Bowden's description, Garrison tirelessly worked to serve his country and would do anything for his soldiers. Some of Garrison's subordinates have also spoken publicly about their former commander.

Staff Sergeant Dan Schilling, an Air Force combat controller who took part in Operation Gothic Serpent, shared his feelings about Garrison in the book *The Battle of Mogadishu: Firsthand Accounts from the Men of Task Force Ranger*. On page 187 of the text, Schilling stated, "I should pause here for a moment to say a few words about General Garrison. Many know his record and command history. I'm not the person to expound on his exploits; in fact I don't know the man very well. But I will say he is the finest general officer I have ever worked for and probably ever will. He understood his men and how we thought, what we wanted and needed, and understood the situation anywhere he was, immediately and completely. He is the finest leader an operator could ask for. It was a shame that his career was derailed after our deployment; it was a criminal act committed by political cowards." By September 1996, Garrison had retired at the rank of major general and settled into a ranch near the community of Hico, Texas.

So how did I meet and date such a famous man? It was during 1977, while I was working for the CDC and our team was sent to Kansas City, Missouri. I worked with a female team, and for most, the daily routine, including evening room service for dinner, then reading a good book. What? I wanted to go out and explore the world! I flew to Memphis, Tennessee, over the President's Holiday weekend to visit my college roommate, Marybelle, since her husband was in optometry school there. On my flight back to Kansas City, I was sitting next to a nice gentleman, and we struck up a conversation. I told him I wanted to find a fun friend to explore the area before our team was headed out, and he told me he had just the friend, Wild Bill Garrison. He did qualify his remarks to say that Bill was not interested in settling down but was a good guy. I also had no interest in settling down, so what the heck? They were at the United States Army Command and General Staff College at Fort Leavenworth, Kansas, a graduate school for United States Army and sister service officers, interagency representatives, and international military officers (Wikipedia).

The following week, while in my room, I got a call from Major Garrison, and he asked me if I wanted to join him for a drink. Sure, I said. When? Right now. He was in the hotel restaurant/bar waiting for me. Mind you, that is a forty-one-mile drive to meet a stranger who might not be in her hotel. So we had drinks. He told me that the nice guy on the plane really liked me and would have asked me out himself if his wife were not picking him up at the airport. What? Is that how Army officers behave? He confirmed he had no wife and was quite single. Later that week, he took me to the officers' club and we had a lovely dinner. When our team was sent east across Missouri, he would come and see me, primarily on weekends. He could not believe he had actually met a twenty-three-year-old young lady who had graduated from college as a virgin! My rules. He remained an officer and a gentleman.

By Memorial Day, our team was being sent to Los Angeles, and I called Bill to give him the news. The phone had been disconnected. What? He disappeared. He had left an APO address where he could be reached, so I sent a scathing letter with my Minnesota home address, saying thanks for nothing. "I thought we had something going and you just left?" That letter did reach him, and he called me about six months later to say he was back in the USA. As an officer involved with special operations, he could not tell me where he had gone. His life was pretty top secret. What? Now I was interested.

He indicated he had been out of the country, learning to fight a new enemy called terrorists. (Remember, this was only 1977.) I told him I was dating a guy (my ex-husband) but I could meet him some-place like Disneyland to just catch up. He told me he had been around the world and back many times and had no interest in Disneyland. He wanted to see me. I asked if we could be friends, and he said he was too attracted to me to be my friend. Oh dear. I had to say goodbye. I couldn't date two guys at once and felt obligated to be honorable in my Santa Barbara relationship. So we said goodbye.

Seven years later, I found myself going through a divorce (1984), and I was watching *ABC World News Tonight*, and dang it, if I didn't see Bill Garrison getting ready to lead his troops into some type of special battle. He had injured his leg while doing some parachuting. So I sent a get-well card to that same APO address, and he got it. He called me and said he was now working with the CIA and Pentagon in Washington, DC, for a while. As it turned out, I was heading to Washington, DC, for one of my USC graduate classes (they have a Washington, DC, campus), and he offered to have me come as his guest, so I did. When I arrived in Dulles Airport, he came to get me and said he wanted to take me out for drinks to meet some of his friends. One of them blurted out, "You must be pretty special if he wants to marry you." What? My divorce had just been finalized, and I had no intention of jumping into another marriage at this stage in the game. So I never got that official proposal, since Bill already knew where I stood. We did have a nice week together and did the same again one month later, when I returned to finish my class. When I told a close friend at the hospital where I worked, she said, "You would make a great officer's wife!" But I was too fragile from all my ex-husband had put me through.

So we kept in touch from a distance, and when I decided to take the Scottsdale job in the fall of 1987, I had some extra time off before

my move and he asked me to come and see him at his home in
Fayetteville, North Carolina, the home of Fort Bragg, where he was
stationed. Again, we had a lovely time, and he even showed me some
neighborhoods with beautiful homes. He did not want to live on
base. He was moving up in rank and was now a brigadier general.
Wow. What did this high-ranking officer see in little old me? So off I
went to Arizona. I did have dinner with him one time when he was
in Tucson, but we never saw each other again—just occasional phone
calls. He once said if I had just realized that he was the best guy for
me, we could have been married and had five children by now. What?
He was already thinking of me as a mother for his children? We never
talked of such things. But he let me know that he had thought I was
the best one for him. To tell you the truth, his occupation scared me
to death! Eighty-Second Airborne Special Operations are trained
killers who handle a lot of black ops across the world. They are in
constant danger, and they may not come home from their next
deployment. Many times their families do not even know where they
are. I was not sure this "lifestyle" would be a good fit for me. In retrospect, I think I would have made a great general's wife but could
not wrap my head around the whole picture at that time. My loss,
maybe?

I have to reminisce about a few things he did say to me. Although
he was not fond of working with the CIA, at one meeting, President
Reagan came in the room, so they all got to meet him. Bill said everyone loved the guy—he was a very good commander in chief. Another
time, he said they had been sent to Los Angeles to help train the
LAPD officers in using antiterrorism tactics to fight the gang wars in
the city. Daryl Gates became a good friend to him. What? That guy
was pretty famous, and it might have been cool to meet the guy. I
learned a lot about world politics before CNN even came on the
scene. Bill knew I was a strict Catholic and said he did not attend
church, but the chaplains he worked with were great, including several Catholic priests. They say there are no atheists in foxholes, so
maybe he was right. I can only think that God had another plan for
me, so He sent my life in another direction. Sorry, General Bill. You
were truly one of the most amazing guys I had ever had the privilege

of knowing. My only regret is that you may have had to go through that terrible congressional hearing alone. I wish I could have been by your side. I hope Texas retirement is good for you.

CHAPTER Z

Zimbabwe (Air Mail and Orphans)

Yes, I skipped *X* and *Y*—I could not think of any good persons, places, or things for those letters. Maybe my next book. So I get to end with *Z* for Zimbabwe. It is a country in South Africa that used to be called Rhodesia. Yep, the home of my high school foreign exchange student! I now sit on a board that serves orphans in this country called Renewed Hope, so I think maybe God is bringing me full circle. I mean, really, Lord? I have only been to two countries in all of Africa, and this is the third one—a place I hope to visit and do some missions work for the poor orphans. Yes, it is on my bucket list to get to Zimbabwe, no matter who is in charge.

So what is the history of Zimbabwe? Here is the summary from www.wikipedia.com. Rhodesia was an unrecognized state in southern Africa from 1965 to 1979, equivalent in territory to modern Zimbabwe. Rhodesia was the de facto successor state to the British colony of Southern Rhodesia, which had been self-governing since achieving responsible government in 1923. The *Atlantic Magazine* ran a great article about this country in December 2003. The title was, "How to Kill a Country: Turning a Breadbasket into a Basket Case in Ten Easy Steps—The Robert Mugabe Way." That is the summary. Here is part of the rest of the article:

> Nearly forty years ago Ian Smith, the Prime Minister of Rhodesia, became the first and only white colonial ruler to break away from the

British Crown. He was tired of London's nagging about the subjugation of Rhodesian blacks. In 1965 Smith declared independence. "The mantle of the pioneers has fallen on our shoulders," he said, calling on white Rhodesians to maintain standards in a "primitive country." Smith saw himself as an apostle of Cecil John Rhodes, the British magnate who gave Rhodesia its name, and who in the late nineteenth century duped black tribal leaders into signing over the fertile land to white pioneers. Although Rhodesia in 1965 was home to just over 200,000 whites and four million blacks, Smith shared Rhodes's belief that black majority rule would occur "never in a thousand years."

Smith was, of course, wrong. In 1980, after a civil war that cost thirty thousand lives, the black majority took charge of the country, which was renamed Zimbabwe. Robert Mugabe, the nationalist leader whom Smith had branded a Marxist terrorist and jailed for more than a decade, a man who had once urged his followers to stop wearing shoes and socks to show they were willing to reject the trappings of European civilization, became president.

In the forty years since that time, everything has gone downhill. So Rhodesia basically came to an end in 1979. I sent airmail letters to that country from 1972 to 1976 and then found out that Brian's parents had fled to Cape Town, South Africa, when the civil war was getting ready to start. When unrest hit South Africa, they returned to their home in England and settled in the area where Brian lived in Cumbria. Bill had a good friend named John who led Promise Keepers at the church where we met. He also grew up in Rhodesia and served in the Army there (a white British businessman). The same happened with his family, and his parents fled to New Zealand. You remember how we visited them during our honeymoon? We put John and Brian at the same table at our wedding reception. How good is God that they had so much to share! What are those odds? Only God could orchestrate such a meeting.

Now Brian is a retired doctor living in northern England. I am a retired person with varied professional experience from health-care administration and marketing to grant writing for nonprofits and education, so perhaps God will allow us to meet up in the country where he grew up. He has a son getting his PhD in African history and a daughter who is also a doctor, so it might make for an interesting missionary team, don't you think? From Minnesota with Manna—with a Rhodesia connection that could end up in a reunion in Zimbabwe? What an interesting way to end my A–Z book!

EPILOGUE

So I made it from A–Z of persons, places, and things that had a great impact in my life. Some might say I was too transparent about all the lumps and bumps of my life as well as that of my immediate family. Yet I wrote each chapter with the goal to encourage all readers that we all go through tough times in our lives, but with the help of God, we can get through them and often end up on a path that we never expected. It is also encouraging that God's book (the Bible) is filled with many such stories, a real inspiration that God can use anyone for His glory! For those who may look at me and think "She has it altogether," they now know that is not the case. Some might even say, "Is this really all true?" Yes, it is. As they say, truth can be stranger than fiction.

I remember when I was growing up, I was not sure what I wanted to be, but I knew what I did *not* want to do with my life—spend it in a small mining town in Minnesota, working for the same company for years and then, after retirement, dropping dead far too young. My goal was to have a life filled with variety—be careful what you wish for! Now that I have reached retirement, I look at friends who did spend one long career, doing one thing, and are now comfortable in their retirement with an income that actually exceeds their earning years. My path was never that smooth, and I had to piece together a retirement from various sources, but I have. I cannot afford to look back and say, "If only I had stayed with that county job for at least twenty years," since it is often the low times in life (i.e., job losses) where we can grow the most. Thank You, Lord!

I remember hearing a presentation by the actress Suzanne Somers about her life story that she put into a book called *Keeping Secrets*. Here is a summary from www.goodreads.com of this first of several books that she wrote.

> This is the story of the Suzanne Somers the world never knew...the shy, frightened child trembling at her father's drunken rages, the troubled teenager who became a pregnant bride, the young model struggling to support her son, the rising star still haunted and controlled by her past. It's the story she wrote for America's millions of adult children of alcoholics, people who don't drink, yet suffer from and need help against the ravages of this insidious disease. And it's a story of incredible courage, a candid, sometimes shocking autobiography of a woman who dared to face the dark side of her soul and triumph over it.

She went on to write a second book, called *After the Fall: How I Picked Myself Up, Dusted Myself Off, and Started All Over Again*. Amazon.com summarizes this book as follows:

> In this moving and inspiring follow-up to her New York Times best-selling memoir, Keeping Secrets, Suzanne Somers revisits her years before and after Three's Company and reveals with fearless self-examination how the dizzying rise and fall of her television career mirrored the chaos and conflict in her personal life. With her usual candor and perspective, Suzanne takes readers inside the rehearsal hall of Three's Company and offers a never-before-seen look at the competition, jealousy, and greed that accompanies a hit TV show. Wow. I love such honesty.

Now, my life is not famous, but I certainly had to start all over again many times. I hope that the people I have mentioned in this book will take every word I wrote as a piece of encouragement to the next person facing struggles like divorce, depression, suicide, job loss, lost relationships, membership in many different churches, and an around-the-world adventure that taught me more than any book could ever do. When I tell fellow Christians that I did not even own my first Bible until I was thirty-six years old, they marvel, How did I survive those early years? I can only say that was when God carried me.

My dad was a Democrat all his life until Ronald Reagan was elected as president. He then became a Regan Democrat. I am sure we both voted for Jimmy Carter in 1976, but never again—we saw the light about who really made a good leader of our great country. I am not a registered Republican either, because I think they also have some poor candidates, but I vote for the person with the best policies, those that honor God and follow high moral standards. Yes, I have become one of those Christian conservatives, and I will happily wear that badge to my grave!

I have to thank all my teachers along the way, including actual teachers, K-12, college, and grad school; each of my brothers and sisters in unique ways; various family members; my close friends along the way, from high school to college and beyond; the many men in my life who loved me but also respected me and never forced me to waver on my moral values; many work colleagues and employees; those Bible-selling book guys from the South; as well as my fellow European adventurers during the bicentennial. I have now taken many Bible studies and love the work of many Bible teachers, especially Beth Moore. She makes Bible studies fun! (She also had a challenging time in her teens and early years.) Our annual Christmas card list usually includes nearly two hundred names, even after we remove some who have died or moved away—people think we are nuts! But I love writing our annual family Christmas letter to reflect on all the ways we have been blessed in the previous year.

Yes, from Minnesota with Manna. I have to thank my Lord and Savior, Jesus Christ, who was always there for me even when I did not know it or know Him. We are taught as Catholic children that we have guardian angels. Our favorite nightly prayer was, "Angel of God, my guardian dear, to whom God's love entrusts me here. Ever this day be at my side, to light and guard, to rule and guide." Perhaps I do have a guardian angel.

Finally, I hope my writing has caused my readers to say, "I never knew that," when I share things like historical stories or just fun, did-you-know things. I pray that everyone can be a lifelong learner and never stop enjoying the wonder of the world around us. I have been blessed in so many ways. I recently heard, "When the Lord starts blessing, the devil starts messing." I have found this to be true, so be sure you have on your full armor of God. My desire to write this book started in 2006, when we left California, but I think God knew I had to mature a bit more before I could put the story together in a way that did not focus on *my* life but rather the path on which *he* has led me. I plan to donate the net proceeds from my book to charity, especially Christian charities. So if you liked what I wrote, do share with a friend and spread the joy and encouragement I tried to share. God bless us, one and all (Tiny Tim).

PHOTO MEMORIES
FROM MY LIFE

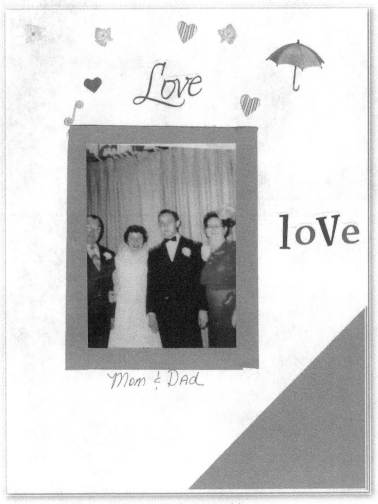

Dick and Elaine Wedding

Kathy and brother Paul early years

Pride & Joy

Kathy early years

Bride and Groom Feb 1995

Kathy Bride 1995

Bill brother Jack-Kathy sister Sue
Best Man & Maid of Honor

Kathy-Mom-Sisters-Feb 1995
Joan and Sue

Bill-Katie-Karen-Jack Feb 1995
Bill's Brother, Mom and Sister

Many nieces and nephews in our wedding party—pure joy!

Kathy and 3 brothers at wedding
Paul, Tom and John

Kathy and Uncle Stan Feb 1995

Our dog Kelly at our wedding

Uncle Don-Aunt Jean—Feb 1995

Happy Birthday
#50

January 13, 2004
Celebrated
January 10th, 2004

Born 1954

For You on your Birthday

KK 50th birthday

friends and family

Dec 2010- Pearl Harbor Trip- New Arizona Memorial

Hawaii Dec 2011

CPSIA information can be obtained
at www.ICGtesting.com
Printed in the USA
LVHW030325030221
678219LV00001B/72